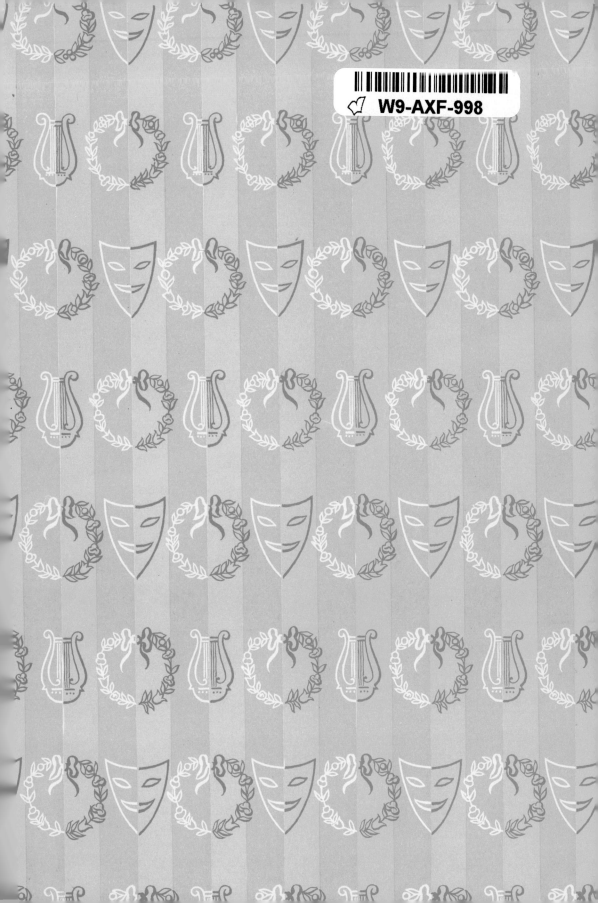

THE MAGNIFICENCE OF ESZTERHÁZA

MÁTYÁS HORÁNYI

# THE MAGNIFICENCE OF ESZTERHÁZA

Barrie and Rockliff
1962

Original edition

HORÁNYI MÁTYÁS

Eszterházi vigasságok

Akadémiai Kiadó, Budapest 1959

Supervised by

DEZSŐ KERESZTURY

and

JÓZSEF UJFALUSSY

Translated

by

ANDRÁS DEÁK

Not to be sold in the Soviet Union and in the countries
of the people's democracy



Joint edition

First published in English 1962 by

Barrie and Rockliff (Barrie Books Ltd.)

2 Clement's Inn, London WC 2

and Akadémiai Kiadó Budapest

Publishing House of the Hungarian Academy of Sciences

Responsible for production and publication

GYÖRGY BERNÁT

Director of the Publishing House of the Hungarian Academy of Sciences and of the Academy Press

*

Responsible editor

BARBARA FARAGÓ

*

Technical editor

MIHÁLY FARAGÓ

Printed in Hungary at the Academy Press, Budapest

# CONTENTS

# PREFACE

Life in the court of Prince Miklós Esterházy 'the Magnificent' has so far been investigated chiefly by musicologists in connection with research into the life of Joseph Haydn, the quondam conductor of the Esterházy orchestra. Most of the data regarding the history of the Esterházy theatres are likewise contained in musicological works, chiefly the work of C. F. Pohl, the author of the first important monograph on Haydn,[1] and J. Hárich who, in his book dealing with the history of the 'Esterházy Librettos', presents a good survey of musical life in the princely court.[2] Essays written by E. Csatkai, A. Zádor and F. Probst contain additional contributions to the subject.

The present book, by publishing the hitherto unknown documents of the archives of the Esterházy family regarding theatrical life at their court, and by describing scenic properties that used to belong to their theatres, continues this work.

The author is deeply indebted to the managers of the Országos Széchényi Könyvtár (National Library, Budapest) and the Österreichische Nationalbibliothek (National Library, Vienna) for their valuable assistance in his researches.

*Budapest, August, 1959*

# AUTHOR'S FOREWORD TO THE ENGLISH EDITION

Although the text of this edition is not essentially different from that of the Hungarian original and the German version, it nevertheless includes a number of additional details and has undergone some modifications in the light of obvious recent literary works on architecture and musical history. The most significant modifications are the omission of passages from Bessenyei's poems, and the transfer of all notes to the end of the book. In excluding Bessenyei's verses from this edition we were led by the consideration that the poetical flourishes and the special flavour of these poems, written in archaic Hungarian would lose all their poetical value and become unintelligible or meaningless to the English reader if one tried to translate them. Our reason for regrouping the notes was that we have amplified them by adding a few special explanations for the benefit of the English-speaking public, and also because their inclusion in the text would have tended to break the flow of the story. These explanations, as also the map—the latter a special feature of the English edition — have the object of facilitating orientation in the labyrinth of Hungarian names and Hungarian history. Foreign names and titles are given in the orthography of the original sources.

A recent essay by J. Hárich* has enabled us to establish the authentic opera programme of the Esterházy-theatre between 1780 and 1790.

* Hárich, J., Das Repertoire des Opernkapellmeisters Joseph Haydn in Eszterháza (1780—1790). Haydn-Jahrbuch. Universal Edition, Wien. (By the autbor's kind permission, on the basis of the manuscript.)

# SURROUNDINGS OF ESZTERHÁZA AND KISMARTON

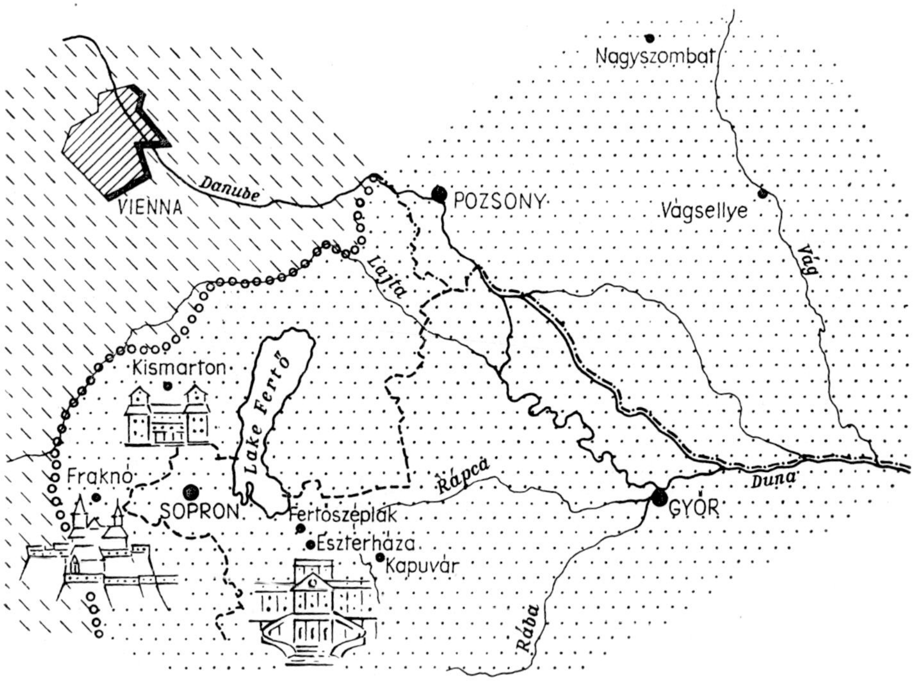


oooooo *Eighteenth century frontier*

----- *Present frontier between Austria and Hungary*

–·–·–· *Present frontier of Czechoslovakia*

*Hungary*

*Austria*

# INTRODUCTION

Play-acting in the Hungarian language began at the end of the eighteenth century. It was preceded by an advanced foreign theatrical culture which served as the model and school for Hungarian dramatic art. There were three sharply separated fields in which this theatrical culture flourished: on the stages of schools, at the theatres in the towns and in the private theatres of the aristocracy. While urban and scholastic miming have been the subject of significant works of scholarship, hardly any attempt has been made to investigate the history of the private theatres of the aristocracy. The situation is similar as regards Austrian and Bohemian theatrical history of the eighteenth century which was closely connected with the contemporaneous development of Hungarian acting. This disregard of private theatres was only natural if we remember that the principal sources of the history of court theatres, the archives of aristocratic families, were until quite recent times in private possession and therefore hardly accessible to research workers. This will explain why theatrical history knows so little of, say, the activities of the aristocratic group which directed the court theatres of Vienna at the outset of the nineteenth century or, again, of the activities of the recently restored castle theatre of Krumlov, in Czechoslovakia. And yet, theatrical life at the residences of the great landlords was not merely a characteristic feature of the final bright period of the *ancien régime* but constituted an active factor of that urban theatrical culture which was rapidly developing in the second half of eighteenth century. The ensembles which performed in the theatres of the towns consisted of the same mimes who appeared on the stage of the castles and palaces, and the cultured taste of the aristocratic audiences gave significant impetus to their artistic development.

Researches made so far make it evident that the court theatres of the aristocrats played a very prominent part in Hungary's theatrical history. It was at the residence of the Esterházy family that the country's first two permanent theatres were erected, and for more than two decades their activities surpassed those of the theatres at Pozsony and Pest-Buda. Menninger, Passer, Hellmann and Koberwein, Wahr, Diwald, Seipp, Mayer and many another prominent German mime of Hungary began their careers in the court of the Princes Esterházy. Apart from German play-acting, this court was also the scene of a flourishing Italian opera culture under the guidance of Haydn, and a richly endowed puppet theatre was maintained in a separate building. Count János Erdődy's private opera at Pozsony was the second most prominent aristocratic theatre. After his death, the excellent opera ensemble was engaged by Sebastian Tuschl, an *entrepreneur* in Pest, who, by doing so, laid the foundations of the capital's operatic art. By patronizing non-Hungarian productions, the theatres of the families of Esterházy and Erdődy prepared the ground for Hungarian theatrical culture. It is almost symbolical that Mayer and Ditelmeyer with their wives arriving in the capital from Eszterháza, established the first regular German theatre of Buda precisely in that wooden building which came to be occupied a few years later by the ensemble of László Kelemen which was the first to give Hungarian performances. How closely the Hungarian theatre was linked up with the court theatres of the aristocracy is clearly evinced by the fact that József Chudy, the former conductor of Erdődy's private opera, became the musical leader of László Kelemen's ensemble. The first Hungarian opera, staged in 1793, *Prince Picco*, is Chudy's composition. The stage properties of several palace theatres were acquired by Hungarian theatres in various towns at the beginning of the nineteenth century; the painted scenery of the Batthyány-Theatre at Rohonc, for example, came into the possession of the National Theatre of Pest in 1838.

The most general trait of the private theatres was their feudal and courtly character. They formed part of, and had to adapt themselves to, the courtly household throughout their history. The drawing up of the repertoire, the engagement of ensembles and artists were exclusive prerogatives of the nobleman on whom the very existence of the theatre depended. This explains the great number of *ad hoc* plays or musical compositions written for special festive occasions, and explains further those sudden changes which the private theatres of aristocratic owners had to undergo in the course of their history. The various court theatres were inseparably linked with the personality of this or that aristocratic patron, and — in like manner — the entire era of Hungarian court theatricals was but an adjunct to a short historical period that had neither antecedents nor continuity.

After having put an end to Rákóczi's war of independence, the Imperial Court of Vienna did its best to paralyse Hungary both politically and strategically. The fortresses were razed, military organization was disallowed, and — in order to offer compensation to the Hungarian aristocracy which had been excluded from the political and military leadership of the country — Vienna was intent upon making concessions at the expense of the serfs, and tried to dazzle the peers of Hungary by drawing them into the magic circle of the splendid Imperial Court. Exposed to increasing pressure from Vienna and inclined to opportunism, Hungarian aristocrats became accustomed to spending the greater part of the year in Vienna, and were ambitious to develop a court life in their provincial palaces after the Vienna pattern.

It is worthy of note that a French traveller, by the name of Riesbeck, recognized quite clearly the tendency towards the assimilation of Hungary's aristocracy. Writing of the Vienna court, he says: 'They [the Court] regarded it as indispensable that the Hungarian aristocrats should be held together, converted into courtiers and deprived of all sentiments of true honour.... They thought they had to enslave the whole nation in order to subject it to their rule'.[3] Riesbeck regarded it as a success of this policy that the Hungarian aristocrats were spending such amounts on the maintenance of their extravagant life as to become financially unable to organize and maintain a national army of any consequence.

At a time when life in the Hungarian castles was beginning to flourish, the courts of European sovereigns stood under increasing French influence. Following St. Petersburg, Potsdam, Mannheim and so many other imperial, royal and ducal residences the new castle of Maria Theresa, in Schönbrunn too, was designed in the style of Versailles. The life of the Viennese aristocracy like that of the readily assimilating Hungarian aristocrats was deeply imbued with French taste and *esprit*. The chief symptom of this process was not so much the adoption of social customs and forms of art as rather the increased cultivation of court life which—after Italian and Spanish antecedents — was now patterned after the image of Versailles.

The most noteworthy result of European court life, stamped with French *esprit*, was the development of new cultural centres which were so many representatives of the *ancien régime*. Castles, built more or less after the model of Versailles, belong to the most exquisite architectural monuments of the eighteenth century. Musical and theatrical art reached hitherto unattained heights in these castles which became the repositories of highly significant collections, picture galleries and libraries.

It was at Eszterháza that Miklós Esterházy, the 'Magnificent', the wealthiest feudal landlord of Hungary, established his court in the French style. It was here that the aristocratic ideal of the century, the world of garden fêtes, shooting parties, fireworks and opera performances, a world one knows from Watteau's paintings and French memoirs, came to be realized to its fullest extent in Hungary. Miklós 'the Magnificent' whose alleged motto was 'There is nothing the Emperor can do that I can't',[4] collected at Eszterháza everything offered by the culture and the refined gallic art of living in the eighteenth century. It is emphasized in the introduction to a poem of Bessenyei,[5] describing the festivities of the year 1773, that the grand style of the court of Eszterháza aimed at making people who had been brought up in Paris and London forget the delights offered by those large cities and transfer their admiration to such an extent as to win admiration for Hungary in foreign lands.

Yet, the representatives of just that Hungarian national spirit which received impetus from Bessenyei's literary activities had not only praise for the court of Eszterháza. While the creation of Versailles was not only an unprecedented example of monarchical splendour but constituted also a shining instance of modern state administration and helped to win glory for French national culture, the princely courts established in imitation of Versailles had always remained more or less alien to the national culture of their own country. This was especially true in the case of West Hungary's aristocratic courts, where gallic features were but a veneer laid over strong Austrian influences which drove the Hungarian language and culture almost entirely into the background. Not more than two decades had elapsed since the appearance of Bessenyei's poem when József Pétzeli, raising his voice in favour of the establishment of a Hungarian theatre, felt induced to write that it would be a great glory for the country if not merely foreign but also Hungarian dramas and comedies were performed at Eszterháza. He added that 'it would be right if the Hungarian muses were to make a humble entreaty to His Grace the Prince in this sense', and that Hungarian playwrights would be found in plenty if only patrons were forthcoming.[6] The reformists raised the same idea in a much more decided form in another respect. A contributor to the *Tudományos Gyüjtemény* (Scientific Collection)[7] expressed his regret that the peerless botanical collection in the park of Prince Esterházy at Kismarton was used solely for the purposes of amusement, that the Prince's picture gallery, of European fame, contributed to the glory of the Austrian capital, although — either united with the

National Museum or lodged in the Prince's palace at Buda — it might serve higher aims and might have made his name as immortal as that of Széchenyi.[8]

The Princes Esterházy kept aloof from the movements of both the reform period and the subsequent struggles for independence. They deserve no credit for the fact that, at last and in spite of everything, the real treasures of the households of both Princes of identical name, Miklós Esterházy, have become an integral part of their proper place in Hungary's national culture. The state purchased the picture gallery from the family in 1860 and it was from this that the Museum of Fine Arts in Budapest subsequently developed.[9] The recently restored castle of Eszterháza is one of Hungary's most notable historic monuments, and Haydn's music, performed at Eszterháza, is now the common property of the whole world. The theatre of Eszterháza, though more ephemeral than the other factors of the culture of this court, produced the most immediate effect and must be regarded as an abiding cultural treasure bequeathed to us by the eighteenth century.

# PALATINES MIKLÓS AND PÁL, FOUNDERS OF THE FAMILY'S POWER

The Esterházy family, one of the most important in the history of Hungary, derived from the clan Salamon in the Csallóköz (West Hungary). Miklós Esterházy, founder of the princely branch, was born in 1583 at Galánta as the son of Ferenc Esterházy, Vice Lord-Lieutenant of the county of Pozsony, and Zsófia Illésházy. Though baptized as a protestant, he was educated at Nagyszombat, Sellye and then in Vienna by the Jesuits, and adopted the Roman Catholic faith at a youthful age. Learning that the young man was contemplating taking holy orders as a member of the Jesuit order, Ferenc Esterházy expelled his son from home.

Miklós Esterházy entered the service of his maternal uncle, the Palatine István Illésházy, and served, after the Palatine's death in 1609, under Ferenc Mágoczy, the Commissioner of Kassa. He commanded at the latter place a troup of fifty, later one hundred, warriors of the border. It was here that he made the acquaintance of Orsolya Dersfy, the wife of Ferenc Mágoczy, with whom he contracted marriage in 1611, after the death of Mágoczy.

This marriage laid the foundations of the wealth and power of the Esterházys. Talented but propertyless, Miklós Esterházy received vast estates with the hand of the childless widow and suddenly became one of the country's leading personages.

Orsolya Dersfy died in 1619 and, after a widowerhood of five years, Miklós Esterházy made a second equally good match. His second wife, Krisztina Nyáry, widow of the young Imre Thurzó, leader of the protestants in Upper Hungary, added enormous wealth to the estates of her second husband. By strengthening the Catholic camp, this marriage was looked upon as a significant political success for the Counter Reformation in Upper Hungary.

Familiarity with political and military matters, acquired in the service of Illésházy and Mágoczy, together with his rapidly increasing wealth, helped the young nobleman in becoming, before long, the leader of the Roman Catholic Hapsburg party. He climbed the ladder of official hierarchy with dazzling rapidity and was elected Palatine of Hungary in 1625.

Nearly a hundred years had elapsed since the Turkish conquest of the greater part of the country. The Hapsburg kings, occupied in West Europe, had made no attempts at Hungary's liberation but throughout the period had been opposing any trend towards a strengthening of the Principality of Transylvania which tried to pursue a national policy. In this situation, Miklós Esterházy was the mainstay of the Hapsburg dynasty and the greatest antagonist of the Transylvanian Princes Gábor Bethlen and György Rákóczi.

As a consequence of political bargains and wars, the fortresses, castles and domains situated on the borders of royal Hungary, Transylvania and of the territories occupied by the Turks changed owners with great frequency. Munkács, the centre of the Esterházy estates, was constantly in danger. It so happened that, in 1622, the king ceded the fortress of Munkács to Gábor Bethlen, Prince of Transylvania, and indemnified Miklós Esterházy with the domains of Kismarton and Fraknó.

Miklós Esterházy had nothing to complain of this exchange. His new estates were in territories little exposed to the vicissitudes of war, and his wealth had been increased. Kismarton and Fraknó were henceforth to remain the definitive centres of the Esterházy estates.

The vast estates of Miklós Esterházy formed but the foundation of the family's later wealth. Pál Esterházy, the other great maker of the family's fortunes, who succeeded the early-deceased László Esterházy succeeded to the title in 1652, added much further wealth to the riches of the family by the modernization of farming, by large-scale building, and by acquiring additional huge estates especially in Transdanubia.

By his first marriage with Orsolya, daughter of István Esterházy, he united the two branches and the wealth of the family, while his second marriage with Éva Thököly helped him to acquire a considerable share of the fortune of the Thökölys. Moreover, when Ferenc Nádasdy, his brother-in-law, was sentenced to death and the forfeiture of his property on account of his participation in Wesselényi's conspiracy,[10] Pál Esterházy acquired—partly by way of purchase and partly by way of royal grant — the bulk of the huge wealth of the Nádasdy family. On top of all this the commission entrusted with the redistribution of the country after the expulsion of the Turks allotted 140,000 acres of additional land to Pál Esterházy.

It was not only in matters of wealth that he brought the family to the summit of power: Pál Esterházy came to the forefront also from a social point of view. Like his father, he became Palatine of Hungary, received the title of a prince of the Empire, and the title was made hereditary in 1712 for the firstborn male descendants. His passion for the acquisition of wealth, and his intransigently rigid support of the Hapsburgs' policy during Thököly's and Rákóczi's wars of independence made him so unpopular that it was impossible to entrust him with the negotiations that were to lead to the Peace of Szatmár[11] although, as Palatine, it would have been natural for him to conduct the negotiations.

When making his testament, Pál Esterházy disposed of a wealth that in less than a century had become the largest feudal fortune in Hungary. He alone had acquired twenty-five castles and palaces, and his landed property amounted to approximately one and a half million acres.

# MUSIC AND THEATRE DURING THE LIFE OF THE TWO PALATINES

There exist no detailed descriptions of Miklós Esterházy's household but we know that he must have had good musicians at Munkács. Before definitely becoming his antagonist, Gábor Bethlen, a man of deep culture, asked him in 1619 to send, if not all his musicians, at least his harp-player to a festival at the court of Gyulafehárvár. Péter Pázmány[12] criticized the pomp displayed in the castle of Lakompak, while Miklós Esterházy kept trumpet, harp and clarinet players in his pay at Kismarton.[13] It is likewise from Palatine Miklós's life that the connection between the Esterházy family and the school theatricals of the Jesuits can be dated. Although no plays were yet performed in the school of the Jesuits at Sopron in the Palatine's life, he lent them his orchestra for the celebrations which, with a tableau vivant as the central feature, were held in 1640 to commemorate the hundredth anniversary of the order's existence.

The true forerunner of the Esterházys, in their capacity as displayers of splendour and patrons of art in the eighteenth century, was Palatine Pál. The Prince himself was no mediocre artist, poet and composer. A song book, *Harmonia Coelestis*, composed and published by him in 1711, constitutes an important document of Hungarian musical history. Pál Esterházy maintained a large orchestra and employed prominent conductors at his court of Kismarton. He engaged Carlone, an Italian architect for the reconstruction of the castle of Kismarton in the sixties of the seventeenth century, and entertained there among others Emperor Leopold and the Queen of Poland as his guests.

Not only the development of the orchestra received an impetus at the time of Palatine Pál's life, but the family's theatrical connections, too, became stronger and more pronounced under his patronage.

Palatine Pál's interest in theatricals may have already been aroused during his studies at Nagyszombat. His diary shows that he took an active part in the school performances, and he seems to have been a gifted actor.

We know from his notes that he performed a Hungarian dance at Pozsony in 1647 in the presence of the royal couple on the occasion of the coronation of Ferdinand IV, and that, later, he represented King Joas at a school performance: '. . .equipped with two naked swords, I had to do a heyduck's dance of which I used to be a consummate master. That dance pleased the Emperor and the Empress very much: the musicians belonged to Messire Ádám Forgách, and Hanzli was the name of the violinist. And then we had to go from Pozsony to Nagyszombat where the Jesuit fathers gave a great and beautiful tragedy of King Joas who was persecuted by Athalia, his step mother. I had to play the part of Joas. It was a part of nearly four hundred lines. And Athalia was killed there, and his son Joas, who symbolized Ferdinand the Fourth was crowned.'[14]

The young Pál Esterházy continued to play theatrical parts in the next year. His diary contains details in this respect: another tragedy was played when — in the presence of Lippay, the Archbishop of Esztergom, Primate of Hungary — the seminarists were first brought to the seminary. The principal role, Judith, was played by Esterházy. He was dressed for the part by the wife of Mihály Thurzó and adorned with rich jewelry. Father Keresztes, Rector of the seminary, had Esterházy's portrait painted in the role. The part consisted of nearly five hundred lines and brought the young actor three awards. The old woman, attached to Judith, was represented by a very ugly-faced student who played excellently and made the audience laugh.

This was during Lent. On Good Friday, Pál represented the Genius of Divine Love in the procession and had to declaim 'verses' in the theatre: his hands were attached to the branches of a green tree, symbolizing the love of our Lord.[15] The picture representing Pál Esterházy in the role of Judith is still to be seen at Fraknó.

The academic year over, Pál attended the palatinal election at Pozsony and returned thereafter to Nagyszombat where again he had to play a female part in a school drama. His voice and stature seem to have fitted him for such roles. He represented St. Catherine on this occasion and had to declaim more than five hundred 'lines'. He was dressed again by the wife of Mihály Thurzó and received two awards.[16]

Returning to Nagyszombat from the wedding of his elder brother László in 1650, Pál was cast in the role of the crucified Jesus Christ in a performance given during Lent. We find notes concerning a student's trick in his diary in connection with this performance: '. . . a play was given in Lent about a man called Gualbertus who for the sake of God

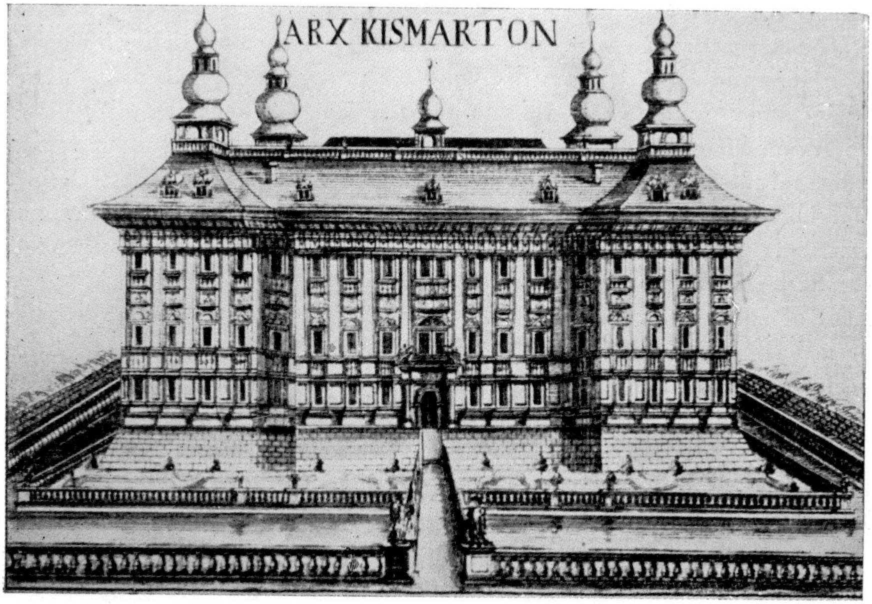


1. The Esterházy Palace of Kismarton at the beginning of the eighteenth century

forgave his enemy: when he was kneeling before the Cross it bent down to thank him for his mercifulness. I represented the Crucified and at my two sides Messires János and Miklós Draskovit, clad in the garb of angels, were holding torches. But János Draskovit, wanting to have his joke, brought the burning torch close to my hand which was attached to the Cross so that, at last, I had to shout and scold him, which made people laugh and aroused the wrath of the master against János Draskovit; and this play was given during Lent.'[17]

The last entry in the diary concerning Pál's histrionic activities dates from 1651 and refers to a play in which he represented St. Francis Xavier.[18]

We possess no data that would point to Palatine Pál as having engaged actors for his court, but it is certain that — possibly in memory of his youthful play-acting — he patronized performances in the Jesuit schools. Relying on the evidence of their chronicle preserved in the National Library, Vienna, E. Csatkai relates that the Jesuits of Sopron arranged the first theatrical performances on Corpus Christi day or during the Lent of 1664, and that Pál Esterházy lent them his orchestra for the occasion. Henceforth, Palatine Pál became an ardent spectator of the performances and even established a fund, the interest of which was used for rewarding the best student-actors. The Jesuits, of course, endeavoured to please their great patron by the choice of their plays. The first play with a Hungarian historical subject, performed in 1697, was about King Sigismund brought back to the throne by his Palatine.[19]

We possess a further valuable proof concerning the close connection between the Esterházys and the Jesuits of Sopron. The latter produced an occasional play, *Serena Domus*, on 31st July 1702, whose musical accompaniment was composed by Franz Rumpeling, the new conductor at Kismarton, who had been engaged a year before. Rumpeling's music was executed at the performance by the Prince's orchestra. The plot of the play deals with the conversion to the true faith of Pál Esterházy and his wife, the ancestors of Palatine Pál. The libretto of the play, printed in Latin and German on four leaves, bears the following title: '*Serena Domus Estorasianae fulcra in Paulo Estoras et Serena Conjuge ad lumen verae fidei per D. Adalbertum traductus.* Ab illustrissime... Episcopalis Gymnasii Soproniensis Juventute in Scenam data Anno MDCCII. Mense Julio die 31. Musicam composuit D. Franciscus Rumpeling Capellae Celsissimae Magister. Vienna, Austriae.'[20]

Palatine Pál patronized school theatricals not only at Sopron but also at Nagyszombat. He had, in 1692, a new stage erected for the Jesuit college of Nagyszombat and equipped it with Venetian scenery.[21]

2. Palatine Pál Esterházy as Judith in a school drama. Oil painting, 1650

Apart from school theatricals, Pál Esterházy had ample opportunity of becoming acquainted with Italian opera. He spent much time in Vienna and sent from there frequent reports to his wife on the performances he had attended during his visits, together with the librettos of the operas. The following passage is, for example, contained in a letter written on 23rd February, 1662: 'We had much fun here, I attended a comedy last Monday evening... there was a nice comedy on Tuesday also, and you will find both enclosed in the Italian language.'[22] A total of fourteen librettos have been preserved in the library of the princely family.

According to J. Hárich,* a stage had also been erected in the castle of Kismarton, presumably in the present 'Haydn Saal'. It served for the performance of popular musical plays at Christmas and Easter. The equipment of this stage forms an item among the objects marked as being out of use in an inventory from 1721.

* Hárich, J., Das Repertoire des Opernkapellmeisters Joseph Haydn in Eszterháza (1780—1790). Haydn—Jahrbuch. Universal Edition, Wien.

# THE HOUSEHOLD OF PÁL ANTAL ESTERHÁZY

Palatine Pál having died, the title devolved upon Mihály, his son from the first marriage, and — after Mihály's death — upon József who bore the title only seven and a half months in 1720.

Palatine Pál's orchestra continued to work during Mihály's tenure, and — for instance — executed in 1715, on the Prince's name-day, *Das wahre Ebenbild Eines Vollkommenen Fürsten,* a cantata composed by Wenzel Zivilhofer who conducted the princely orchestra at that time. The libretto of this cantata is the first known piece in the long series of Esterházy librettos. Prince Mihály introduced, according to J. Hárich,* the performance of oratorios on Good-Friday for which even printed librettos were provided. It also happened that singers from Vienna performed in the castle, for instance in 1716, on the name-day of Prince Mihály's consort, Anne Margit Blandrat. The subject of their performance is unkown.

Pál Antal was only ten and Miklós seven years old when József died. It was Prince József's widow, Maria Octavia Gilleis, who superintended the education of the children and the management of the family property during nearly fifteen years. She substituted German for the Hungarian language in the princely offices as from 1721, and ordered the two boys to be taught in the German and French languages. This was, to some extent at least, the reason why the hitherto Hungarian character of the princely court was lost under the rule of Pál Antal and Miklós.

In marked contrast to his illustrious forebears, Pál Antal, instead of initiating large-scale constructions, was determined to raise the life in the palace of Kismarton to a European level. The Italian garden of the castle was reconstructed in the French style according to the plans of Louis Gervais, and considerably enlarged by abolishing the old game

* Hárich, J., Das Repertoire des Opernkapellmeisters Joseph Haydn in Eszterháza (1780—1790). Haydn-Jahrbuch. Universal Edition, Wien.

reserve. The park was adorned with stone statues carved by Jacob Schletterer, a disciple of Rafael Donner.[23]

It was during his studies at the University of Leyden that Prince Pál Antal laid the foundations of the Esterházy library. He spent much money on books and sent home a mass of material which he subsequently continued to add to. Besides historical, political, geographical and medical works he collected a great number of French works of fiction. The catalogue of his library already filled a large folio in 1738.[24]

It was likewise Prince Pál Antal who assembled the first permanent members of that orchestra which was to become so famous under Miklós the 'Magnificent', and it was he who engaged Haydn in 1761. That musical life was very active in his court is shown by still extant oratorio librettos, the music of which was composed by Gregorius Werner, conductor of the Prince's orchestra. In 1759, Prince Pál Antal sent the tenor, Carl Friberth, and the violinist Luigi Tommasini, who was to become so famous, on a study tour to Venice.[25] With a view to developing the court orchestra, the Prince started a collection of musical scores. Prince Pál Antal sacrificed vast sums for the acquisition of the masterpieces of ecclesiastical and secular music from Vienna, Dresden and Italy. The church-music manuscripts are still in the castle of Kismarton, while the opera collection, that has since become world famous, belongs now to the National Library, Budapest.

In 1756 and 1759, Prince Pál Antal had catalogues made of the musical material by Champée, a member of the French theatre in Vienna. Together with part of the Esterházy archives and library, the two catalogues were destroyed during the siege of Budapest in 1945, but their contents are known from the reconstruction made by J. Hárich.[26] As far as can be judged from the notes, the operas were never performed. The scores were deficient, the singing parts were not separately indicated, and only their instrumentation for three to six instruments was prepared (violin, flute, oboe, bassoon, viol, bass clarinet). These compositions were presumably meant to be played only for the diversion of guests at dinner time.

A development of the chorus and orchestra and the collection of scores nevertheless prepared the ground for stage music. Considering that the first theatre in the park of Kismarton owes its existence to Prince Pál Antal, his patronage of the chorus, orchestra and manuscript collection appears to have been deliberate and well-planned.

The Prince's interest in theatricals can be traced as far back as the thirties of the eighteenth century. School dramas performed by the Jesuits

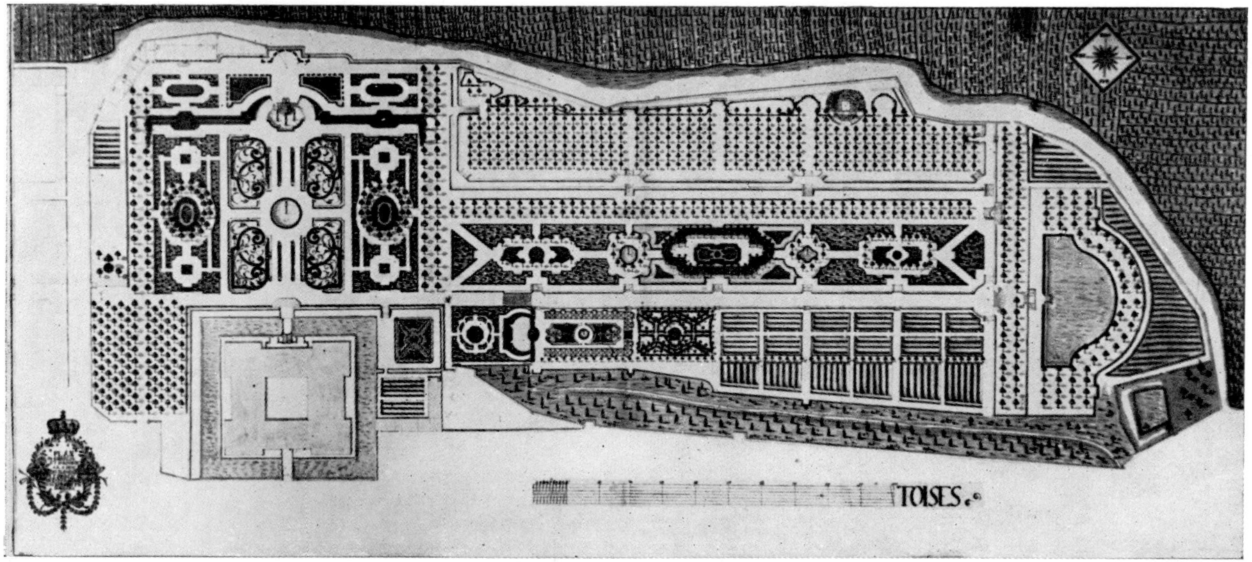


3. Louis Gervais, Plan of the French park of Kismarton, 1760

of Sopron in 1735 and 1744, respectively, presented two heroes of the Esterházys' history: Mihály who fell on the ramparts of Buda, and Lajos who showed his mettle at the siege of Győr.[27] These performances and, no doubt, others as well, were attended by Prince Pál Antal and — like Palatine Pál before him — he, too, may have lent his orchestra for these theatricals. Another proof of his interest in matters theatrical is the fact that he brought opera librettos for his library when returning from France and Italy.[28]

The first theatrical document of Prince Pál Antal's own court dates from 1749. According to a bill presented by G. Maria Quaglio on 6th August, 1749, he executed *Theater Mahlerey* for the fireworks of 4th August, and received money to cover the expenses of a lighting apparatus and firework machinery (spese della Machina d'illuminazione e Jiuoco artificiato). The scene of the presentation was, according to the bill, the place 'near the so-called Paris mill' (bei der so genannten Paris Mihl), situated south of the castle outside the park. G. M. Quaglio, described as a painter in the document entitling him to draw 250 florins[29] for his work but indicated as an engineer in his signature on the receipt, came from an illustrious theatrical dynasty. Carlo Quaglio was employed at Eszterháza in 1761, while other members of the family worked in Vienna and Munich as well-known scenewrights.

Quaglio's bill does not offer sufficient evidence for us to decide whether, apart from the spectacles presented near the 'Paris mill', other prose or musical performances were given at the court of Kismarton during this epoch. The events of the next decade show in any case that the time for such performances was ripe.

Heading an imperial delegation as Envoy Extraordinary, Prince Pál Antal went to Naples on 17th October 1750. On 13th May of the next year, the birthday of Maria Theresa, he had a cantata, *Gli orti esperidi*, composed by Niccolo Conforti to the libretto of Metastasio, performed, while another cantata, *Endimione*, composed by Niccolo Conti likewise to the libretto of Metastasio, was executed on 26th June, on the occasion of his official entrance to Naples.[30]

His experiences in Italy, and the opera performances enjoyed in Naples and Rome in particular, may have ripened the Prince's resolution to introduce stage music into his own court. It was on 22nd April 1755, Prince Pál Antal's birthday, that the first musical work was performed at Kismarton, presumably with the participation of singers from Vienna. The libretto contained four leaves and bore the following title: 'Ecloga pastorale da Cantarsi in occasione del Giorno Natalizio di Sua Altezza il

Sig$^{r}$ Principe Esterhazi . . . La poesia è del Sig. Ab$^{e}$ Gio. Claudio Pasquini. La musica, del Sig. Francesco Maggiore'. An ensemble of eleven members under the leadership of Giovanni Francesco Crosa gave guest performances at Kismarton between the 16th and 23rd July of the next year. While offering some information about the accommodation of the ensemble, the document concerning this guest tour says nothing of the programme.

Documents regarding the construction, in 1761, of a 'new theatre' or stage (neues Theatrum) contain[31] two references to a certain 'old theatre' which may have meant the stage in the castle ('wegen dem Neu und alten Theatro'; 'Tagwerk bey ausbesserung des alten Theatri') of which nothing is known to us. Since it is not indicated in a plan of the park in 1760, it is quite possible that this, too, was inside the conservatory.

Presumably, it was in this 'old theatre' or on this 'old stage' that the ensemble of Giovanni Francesco Crosa acted. No further records concerning new performances until 1762 are available but it is to be supposed that the 'old theatre' was not always empty during the summer seasons. The fireworks, first presented in 1749 near the 'Paris mill', seem to have become customary, for Christian Koepp was entrusted with the repair of the firework scenery of the 'hochfürstliche Pariser Mühl' in 1761, i. e. twelve years after the original performance.[32]

*

Theatrical and musical life at the court of Kismarton developed very rapidly from 1761.

The engagement of Josef Haydn as assistant conductor must be regarded as the cardinal point of this development. That the opera performances of the princely court rose to European fame was due to him above all.

Although Haydn's contract, signed on 1st May 1761, contains no reference to the theatrical affairs of the Prince's court, it is nevertheless a significant document which throws light on the severe formalities of court life at Kismarton and the possibilities that were open to Haydn, the new conductor. It demanded full compliance and utmost loyalty from Haydn to the Prince and from the musical staff towards Haydn. We learn from the contract that both Haydn and the members of the orchestra had to don full uniform prior to appearing before the Prince, and that Haydn was bound to report every morning and afternoon in the Prince's antechamber in order to receive from 'and discuss with' his master instructions concerning the orchestra. The contract refers to the advanced age of Gregorius Werner, the chief conductor, as the reason of Haydn's engagement, and — except in matters of church music —

gives him a free hand in the leadership of the orchestra. Availing himself of the possibilities so offered, Haydn lost no time in amusing the princely court with, in addition to his many other compositions, comic operas.

Besides the engagement of the new conductor, another significant event in the history of the Esterházy court theatres was that, a month after Haydn's engagement, Prince Pál Antal began the construction of a new theatre in the huge conservatory of the park[33] and gave orders for the restoration of the 'old theatre' and the 'Paris mill'.

Apart from numerous Viennese and local joiners, locksmiths, turners, cartwrights, ropemakers and other artisans, also three painters from Vienna and one from Kismarton co-operated in the works of construction: Carlo Quaglio, Johann Gefall, Franz Purgau and J. Pögg. The latter was to remain the assistant of all scenewrights employed by the court during a number of decades.

Of all the artisans who collaborated in the works of construction Carlo Quaglio was, to our knowledge, the only theatrical expert. According to extant documents, he undertook to perform engineering work and painting. It is not impossible that he was the designer of the whole conservatory theatre or that, at least, he conducted the work of construction. This seems to be borne out by a bill drawn up by Sebastian Rössler, a locksmith and watchmaker of Kismarton, which refers to the delivery of forked cylinders, hooks, rings and iron bars: it was approved and passed ('richtig gefunden') by Quaglio's signature.[34]

As regards the arrangement of the theatre in the interior of the huge conservatory and the technical equipment of its stage, there is too little information surviving, to enable us to form any idea of its comparative size and quality. The most obvious basis of comparison is offered by the construction of the small castle-theatre at Krumlov which was erected five years later, likewise with the participation of Viennese artisans.[35]

The dates of the bills and invoices make it clear that the new theatre could not be finished before September, so that, presumably, its inauguration took place at the beginning of the next summer season, i. e. in May, 1762, by which time the Prince was dead.

# THEATRICAL LIFE AT KISMARTON
## 1762–1768

Upon the death of Pál Antal Esterházy on 18th March, 1762, his brother, Miklós, only three years the junior of the deceased Prince, succeeded to the title. During his tenure, the court of the Esterházys achieved European fame and became the most significant cultural centre of West Hungary. The celebrations held at the installation of Miklós 'the Magnificent' on 17th May constitute an event of historical importance in the annals of the Esterházy theatres. Besides a display of fireworks next to the 'Paris mill', the day was made memorable by the performance in the castle's ceremonial hall, of Haydn's first compositions written at Kismarton. There were four of them: *La marchesa Napoli*, *La vedova*, *Il Dottore* and *Il Sganarello*, presented by an Italian company. Only fragments of *La marchesa Napoli* are still extant (in the National Library, Budapest), and the roles indicated therein, Colombina, Sganarello, Pantalone, allow the conclusion that Haydn's comic opera was based on a Commedia dell'-Arte subject. The fragment mentions six performers altogether (including in addition to the above: Sra. Barbara, Leopoldo, Sra. Augusta).

The other three comic operas have disappeared without a trace and only their titles are known to musical history from Haydn's first *Entwurfkatalog*. It is rather improbable that, as regards size, they were on a level with *La Marchesa Napoli*. Not even later, when the princely opera ensemble had become very active, did Haydn compose more than a single opera buffa each year. It is in Haydn's own handwriting that the word 'opera' is prefixed to the title *La Marchesa Napoli* in the *Entwurfkatalog*, while the word 'comedie' — subsequently added to the other three titles — seems to have been written by somebody else. It can be presumed therefore that the three compositions in question were just short scenes written as intermezzi, neither is it impossible that they were 'divertissements' within *La Marchesa Napoli*.

Nothing is known to opera-history of the performers, beyond what is indicated in Pohl's notes (these unfortunately, are without any reference to sources). He mentions that, from the 12th May, Italian comedians (Welsche Komödianten) had been staying in the 'Griffin' where they remained right to the end of June.[36] It seems that these comedians belonged to that Italian ensemble which used to give performances at Pozsony at that time. We are led to this conclusion by the following facts:

On the 1st July, that is at the termination of the Italian guest performances, the Prince engaged a scenewright who also undertook that he, his wife and daughter would appear in singing parts.[37] The scenewright is referred to as Le Bon in the contract but the signature says Hieronymus Bon. This Bon cannot possibly be anyone but the director of the opera company at Pozsony; he is first mentioned in 1741 as 'Hieronymi Bon, Impresario der Wellischen Opera',[38] while — in 1759 and 1760 — he and his whole family appeared in the cast as indicated in the libretto of the operas *Leucippo* and *Don Calandrano*: Anna and Rosa Bon, and he with his original Italian name: Girolamo Bon. His recommendation of *Don Calandrano*, addressed to Károly Erdődy-Pálffy, was signed by him as painter, architect and director: 'Girolamo Bon, pittore Architetto e Direttore dell' Opera.'

Apart from name, occupation and family data, we have other proofs to show the identity of the Bon of Pozsony with the Bon of Kismarton. The cast of the *Leucippo* and the *Don Calandrano* included also two tenors: one of them, Carl Friberth, had been a member of the Esterházy chorus since 1759, the other, Leopold Dichtler, since 1763. The fact that Friberth was in a position to play a part in Bon's ensemble in 1759 and again in 1760 shows that he must have been granted leave from Kismarton during these years, and shows at the same time the resourcefulness of the little opera company.

The ensemble performing at Kismarton in May and June, 1762, i.e. immediately before the contract was concluded with the Bon family, seems, therefore, to have been this company, already more or less engaged by the Prince. It was by the members of this ensemble — strengthened by the addition of singers who had been in the Prince's service already — that Haydn's composition or compositions were performed.

The data from Kismarton and Pozsony help to fill gaps in the biography of a versatile and prominent Italian artist. As far back as 1735—6, Bon was the leader of a company of singers and dancers which toured Germany. He and his wife were engaged by the Court Theatre of St. Petersburg in 1735. No data are available about the time between 1737 and 1742, but their emergence at Pozsony seems to prove that they had spent the intervening time in Central Europe and not in Russia as used to be sup-

4. Portrait of Joseph Haydn

posed. Bon and his family were once more in St. Petersburg between 1742 and 1745. The scenery for the operas *La clemenza di Tito* and *Scipione* was designed by him, and his wife was engaged as singer of the Tsar's opera until 1746. After the Russian capital they also performed at Berlin, Dresden, Potsdam and Antwerp. Bon published a few compositions of his own at this time, and produced Italian operas at Frankfurt in 1754, Pergolese's *La serva padrona* among others. After a short stay at Bologna, he occupied the chair of Professor of Architecture and Perspective at the Academy of Fine Arts of Bayreuth from 1756 to 1761. This is the last biographical item hitherto recorded by literature.

Bon's appearance at Pozsony seems to show that the 'pittore Architetto' used his summer vacation for guest tours and that the loss of his tracks at Bayreuth in 1761 was no indication of his decease. The last record concerning his presence at Kismarton is a list of the musical staff from 1765 where his name occurs together with that of his daughter.[39]

Not a single piece of Girolamo Bon's original scenery has been preserved but it is known that his most beautiful scenes represented groves dotted with ruins, in the neo-classical style. His important position in St. Petersburg and Potsdam, as also his professorship at the Academy of Fine Arts at Bayreuth make it obvious that Bon must have been a great master.

His Arcadian groves of ruins, his professorship of perspective and his Kismarton contract of 1762 inevitably give rise to the idea that the set-pieces which are in the custody of the National Library, Budapest and labelled as the works of an unknown painter may have been by Girolamo Bon. Together with the works of Carl Maurer, a later scenewright of the princely family, the two paintings in question were transferred in 1949 to the Department of Theatrical History of the library from Rudolf Bedő's collection. Both bear the date 1762. The delicately coloured designs reveal the work of a well-trained hand; the scene which represents a long vista in perspective could serve as the most typical example of perspective representation, while the Arcadian scene showing a grove with ruins reminds the spectator of descriptions of Bon's best works. Even if these two pieces were not meant for Kismarton, it can be taken for granted that Haydn's first compositions, staged at Kismarton, were played in scenic surroundings designed by Bon.

The emoluments of the Bon family consisted of an annual salary of 600 florins and full board. Considering that Haydn, the conductor, was hitherto receiving a yearly salary of 400 florins, the payment given to the Bons must be regarded as an indication of the esteem in which they were held.

5. Portrait of Miklós Esterházy. 1770, L. Guttenbrunn—Ch. Pechwill

The conclusion of a contract with Girolamo Bon was only the first step in that general reorganization concerning matters of art which followed the succession of Miklós 'the Magnificent'. *Instructio et Conventio Musicorum* was the title of a decree which, issued by Prince Miklós a few days afterwards (5th July 1762), regulated the duties and emoluments of the orchestra he had taken over from his predecessor. Salaries were considerably raised: most members of the orchestra were to receive 240 florins a year, while Haydn's salary was raised to 600 florins. Apart from salary in cash and emoluments in kind, every member was entitled to a new uniform every year.[40]

Unfortunately, we find in the *Instructio* no mention of services to be performed by the orchestra and the singers on the stage, although the new lord of the princely court seemed to be much addicted to stage music as was shown within half a year by those famous celebrations and feasts which inspired Bessenyei to write his well-known epic poem.

To celebrate the wedding of his son Antal with Countess Maria Theresa Erdődy, Miklós Esterházy arranged a series of festivities in the castle of Kismarton which started on 10th January 1763, and lasted three days. It was on this occasion that Haydn's first larger composition for the stage, *Acide*, was performed. The libretto, printed for this occasion, includes the cast which shows that the Prince did not engage a separate opera ensemble and that, as was to be the rule, his own permanent staff of singers had to comply with the task. The choir of Kismarton consisted at this time of six members all in all, five of whom had to appear in the *Acide*.

The *Wiener Diarium* published a report on the festivities.[41] The first day began with a solemn service in the church, after which different open-air spectacles were given for the amusement of the people. The performance of *Acide* was fixed for the time after lunch. The members of the orchestra appeared at the performance in dark red, gold-laced gala uniform. A ball in the richly decorated ceremonial hall of the palace concluded the first day. A great banquet, various entertainments and a fancydress ball in the evening were the items of the second day, while a comic opera (the report does not say which) was performed on the third.

The programme of this first series of festivities was to become typical for all subsequent arrangements in the court of Miklós Esterházy. Visits of distinguished guests or family feasts were always celebrated by a rich variety of amusements lasting a number of days. Opera performances, banquets, shooting parties and fancy-dress balls were invariably supplemented by the appearance of the 'people', i.e. the domestic staff and the

6. Scene designed by Girolamo Bon (?), 1762

inhabitants of the surrounding villages. They were regaled with plentiful food and drink near the castle and entertained by strolling players who performed their tricks in booths erected in the park. The spectacle of the dancing and carousing people, dressed in their Sunday best, constituted a permanent item of the amusements offered by Miklós 'the Magnificent' to his guests.

*

Miklós Esterházy travelled to Frankfurt-on-Main at the beginning of 1764 to represent the Bohemian Elector on the 3rd April, at the coronation of Archduke Joseph, Maria Theresa's son, as Roman Emperor. Like the other delegates, Prince Miklós arranged splendid illuminations in honour of the occasion, and in addition regaled the gaping citizens with food and drink. Goethe, fifteen years old at that time, stood among the marvelling citizens, and remembered long afterwards the spectacle presented by Miklós Esterházy. Commenting upon it when recalling childhood memories in the *Dichtung und Wahrheit* he describes the admiration aroused by the various dazzling shows and the wonderfully lighted edifices, all the spectacles presented by the delegates who were vying to outdo one another. It seems that Esterházy succeeded in excelling all his rivals. The young Goethe and his companions were charmed by the inventiveness of the Prince and the manner in which he presented his show. Goethe and his youthful followers strolled about the whole town but were glad to come back to Prince Esterházy's 'fairyland'. Wishing to celebrate the day in an adequate manner, the Prince neglected his own unfavourably situated quarters, and adorned the long avenue of linden trees in the Rossmarkt with a colourfully illuminated portal at the entrance and with sumptuous decorations at its other end. The whole garden was lit up with lamps. There were lighted pyramids and spheres on transparent pedestals among the trees. Hanging lamps were suspended from sparkling garlands running from tree to tree. Bread and sausages were distributed at several places, nor was the host less lavish in offering wine to the passers-by. Goethe walked to and fro, accompanied by Gretchen, and felt as if he were in the Elysian fields where crystal cups could be plucked from the trees which are instantly filled with the desired wine, and where, from the trees fruit could be shaken which would turn into any desired delicacy. It is in this vein that Goethe commemorates the day in Book 5, Part 1, of the *Dichtung und Wahrheit.* Not only the splendid sights but also the person of the Prince himself made a deep impression on the mind of the young Goethe. Prince Miklós is described in the

7. Scene designed by Girolamo Bon (?), 1762

*Dichtung und Wahrheit* as a man of good, though not high, stature, vivid, dignified and noble, without any trace of coldness or pride who, reminding Goethe of Marshal Broglio, seemed especially attractive to the youthful poet.

The first two festivities arranged by Miklós Esterházy showed that spectacular events were to play a great part in his household. His lavish extravagance in all things augured the establishment of a court life that promised to be more luxurious than that under any of his predecessors. Each of the Palatines Miklós and Pál had an old castle reconstructed, Fraknó by the former and Kismarton by the other. Prince Miklós created a most magnificent and lordly residence to replace that hunting seat which had been built in 1720 under the guidance of Anton Erhard Martinelli and contained twenty rooms and two ceremonial halls.

The works of construction started in the fifties already under the supervision of Prince Miklós though still in Prince Pál Antal's lifetime, but most of the work was finished after the latter's death. We shall have occasion to give a detailed description of the new castle later in this book, but here we shall content ourselves with pointing to the almost symbolic similarity between the establishment of the palace of Versailles and that of the 'Hungarian Versailles'.

Versailles was built on the gentle slope of an otherwise flat woodland and moorland near Paris. The first building, a small hunting lodge, had been erected in 1624 for the convenience of Louis XIII and, according to Saint-Simon, its purpose was to save the Sovereign from having to seek accommodation in a decrepit wind-mill and resting on a bed of straw. Louis XIII formed the habit of visiting this hunting seat more and more frequently: he used to relax there after military campaigns, arranged feasts in the lodge and sometimes even invited his Ministers to conferences there. When, not long afterwards, the hunting lodge became too small, its enlargement and reconstruction was taken in hand in 1630 according to the designs of Philibert Le Roy. The work of further enlargement was begun in the sixties of the seventeenth century under Louis XIV who added new buildings to the four-towered and moat-protected hunting seat finished under his predecessor and, surrounding it with a huge park, developed the place into Europe's most sumptuous royal residence.

When, a century later, Miklós 'the Magnificent' gave orders for the transformation of the hunting lodge in the water-logged forest of Süttör into a palatial residence, many people were quite as sceptical as was Colbert when Louis XIII set about the realization of his Versailles projects. However, the castle of Miklós 'the Magnificent' was shortly finished, and it was soon afterwards that the Belgian Prince Ligné — an idealistic courtier of the age, an adventurous writer and military leader in Hapsburg service — wrote of it with enthusiasm. According to him, Prince Esterházy, the Lord of the castle in the vicinity of Lake Fertő, 'the world's most beautiful lake, is destined to play the role of Hungary's Neptune who ought to launch galleons and gondolas on the lake, the shore of which should be embellished with stairs, terraces, the idyllic sight of antique temples and enlivened with grazing flocks'.[42]

*

Court life went on undisturbed at Kismarton during the construction of Eszterháza. Although no new libretto, printed for the use of the Prince, exists before 1767, musical and theatrical life is known to have suffered no interruption. We learn from a carrier's bill[43] that a 'Comique Banda' arrived from St. Pölten at Kismarton on 1st April 1765. It likewise appears from the bill that the company in question was the well-known 'Schulzische Comique Compagnie' led by Josepha Schulzin.

This ensemble had originally been created by Schulz, an excellent actor, who emerged in 1718 at Danzig, served for two decades in the court of Munich and then gave performances with his own company in many places, among others in Munich, Straubing, Freising, Regensburg, Prague, Nuremberg and Pozsony.[44] To this ensemble belonged, among others, Menninger and Marinelli who were subsequently to become famous theatre managers. On Schulz's death, his widow, thirty years old at that time, married Menninger who thus succeeded to the managership. His company also appeared in Pest in 1770.[45]

Schulz had already passed away when the company appeared at Kismarton in 1765, and it remained under the management of his young widow. Presumably, the repertoire consisted mostly of improvised plays and buffooneries. This can be inferred from the company's repertoire at Pozsony next year which is said by Karl Benyovszky to have contained very few 'regular' plays.[46] According to a letter of Josepha Schulzin, even Menninger himself was 'a brave buffoon'.[47] The performances at Kismarton lasted from the beginning of April to the end of May during which time the ensemble received a weekly salary of 100 florins and a bonus of 200 florins.

It was in the following year, 1766, that Haydn composed a new comic opera in two acts, *La Canterina*. According to its libretto, printed at Pozsony, the opera was first performed during the carnival of 1767. As the libretto reveals nothing about the place of performance, theatrical litera-

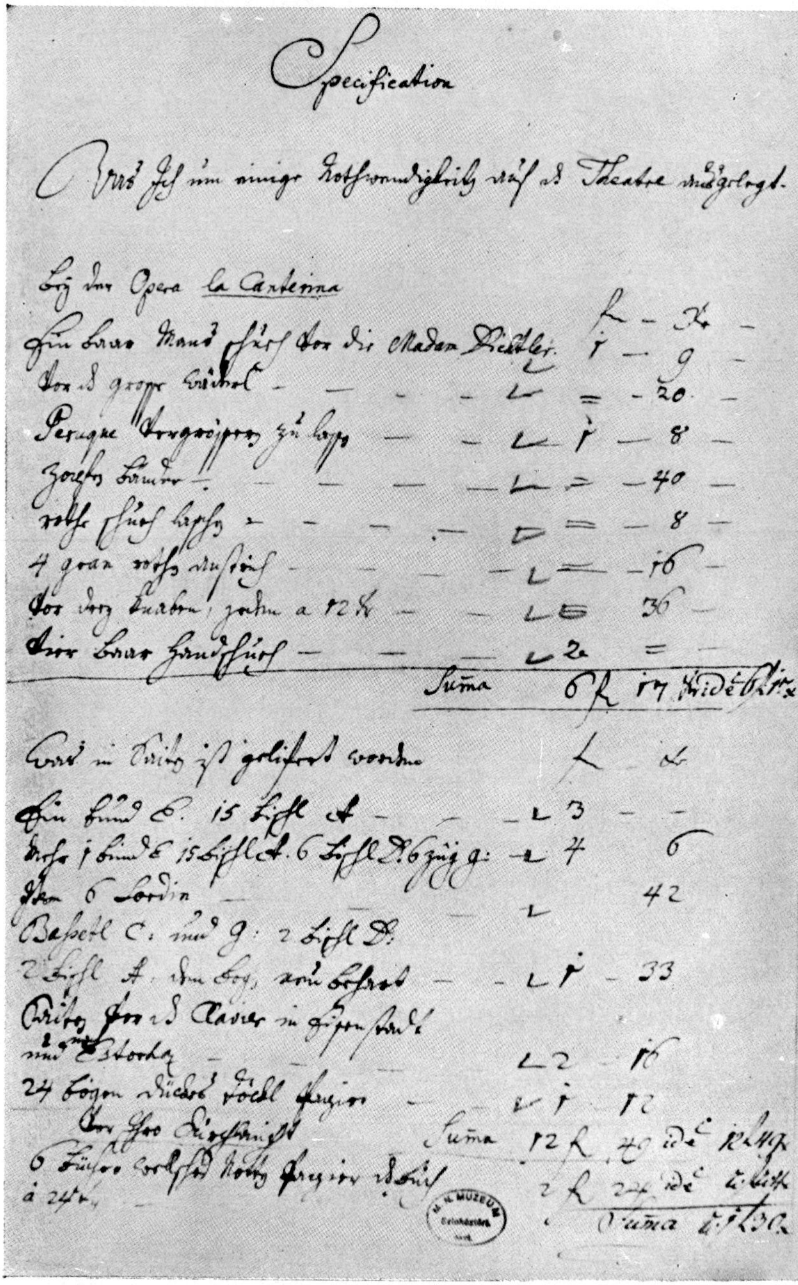
Specification

8. Haydn's statement of expenses for stage properties required for the performance of *La Canterina*, 11th September 1766

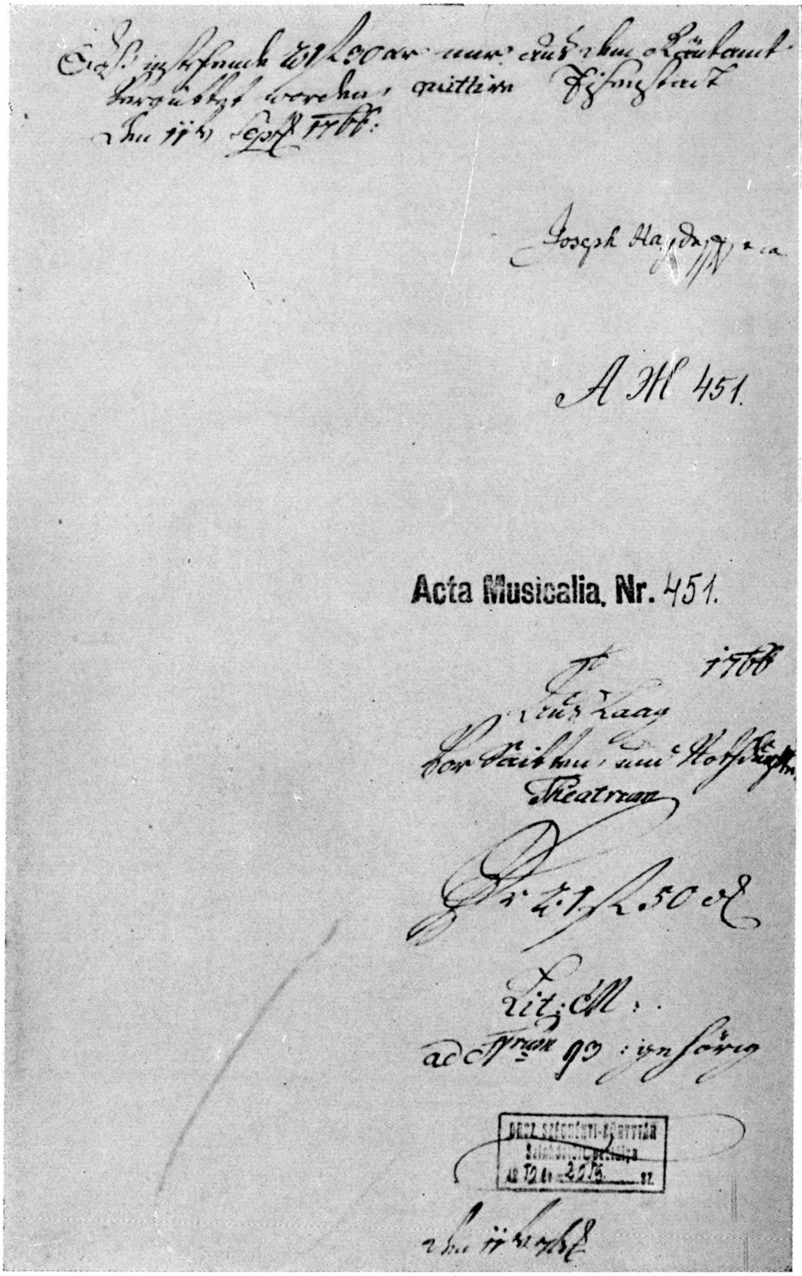


9. Haydn's statement of expenses for stage properties required for the performance of *La Canterina*, 11th September 1766

ture had to resort to conjectures. All Pohl ventures to say is that one has to deal probably with a parlour show.[48] Larsen and M. H. Scott, presumably relying on the evidence of the cast which includes the names of artists from Eszterháza, favour the supposition that the performance was given at Eszterháza. We possess two mutually supporting arguments for the elucidation of the question:

1. The libretto was printed in 1767, and, according to its front page, the opera was performed during the carnival for the entertainment of Royal personages (...rappresentata nel tempo di carnevale per divertimento delle loro Altezze Reali). Prince Miklós Esterházy had no claim to the title 'royal', and he had never, not even by mistake, been designated as such.

2. It is repeatedly mentioned in the diary of Khevenhüller-Metsch during February, 1767, that Maria Theresa with her court had visited Pozsony and spent much of her time in the company of Hungarian aristocrats such as Pálffy, Batthyány, Csáky and Esterházy. Prince Esterházy gave a concert on the 15th February in which he played his favourite instrument, the barytone. Relating to the 16th February, Khevenhüller's diary contains the following note: 'In the evening, an opera buffa was performed in the Bishop's Garden by Prince Esterházy's famous composer and conductor, Mr. Haydn, and the Prince's musicians (who may cost him some 20,000 florins a year)'.[49]

Thus, everything seems to fit in: the date (carnival, 16th February), the indication 'opera buffa', the expression 'Altezze Reali'; moreover, if the orchestra, headed by Haydn, made a trip to Pozsony for the performance of an opera, it is natural that the singers indicated by the cast should have gone also.

All these data justify the conclusion that *La Canterina* was performed at Pozsony in a building in the Bishop's Garden which used to serve theatrical purposes. It is, however, by no means sure that this was the *première* of the opera in question. A list, signed by Haydn, which tabulates the expenses of the stage requisites needed for the performance of *La Canterina* bears the date 11th September, 1766.[50] The guest performance at Pozsony must surely have been preceded by painstaking rehearsals at Kismarton, and it is hardly probable that not even a single performance of the opera should have taken place at home.

The cardinal point in the history of the princely theatre was the accomplishment and opening of the opera-house at Eszterháza in 1768. The Esterházy librettos rate as bibliographical rarities, and it is in the libretto of Haydn's new opera, *Lo speziale* — which was printed by the firm of Siess at Sopron — that Eszterháza is indicated as the place of the performance and the autumn of 1768 as its time. There exists no source to tell us whether the inauguration of the new theatre took place amidst splendid ceremonies and was fêted by special receptions. It is quite possible that the Prince wanted to await the accomplisment of all work of construction before arranging celebrations for his illustrious guests at Eszterháza. It was still from Kismarton that the singers and the members of the orchestra made a trip to Eszterháza for the performance of *Lo speziale*, and the definite removal to the new residence did not take place until 1769. This delay may have been occasioned by the fact that the 'music house', erected for the accommodation of the singers and musicians, had not been finished at the time. That the members of the chorus and orchestra were really still at Kismarton in 1768 is proved by a letter written by Haydn and dated from Kismarton 22nd December 1768: 'True, if the whole orchestra will move to Eszterháza next year . . .' The travel bill of 16th May 1769, in which Haydn lists the expenses of his trip to Pozsony for the engagement of new female singers, was still drawn up at Kismarton.[51]

Before narrating the history of the theatre of Eszterháza we will first describe the princely residence as it is known from descriptions made in the eighties of the eighteenth century, that is in the heyday of court life at Eszterháza.

# ESZTERHÁZA CASTLE, PARK AND THEATRE BUILDINGS

The names of Eszterháza's architects were long shrouded in obscurity. It is learned from a recent essay of I. Cs. Katona[52] that the construction of the castle at Süttör, originally begun under the guidance of the architect Martinelli, was continued first according to the plans of Johann Ferdinand Mödlhammer and then according to those of Melchior Hefele, and that Nicolaus Jacoby, the engineer who had prepared the engravings of the *Beschreibung* (see Ill. 26), played a certain role in the actual work of execution. Mödlhammer's plans were used for the garden façade and those of Hefele for the main front facing the court.

Available documents afford only a general idea of the pace at which the works of construction advanced. The ducal apartment of the old hunting lodge was renovated in 1754, and works of amplification were begun in the following years. Miklós 'the Magnificent' gave the half-finished castle the name of Eszterháza in 1765, and a letter he wrote in 1766 was dated from 'Schloss Eszterház'. Not more than the main building could have been finished at that time. The equipment of the castle, the erection of the subsidiary buildings and the development of the huge park still required a considerable time. Even as late as 1781, Márton Dallos remarked that 'the works are continued without interruption'.[53] Indeed, the large cascade in front of the main building, one of the ornaments of the park, was not finished until 1784. The plans of the waterfall, kept in the National Archives[54] were only prepared in 1782; the author of the *Excursion* (see Ill. 15) only saw it in the course of construction in the spring of 1784 and had to go to the sculptor's workshop to admire the allegorical groups that were to adorn the setting of the waterfall. A print made by Jacoby in 1784 for the *Beschreibung*, the most detailed description of Eszterháza, already indicates the cascade on the map of the park.

We possess very few facts concerning the progress of construction during its course of two decades. The opera house was opened in 1768, and the 'music house' must have been finished by 1769. A poem of György

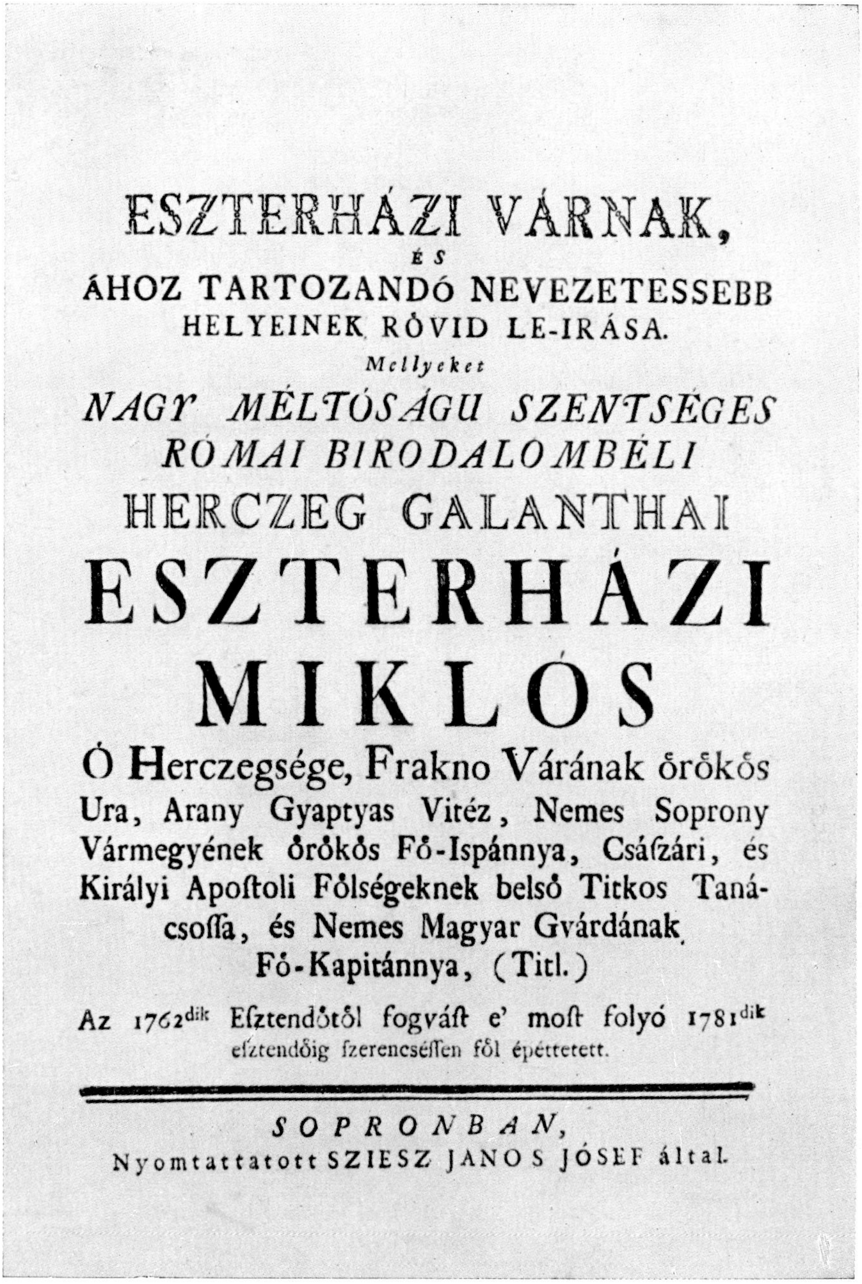
ESZTERHÁZI VÁRNAK,

ÉS

ÁHOZ TARTOZANDÓ NEVEZETESSEBB HELYEINEK RÖVID LE-IRÁSA.

Mellyeket

*NAGY MÉLTÓSÁGU SZENTSÉGES RÓMAI BIRODALOMBÉLI*

HERCZEG GALANTHAI

ESZTERHÁZI

MIKLÓS

Ő Herczegsége, Frakno Várának örökös Ura, Arany Gyaptyas Vitéz, Nemes Soprony Vármegyének örökös Fő-Ispánnya, Cſáſzári, és Királyi Apoſtoli Fölségeknek belső Titkos Tanácsoſſa, és Nemes Magyar Gvárdának Fő-Kapitánnya, (Titl.)

Az 1762dik Eſztendőtől fogváſt e' moſt folyó 1781dik eſztendőig ſzerencséſſen föl épéttetett.

*SOPRONBAN,*

Nyomtattatott SZIESZ JANOS JÓSEF által.

10. Title-page of Márton Dallos' poem

Bessenyei, written on the occasion of Prince de Rohan's visit in 1772, refers to the various 'temples' of the park. The puppet-theatre and the Bagatelle are mentioned in a French report on the Queen's visit in 1773, while it is a report on a visit of the Imperial court to Eszterháza in 1775 in which the Hermitage occurs for the first time.

Only after the completion of the great cascade does Prince Miklós seem to have regarded the construction of his new residence as finished. That this was so is substantiated by the fact that an anonymous description of Eszterháza — a very detailed one which may have been prepared upon the Prince's instruction — was published in the year 1784.

The castle, its annexes, the park, the game reserve and even the surrounding villages are all parts of a single grandiose composition. Its east-west axis is formed by the road connecting the villages Széplak and Süttör, its north-south axis is an avenue which, several miles in length, leads from the central point of the main building across the park and the game reserve to the precincts of Fertőszentmiklós. From the same central point run two avenues, one to the right and the other to the left of the said broad walk, which traverse the park and the game reserve along a length of several miles and divide, by crossing a number of smaller transverse roads, the whole plan into geometric figures. The prospect from the starting point of the three avenues, i. e. from the balcony of the palace, is bounded by a church tower at the end of each avenue.

The avenues, starting at the central point of the palace, spreading out fanwise and lost in the infinity of space; the systematic proportions of the whole area; its clear division; the trimmed alleys; the French garden in front of the main building and the symmetrical arrangement of the entire scheme of buildings cannot fail to awaken memories of Versailles.

Both the palace and the subsidiary buildings were situated on the two sides of the avenue between Süttör and Széplak. The palace was on the north side, while on the south side opposite to it, symmetrically arranged on both sides of the French garden, were the opera-house, the puppet-theatre, houses provided for the clerical staff, the stables, one more dwelling house and, finally, the 'music house' towards Széplak and the barracks towards Süttör. Uniform L-shaped buildings for the artisans of the Prince stood beyond the barracks and the 'music house' on both sides of the way.

The park was adorned with a multitude of statues, vases, fountains and a number of buildings: temples of the Sun, Diana, Fortune and Venus, the Hermitage and a Chinese pleasure house. When Maria Theresa expressed her admiration of the latter, Prince Miklós — with a

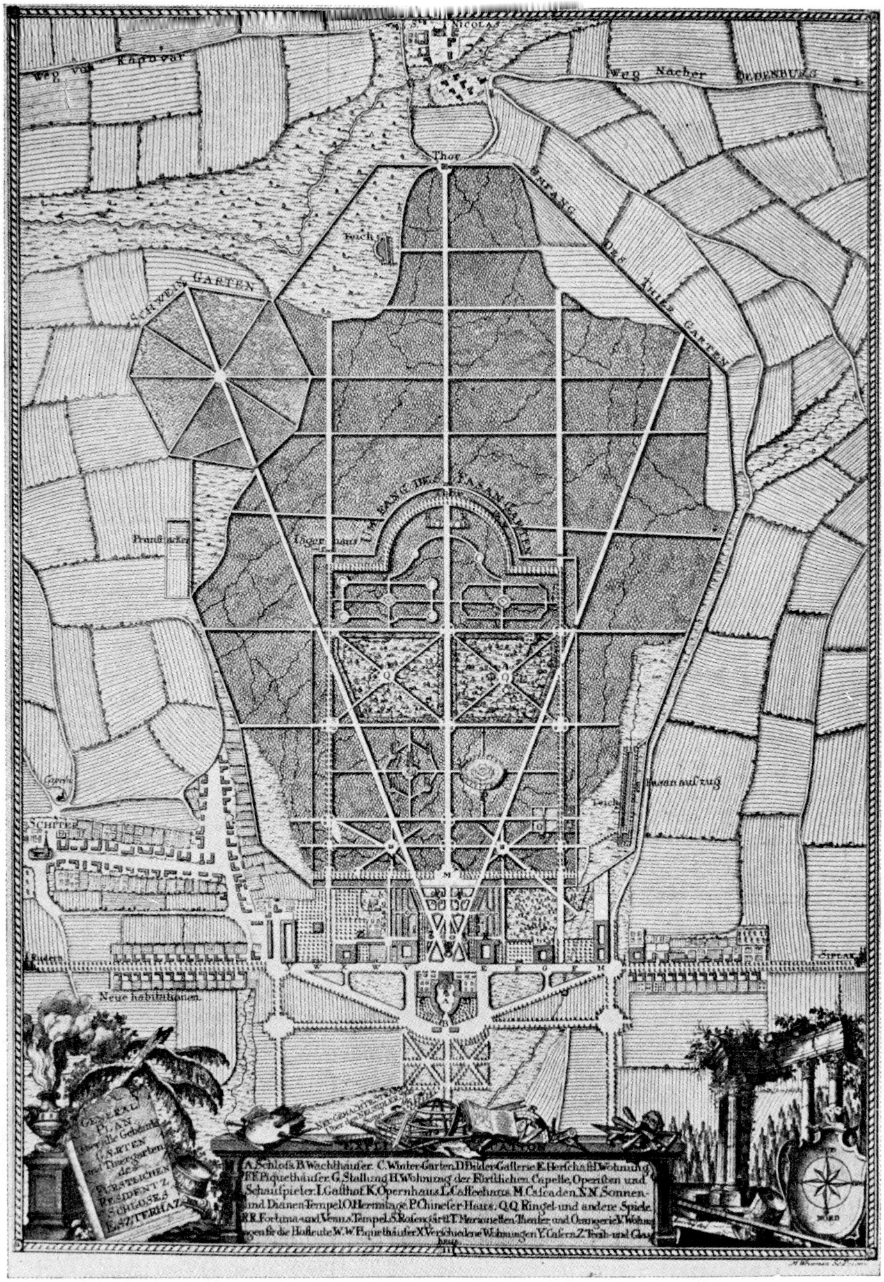


11. General plan of all buildings, garden and zoological garden of the Princely Residence, Eszterháza

lordly gesture — dropped the remark that it was just a trifle, a *bagatelle*, and it was henceforth that the building had come to be referred to as the 'Bagatelle'. The main entrance to the castle formed the northernmost point of the whole grandiose and spectacular scheme of buildings and park. A rococo gate of wrought iron gave access to the central courtyard. From each side of the gate a low colonnade curved round to meet the wings of the main building. The central part of the three storied façade was decorated by twelve half-columns reaching from the ground to the roof, with a window at every floor set between each column. The central structure was flanked by blocks of the same elevation and style but only half as wide. The two wings, each with a central porch, were of a similar design. The projecting porch and pediment at the centre of the façade were crowned by a balustraded belvedere and two curving flights of stairs running from the ground to the balcony over the porch gave access to the ceremonial hall on the first floor. The staircases had rich rococo balustrades of wrought iron, intersected with newel-posts with lamps and putti. A fountain spurting upwards from a beautiful group of statues in the middle of a round basin adorned the huge closed courtyard.

The façade of the palace toward the park was divided into a central part with eleven windows and in the balustrade of the belvedere the Esterházy coat of arms was visible, beneath which, opening from the first floor, there was an iron-railed rococo balcony resting on four Tuscan columns. To the northern and southern wings of the palace two nine-window single-floor annexes were added, one on the east and one on the west side: the picture-gallery and the conservatory.

The decoration and the furniture of the castle's hundred and twenty-six rooms were in a light rococo style. The large and dazzlingly luxurious salon of the first floor and, beneath it in the main axis of the building, the Sala Terrena were the two *pièces de résistance* in this vast series of appartments. The most beautiful quarters of the palace were the rooms used by the Prince and his Consort, the armoury, the so-called Maria Theresa room which accommodated the Queen during her stay at Eszterháza in 1773, the libraries, the concert hall, the porcelain cabinet, the chapel, the picture-gallery and the conservatory. Most of the other accommodation consisted of guest-rooms adequately fitted out for the reception of illustrious visitors.

The architectural execution and the furnishing of the castle's interior revealed the *Zeitgeist* in a tendency to accumulate costly rarities. Zorn de Bulach who visited Eszterháza as a member of Prince de Rohan's suite wrote that the Prince had all rarities sent from Paris.[55] Each of the

PROSPECT DER FÜRSTLICHEN RESIDENZ ESZTERHAZ VON DEN
HAUPT THOR GEGEN NORDEN.


12. View of the Palace from the garden and the wood southwards

two living-rooms of the Prince was embellished with ten Japanese wooden screens coated with black lacquer and adorned with paintings which had cost ten thousand florins apiece. In a room opening from the library, there were the life-sized statues of a fisherman and a fisherwoman, both composed of a special sort of shell. These had cost three thousand florins. The whole palace was crowded with objects and figurines of Chinese, Japanese and German porcelain and various chiming pieces. There were musical spinning wheels, musical chairs and a diversity of chiming clocks. Ornamental pieces made of gold, pearl and shells, paintings, tapestries, crystal chandeliers and candlesticks added to the luxury of the interior decoration.

Concerts were regularly held under the guidance of Haydn in the halls of the castle and, occasionally, even theatrical performances were given in them.

Theatrical history is especially interested in three of the buildings that stood on the south side of the way between Széplak and Süttör: the opera-house, the puppet-theatre and the so-called 'music house'.

Comparatively detailed data concerning the building of the opera house are available. J. de Fernstein's print shows its ground plan, façade, longitudinal section and a cross section each in the direction of the stage and the Prince's box, while a sketch in the National Archives shows the basement and the ground-floor plan of the central heating. This plan conforms to Fernstein's ground plan.

Only the ruins of the opera building are nowadays visible at Eszterháza and so we must rely on these plans if we want to form a picture of the original edifice. The opera-house stood between a house built for the clerical staff and a coffee-house that were on the west side of the French garden before the garden-front of the palace. The opera building had a width of about sixty and a length of more than two hundred feet.

Its façade, built in the classical style and flanked by an ornamental gate on each side, had five windows. A gallery, slightly curved at the centre and resting on double Ionic pillars, ran along the entire length of the façade, and French windows opened into the first-floor rooms. The gallery had a gilded balustrade which made a striking impression even if viewed from a distance. The façade of the first floor was divided by engaged Corinthian pillars and terminated above the cornice in a parapet before the high mansard roof: it displayed a group of trumpeting putti in the middle, was flanked by a vase on each side, and the putti seated at the flanks were linked by festoons.

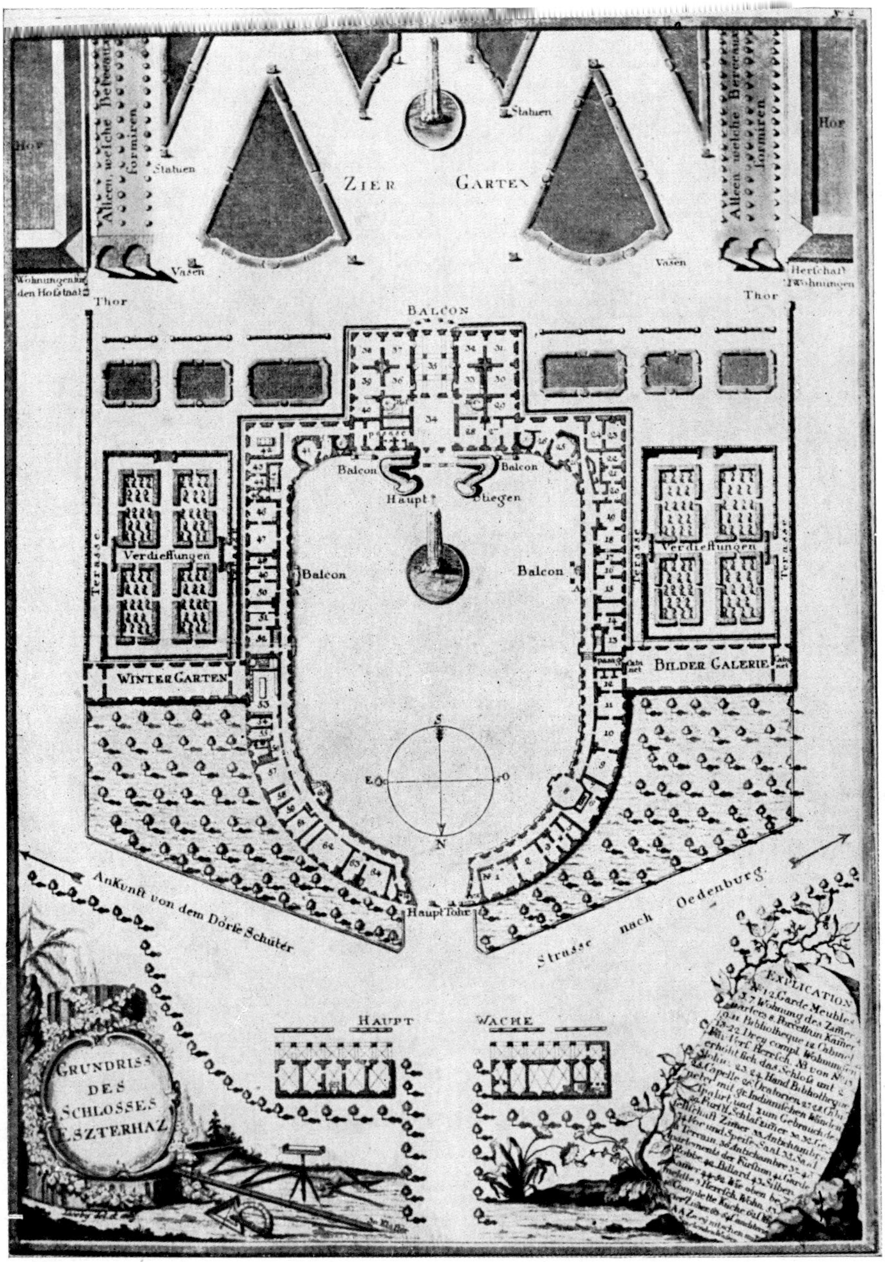


13. Plan of the Palace of Eszterháza

The interior of the building had four principal parts: the foyer, the auditorium, the stage and the wardrobe. A flight of stairs, turning at right angles, led from both sides of the comparatively small foyer to the large oval box of the Prince on the first floor, which communicated with the galleries and through them with the two proscenium boxes. Adjacent to the boxes, there were rooms — lavishly furnished with couches, mirrors, clocks, porcelains and sundry utilitarian and ornamental objects — for the convenience of guests. It was from the first floor that the family and the more distinguished guests watched the performances. The auditorium, large enough to seat an audience of about four hundred persons, was decorated in gold, red and green; it had three entrances from the foyer, while open-air flights — accessible from the ornamental gates on both sides of the façade — led from each side of the auditorium to the galleries. There were three huge windows on each of the sides between engaged Corinthian pillars, and airy allegorical frescoes adorned the ceiling of the auditorium.

The stage had an aperture of about eighty square yards and a depth of approximately sixty feet. The audience was seated in eleven rows divided by a broad aisle in the middle, and the orchestra was placed between the two stage boxes. The plan preserved in the National Archives shows six and the aforementioned print eight successively arranged frames of side scenes and hangings. According to the plan, double and even quadruple frames were used so as to be able to prepare the following scenes. Photographs of the threefold framework of the recently restored castle theatre of Krumlov[56] show this arrangement very clearly: two empty frames of slides and hangings — removable by means of casters — were behind each of the wings looking towards the aperture of the stage.

Behind the last of the diminishing frames 'suggestive of a folding camera' an exchangeable back-cloth closed the upstage, or opened up a further perspective with its painted scenery. It is pointed out in the *Beschreibung* that changes of scene could be effected in a few seconds, and that the stage was provided with lifting and sinking machinery so that gods could be slowly lowered from the clouds. Judging from the evidence of the Krumlov theatre, this operation was probably made by means of armchairs suspended from a device rolling along a longitudinal bar. The floor of the auditorium being level and the front of the stage fairly high, the stage was raked so as to give the audience a better view. Mirrored sconces provided light for the auditorium, while spiritlamps between the wings served to illuminate the stage. Beams of light coming from the wings are well observable in the print by J. de

PROSPECT NACH DEM GARTEN UND WALD GEGEN SÜDEN.

14. View of the Palace of Eszterháza from the main entrance northwards

Fernstein. Beneath the stage, towards the back on both sides, were the dressing-rooms, and behind the stage was the wardrobe with ten huge armoires for the costumes.

Four large tile stoves, fed from outside, and four other stoves in the basement, heated the auditorium: the basement stoves radiated heat through four apertures placed in the middle of the floor of the auditorium in the manner of central heating.[57]

Still another sketch of a theatre-building with the plan of the ground floor and first floor was prepared by the same hand that had designed the central heating.[58] It is not so easy to divine the purpose of this plan. If the prints of the *Beschreibung* are accepted as authentic it cannot have referred to the puppet theatre, for the plan in question shows a building with three windows whereas, actually, the building of the puppet-show has five windows as has the opera house. The most probable explanation is that the designer submitted two alternatives and that the more luxurious plan was then carried out.

The puppet theatre faces the opera building on the other side of the French garden. Its ground-plan has been lost so we have to rely on the data contained in the *Beschreibung* and the *Relation*. It has been noted that, according to a print in the *Beschreibung*, it had a façade similar to that of the opera (Prospect nach dem Garten und Wald gegen Süden). All we know of its dimensions is that, though fairly spacious, it had neither boxes nor galleries. The cave-like ground floor with the glittering surface of its walls and its lateral niches in the form of rocailles, its tiny fountains and frescoes lighted by chandeliers, must have made a strange impression. The rocaille-adorned cave of Tethys at Versailles seems to have served as its model.

The array of buildings towards Széplak beyond the opera-house terminated in the so-called music-house at the junction of the roads leading to Fertőszentmiklós and Fertőszéplak respectively. It was in this building that the members of the Esterházy orchestra lived during more than two decades. An embossed memorial tablet, made by the sculptor J. Bory and mounted on a wall of the building in 1932, honours the memory of Haydn. In addition to the musicians, the singers and the members of the theatrical companies engaged for Eszterháza were lodged in this house.

The building was two stories high, rectangular in shape and had three courtyards partly flanked by arcaded corridors, and rows of windows of different length. Its walls were plastered. Most of the arcades are now bricked up.[59]

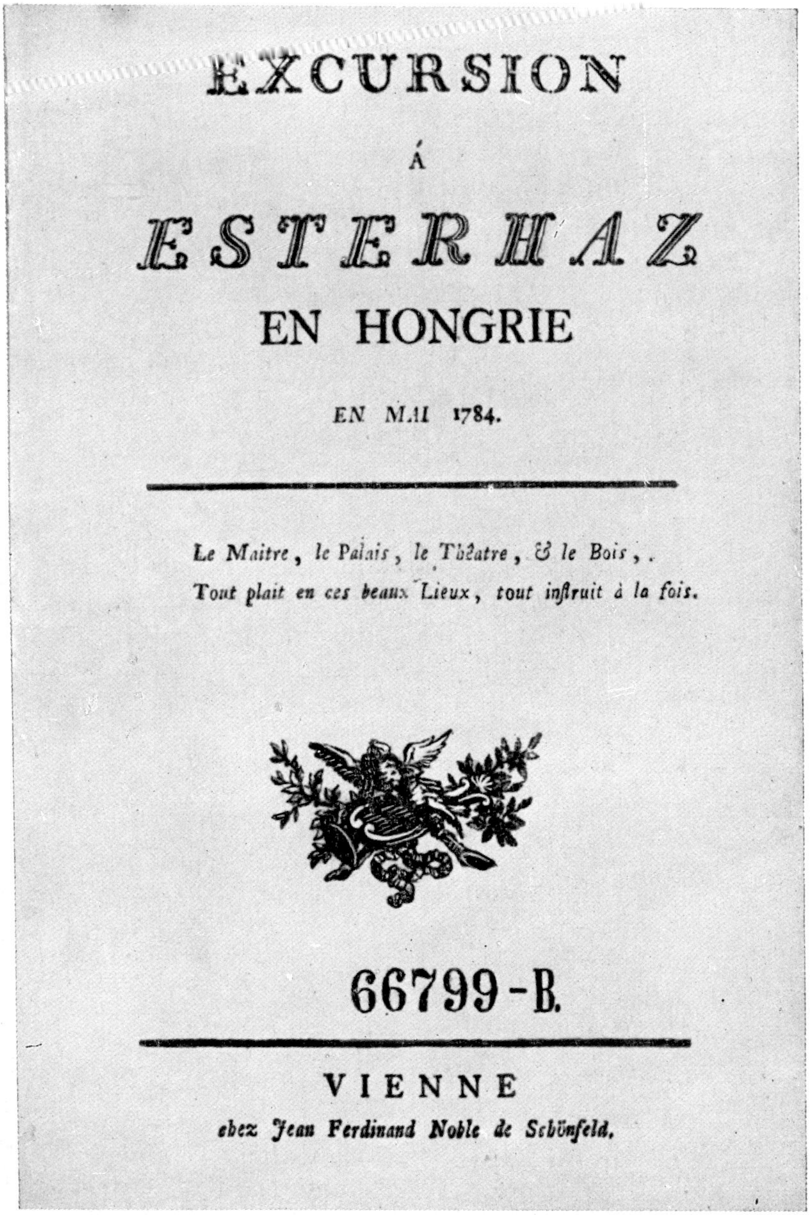

EXCURSION

Á

ESTERHAZ

EN HONGRIE

EN MAI 1784.

*Le Maitre, le Palais, le Théatre, & le Bois,*
*Tout plait en ces beaux Lieux, tout instruit à la fois.*



VIENNE

chez Jean Ferdinand Noble de Schönfeld.

15. Title-page of Eszterháza's French 'Description'

News of the construction of Eszterháza at a cost of thirteen million florins, and of its beauties and splendour soon began to spread. French, German and British travellers described it with enthusiasm and likened it to Versailles. In its brightest period, lasting two decades, it became the most important centre of aristocratic culture in West Hungary. It maintained a steady and permanent contact with the theatrical life of Hungarian, Austrian and Bohemian cities, and was — as regards artistic standards and initiative — frequently ahead of them.

*

# THEATRICAL LIFE AT ESZTERHÁZA
## 1768–1780

The first ensemble to be engaged for Eszterháza was the company of Joseph Hellmann and Friedrich Koberwein. It is from a letter, written from Brünn by the actress Catharina Rösslin on 19th January 1770, that we know of the company's presence at Eszterháza in 1769.[60] The letter contains a request of the actress asking the Prince to re-engage her for the 'Hochfürstliches Theater' in the next summer. She also informed the Prince of having left, together with her husband, the 'Hellmann-Koberweinische Compagnie' and that her new manager was Franz Passer.

The troupe of Hellmann and Koberwein played in Pozsony during the winter 1768-9 and returned there repeatedly during subsequent years. Therefore, if sources from Eszterháza are scanty in this respect, those from Pozsony enable us to form a notion of the company. Sources from Pozsony are, in general, important for the historian also in respect of companies engaged for Eszterháza at subsequent periods because the theatre of Pozsony used to be hired for the winter season by the same company which had played at Eszterháza during the previous summer. Hellmann and Koberwein's engagement for Eszterháza is thus the first link in that long chain of theatrical events which was to connect Pozsony and Eszterháza in years to come.

Apart from Catharina Rösslin and the two managers we know nothing of the members of the ensemble. Miss Rösslin mentions in her letter referred to above that Passer is quite as good in comic roles as Koberwein, while it is known that Hellmann, before embarking on his joint venture with Koberwein, used to be a member of Menninger's troupe. It is, therefore, quite possible that he had already performed before the Prince at Kismarton in 1765. Later, he joined Menninger's ensemble once more and became one of the pillars of the Leopoldstadt company.

At the time, the company of Hellmann and Koberwein must have been one of the best. Miss Rösslin, although having withdrawn from it, intrigued against it and joined Passer's troupe, described her new company to the Prince as being equal to (eben so stark) the ensemble of Hellmann and Koberwein. The latter is registered in the annals of Pozsony's theatrical history as the first to try to make 'regular plays' popular and to make stand against buffooneries. The company's repertoire at this time included the following plays: Schlegel: *Kanut*; Lessing: *Miss Sara Sampson*, *Minna von Barnhelm*; Voltaire: *Schottländerin*; Lillo: *Barnwell*; Gellert: *Betschwester*; Weiss: *Haushälterin. Die Freundschaft auf Probe*; Molière: *Der eingebildete Kranke*; and, in additon, some comedies of Heufeld and Hafner. Hellmann and Koberwein were in permanent contact with theatrical life abroad and maintained especially close relations with Leipzig.[61] That the performances of the company enjoyed general appreciation is borne out by the fact that it had the privilege of appearing repeatedly before Maria Theresa at Schönbrunn and Laxenburg in 1771.[62]

All these facts justify the conclusion that the ensemble of Hellmann and Koberwein was one of the best provincial companies of those times, and it is, thus, not surprising that, impressed by their first performance, the Prince was persuaded to engage them for three years.[63]

The contract was actually concluded on 31st July 1769, presumably during the company's stay at Eszterháza. The company undertook, for three years as from 1st May 1770, to 'perform, with at least fourteen appropriate and experienced persons, a comedy every day at any place and hour to be determined by him (i. e. the Prince), and to take charge of the necessary dresses and plays'.

The Prince, on the other hand, pledged himself to pay a weekly sum of a hundred florins to the two managers and to put seven rooms with heating and lighting at the company's disposal. To provide music and illumination for the performances was likewise the Prince's duty, and expenses of possible necessary trips to Vienna or Pozsony were also to be defrayed by him.

The contract fixed the theatrical season at Eszterháza as running from 1st May to 15th October every year, and contained a clause according to which the engagement could be terminated by either party giving notice four weeks before the beginning of Lent.

Notice was actually given before six months had passed. Personal differences seem to have caused the break. The documents at our disposal suggest the following conclusions.[64]

As early as October, 1769, the two managers were summoned to return the contract and their concession to the chancellery of the Prince. It appears from the protests and written explanations of Hellmann and Koberwein that disagreement arose between the two managers on the

16. Franz Gruss, plan of cascade in the park of Eszterháza, 1782

one side and the 'bonorum director', Kleinrath, on the other side regarding the distribution of the bonus of 200 florins granted at the end of the summer season; the differences of opinion were partly due to contradicting instructions and partly to the fact that the managers regarded the sum allotted to them as insufficient.

Disputes about the allocation of the bonus were further aggravated by a disagreement between Catharina Rösslin and the leaders of the company. Catharina Rösslin, allegedly the mistress of Kleinrath[65] and therefore sure of support from above, felt entitled to special treatment. Things came to a head, Catharina Rösslin quitted the company and, according to the manager, gave Kleinrath an unfavourable report on the company. The atmosphere grew so embittered that Kleinrath declared the managers to be impostors, and the contract was finally dissolved.

So it happened that next year, in 1770, Franz Passer's company and not that of Hellmann and Koberwein was engaged for Eszterháza.

The earliest particulars we know of this company in connection with Eszterháza are contained in Catharina Rösslin's letter of 19th January 1770. She informed the Prince that her new manager was the head of the ensemble that was to perform at Graz throughout the winter, and that it could go to Eszterháza soon after Easter to play there during as many months as was agreeable to the Prince. After 'placing herself, her husband and her manager at the Prince's feet', she goes on to describe the new company. First, she draws the comparison of the new ensemble with that of Hellmann and Koberwein and then continues to inform the Prince that Passer's company is in a position to perform a sufficient number of regular dramas and comedies, plays, operettas, burlesques, pantomimes and spectacular interludes. Miss Rösslin's intervention appears to have been successful: soon afterwards, Passer himself submitted a petition to the Prince,[66] and a contract was concluded on the 5th March.[67]

Passer, in his application, observed by way of introduction that they would behave more decently than did Hellmann and his people, and that he expected a weekly salary not of a hundred but of only eighty florins for his company of twelve members. He declared moreover that his wardrobe would be much richer than that of Hellmann and Koberwein.

The contract was drawn up on the lines of the previous one with Hellmann and Koberwein: Passer undertook to give daily performances wherever and whenever the Prince desired them, and to provide all necessary dresses and costumes. The company, like the earlier one, consisted of but twelve members, but the season was to last from the beginning

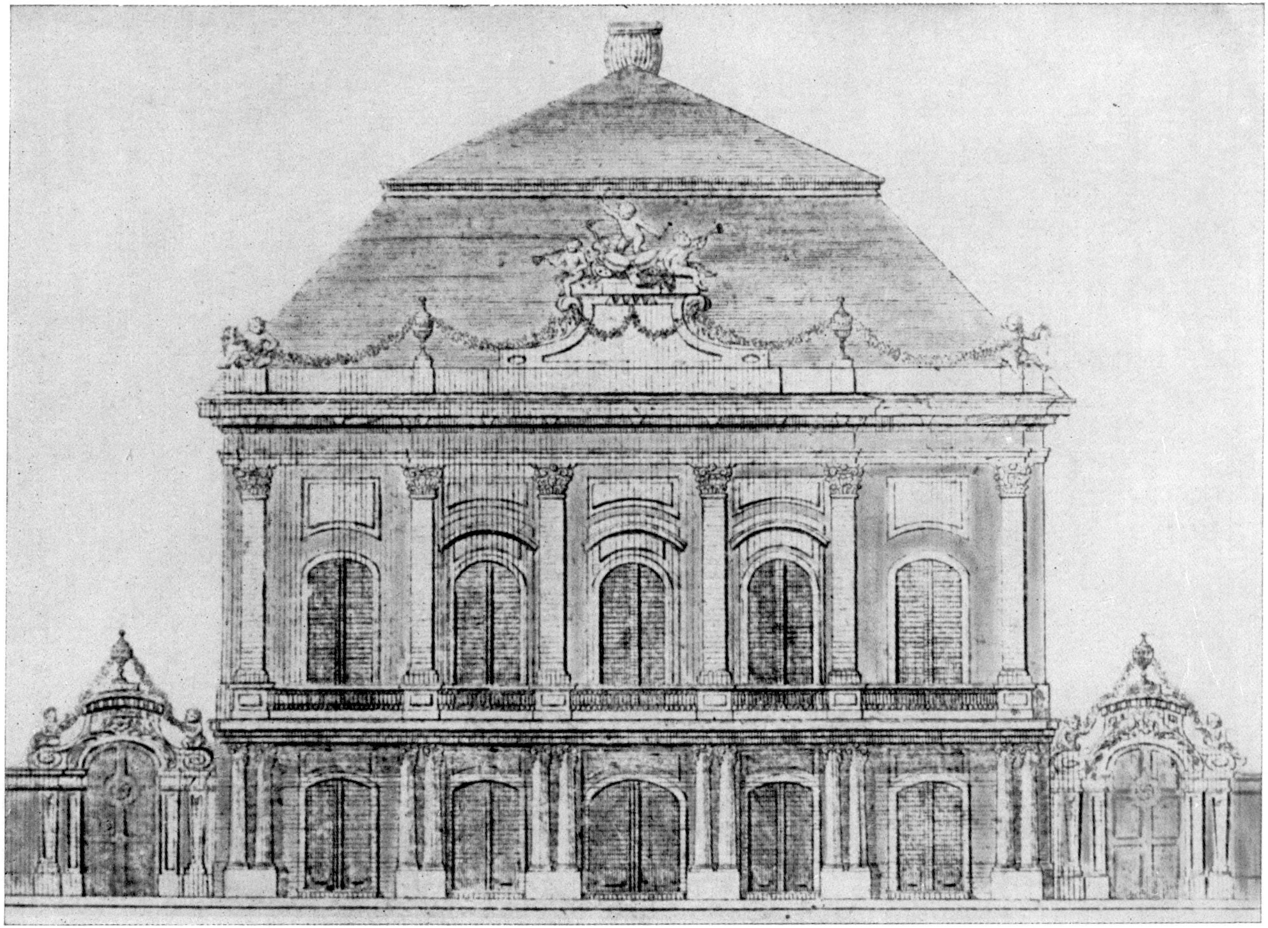

17. Princely Opera House at Eszterháza. Main façade

of May to the end of October (and not, as before to the 15th). The emoluments of the company amounted to eighty florins a week and accommodation (a total of six rooms with table and chairs), lighting and firewood. Music required for rehearsals and performances was to be provided by the Prince.

A statement, dated from the end of October, 1770, affords information about the names of the members[68] by recording the distribution of eighty ducats granted as a gift to the company. Ten persons, namely Pässerin, Rössl, Rösslin, Pärtl, Pärtlin, Scheiblin, Wanerin, Diwald, Tamaso and Heigel received five ducats each, i.e. a total of fifty ducats, while Passer came in for thirty ducats ('Prinzipal ... Reishin und her und Discretion 30 ducaten'). One of the members, Diwald, was to return later to Eszterháza as principal.

Passer's performances are recorded in literature as having contributed much to the transition from buffooneries to regular dramas. However, Benyovszky's remark[69] that Passer 'presented also occasional buffooneries in order to replenish the coffers' seems to show that the public was still much addicted to this genre.

As to the history of the company, suffice it to say that it had played at Sopron and then at Igló and Graz in April and May of the previous year, and performed once more at Sopron at the end of April 1770, where one of the performances was attended by Joseph II.

Singers permanently engaged by the Prince still had, at this time, the main task of singing in the church and at concert-like performances. Operas were rarely presented, that is, only when a new composition of Haydn had to be performed.

The daily routine of the chorus and orchestra was then interrupted by an interesting event. They performed, in March 1770, *Lo speziale*, Haydn's opera which had its *première* two years before, in the private residence of an Austrian nobleman, Gottfried Freiherr von Sumerau at Mariahilf, Hauptstrasse 12, which, at that time, was an insignificant suburb of Vienna.[70] This was the first Viennese guest performance of the Prince's chorus and orchestra.

The day of the performance was 22nd March, and it was soon followed by a concert. The first public appearance of the Esterházy orchestra which, under the conductorship of Haydn, had already earned wide renown was looked upon as a musical event of great importance: the *Wiener Diarium* published an enthusiastic report on the concert (No. 24).

This was the time which the Prince seemed to regard as appropriate for presenting his new residence and court to the aristocracy of Vienna.

18. Princely Opera House at Eszterháza. Section through the Princely Box

The first public appearance of the orchestra was followed in September by the first large-scale celebrations at Eszterháza on the occasion of the wedding of Countess Lamberg, the Prince's niece, to Count Poggi. Both the *Wiener Diarium* and the *Pressburger Zeitung* reported the event in much detail.

The solemn church ceremony began in the presence of the Prince and his Consort and a large company of guests in the palace chapel on Sunday at 5 o'clock on the 16th September. When it was over, the guests moved over to the theatre where a new opera of Haydn, *Le pescatrici*, written for the occasion, was presented by the Prince's singers and orchestra. The performers displayed, according to the similarly-worded reports of the *Wiener Diarium* and the *Pressburger Zeitung*, 'all possible skill and artistry'.

It is characteristic of the theatrical feeling of the age that, the opera over, the Prince's grenadiers marched onto the stage and presented battle scenes. The reports contain details of these scenes: excellently trained grenadiers attacked one another with all the semblance of reality, the theatre was filled with a blare of military instruments, resounding with the boom of cannons, and the whole scene was quite as good as any spectacular play. Both this occasion and the history of subsequent celebrations at the princely residence make it clear that artistic productions of high value, though of a degree which would command our admiration even today and notwithstanding the sincere admiration paid by contemporary spectators and experts, were nevertheless but solitary items in a rich programme filled with banquets, opera performances, shooting parties, fireworks, pantomimes, tattoos and concerts. A series of such celebrations, stretching over several days, may be regarded as a single pageant which had the aim of dazzling the participants by the wealth of spectacle and the accumulation of entertainments. These celebrations were true counterparts to the stupendous but not uniformly harmonious splendour of the castle and its park. As the palace contained all sorts of chambers, from the porcelain cabinet to the rooms panelled with scented wood from all over the world, so were the celebrations a veritable medley of amazing entertainments offered by the Prince to his guests that they might be enchanted with the magic of a fairyland during their stay under his roof.

The thundering military parade, not less than the opera, both had the same purpose of adding to the giddily whirling programme of festivities. This is the reason why contemporary notices do not usually record the titles of plays or operas featuring in the programme but content them-

19. Princely Opera House at Eszterháza. Section through the theatre

selves with mentioning the genre of each item so as to give a comprehensive picture of the whole pageantry.

This happened in connection with the description of the second day of the celebrations under review. The illustrious guests forgathered at 6 p.m. in the foyer of the theatre where, so we learn from the newspaper reports, 'two short German plays with inserted arias were performed by the Prince's permanent company actors amidst repeated and loud acclamations of the audience'. So we know that the performance of Passer and his troupe was favourably received but we are in the dark about what the company played.

The next part of the programme was really like a journey into wonderland: on leaving the theatre, the guests found carriages waiting to drive them through the magnificent park to a round glade amidst rich foliage; there was, so the description says, 'a splendid fountain in the middle and this splendid place was illuminated with such art and taste that one was lost in astonishment'.

And then, suddenly, peasants, both men and women, emerged from among the trees and entertained the guests with folk dances and folk songs. The report of this popular feast reminds us of the celebrations at Kismarton in 1763 and of those at Frankfurt a year afterwards: 'their merriment and high spirits contributed a good deal to the entertainment of the illustrious guests; this popular feast lasted far into the night, and a copious amount of food and drink helped to keep the merriment at a high pitch'.

Although the popular feast in the park finished at a late hour, there was still, according to the report, a full programme provided for the night. On returning to the palace, the guests partook of a sumptuous meal prepared for forty persons, and the banquet was followed by a ball which lasted till dawn. The reporter admires the great pomp, the high spirits, the wonderful illumination, the splendid orchestra, the excellent refreshments and, in general, the host's prodigal hospitality. More than four hundred persons attended the ball.

There was once again a banquet for forty guests on the third day, and the repeat performance of *Le pescatrici* was received with just as much enthusiasm as on the first occasion. A grandiose firework display in front of the palace, admired by the guests from the windows, concluded the day.

The summer season of the Eszterháza theatre still lasted a month after this three-day feast; and as soon as it was finished, preparations for the next season were begun.

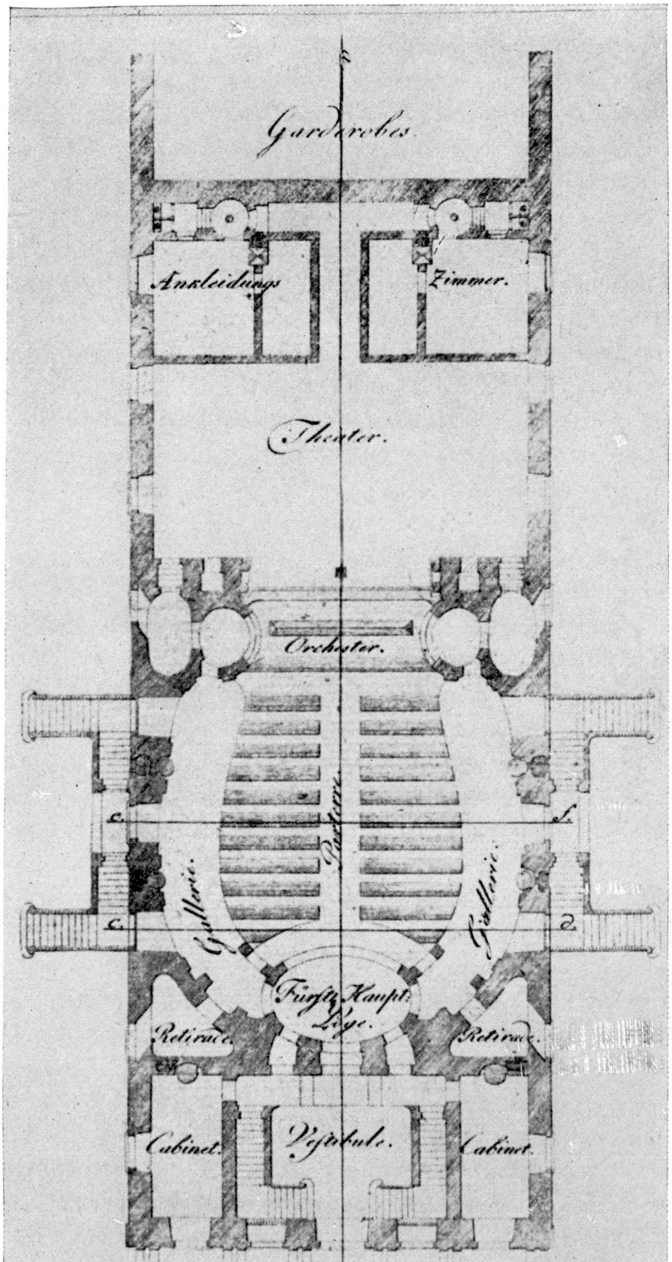


20. Princely Opera House at Eszterháza. Ground plan

Passer seems to have applied to the Prince as early as October for his re-engagement for the next summer season, since, referring to Passer's last letter, the Prince's secretary addressed a letter to him on 18th October in which the secretary informed Passer of the Prince's assent with the condition that the actors would not be less satisfactory than in the last season. The secretary requested a binding promise by return of mail.

Passer's declaration, written at Eszterháza on 31st October 1770, in which he pledged himself to re-enter the services of the Prince as from 1st May, contains important information summing up his activities at Eszterháza during six months. He mentions that the company gave performances both inside and outside the theatre (ausser Theatralischen Aufführung). This remark, in conjunction with later statements, increases the significance of the entertainments arranged in the park.

The company received a letter from Nicolaus Scheffstoss, the secretary, in which the Prince's satisfaction was expressed and which certified that the re-engagement was well deserved.

Returning from Eszterháza, Passer spent the winter 1770–71 at Graz and it was from here that he wrote a letter on 28th December 1770.[71] He informed the Prince that his performances had met with the approval not only of the whole nobility but with that of 'other visitors' as well, and that his reputation was growing from day to day. He wrote further that he would try to raise his company to a still higher level by the engagement of new members and the enlargement of the wardrobe; he requested the Prince to raise, in consideration of these efforts, the weekly salary of the company from eighty to one hundred florins. He added that he would not return to Graz for the next winter season since Count Castiglione had promised to get him to Pozsony.

Passer's next letter,[72] written on 12th January, refers to the reply of Secretary Scheffstoss who had, meantime, advised him that the Prince had given his assent to raise the company's salary. Passer, presumably in reply to a question of Scheffstoss, informs the secretary that he is to remain at Graz during Lent and four weeks after Easter as he is afraid that Sopron could not provide for his ensemble. It seems as if the number of theatre-goers had been unsatisfactory at Sopron the year before. Passer requests the Prince that, in view of his expected engagement for Pozsony, he should allow the company to terminate the season at Eszterháza on the 10th, instead of the end of, October, so as to enable Passer to take his new post at the beginning of the winter season on 15th October.

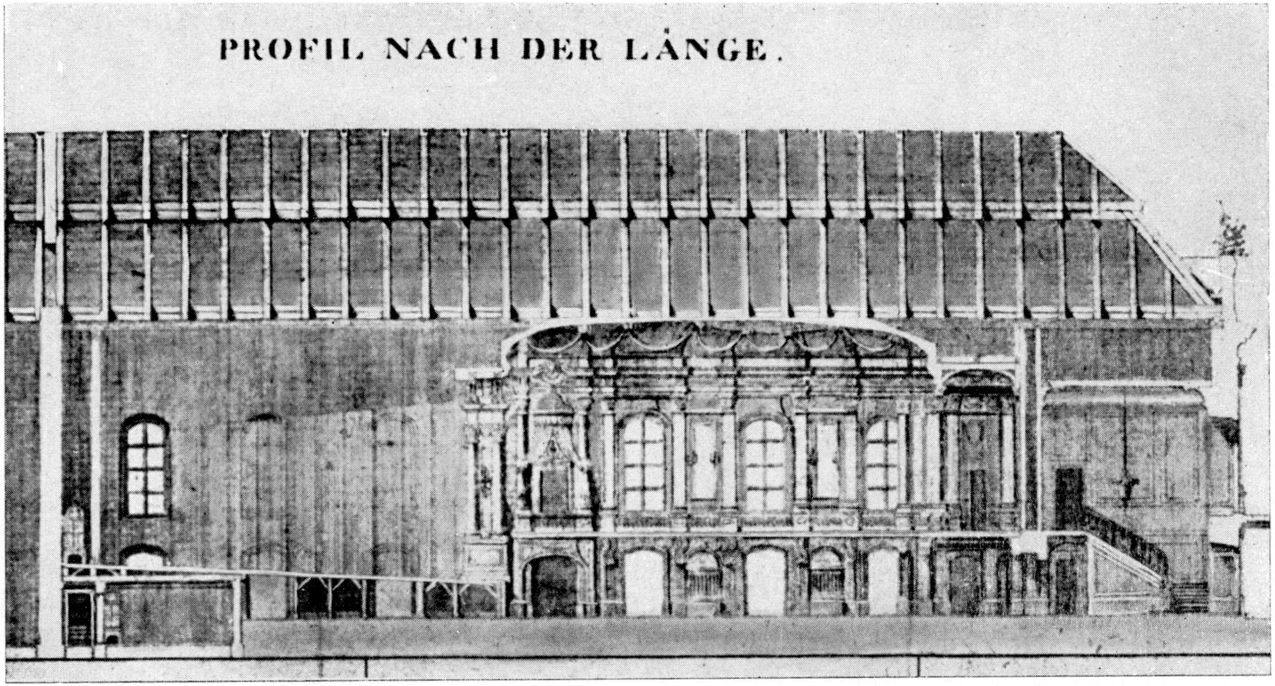


21. Princely Opera House at Eszterháza. Longitudinal section

The secretary's answer to this letter bears the date of 22nd January.[73] Scheffstoss informed Passer that he had to start his performances on the 1st of May and that a contract with a terminal date of 10th October was out of the question; the Prince was, nevertheless, inclined to assent to the departure of the company in good time if Count Castiglione was to ask for it in writing. Scheffstoss further informed Passer that seven instead of six rooms would be placed at the company's disposal and asked him to send a list of the members.

The contract, worded similarly to that of the year before, was signed by Passer on 26th January 1771.[74] It differed from the previous contract only in respect of the increased salary and the extra number of rooms and also in that the Prince had undertaken to provide not only illumination for the performances but stage hangings as well.

That the provision of stage hangings now became the Prince's duty may be due to the fact that it was at this time that a scene painter of Milanese origin, Pietro Travaglia, a disciple of the famous brothers Galliari, was engaged by the Prince for Eszterháza. The contents of Travaglia's contract are unknown, but we know his application, addressed on 8th January 1809, to the Prince's grandson, Prince Miklós II, in which Travaglia solicited the increase of his pension by one hundred florins and supported this request among others by reminding him that he had served the princely family for twenty-seven years.[75] As Travaglia was put on the retired list in 1798, he must have come to Eszterháza in 1771. All stage designs for the operas performed in the heyday of the Esterházy theatre are associated with his name. According to J. Hárich, Stefan Dorfmeister, a famous painter of Sopron, also did scene-painting work for the Prince's theatre during the year 1771.[76]

As in the year before, Passer's company received a bonus of eighty ducats after the termination of the season; the distribution of the sum was noted on the back page of the list of names from the previous year. According to the following statement, there were four married couples among the members of the ensemble:

'The comedians were awarded a premium of 80 ducats in the year 1771 as follows :

| | |
|---|---|
| Partl and wife | 12 |
| Rössl and wife | 12 |
| Simon and wife | 12 |
| Tomaso | 6 |
| Dibald | 6 |

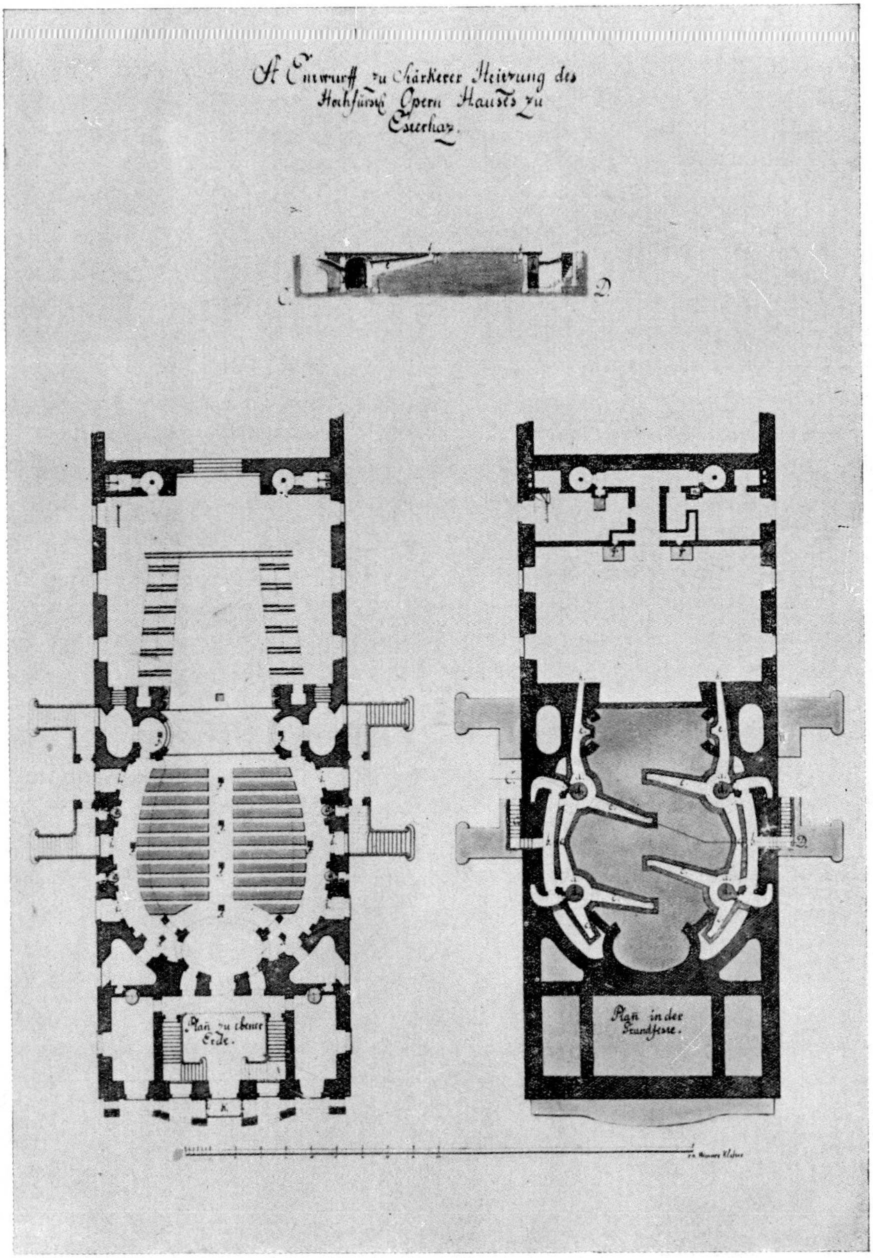


22. Project for the improved heating of the Princely Opera House at Eszterháza

| | | |
|---|---|---|
| Heigl | ........................................ | 6 |
| ——— | ........................................ | 2 |
| ———and wife | ................................ | 4 |
| Passer, the principal | .......................... | 20 |
| Total, 13 persons | .............................. | 80 |

distributed by Passer in persona.'

At the beginning of 1771, probably after the contract with Passer had been concluded, 'Comödiant Prenner', leader of the theatre company at Wiener-Neustadt, also offered, for the second time as it seems from his letter,[77] his services and wanted to present dramas, comedies, plays and operettas at Eszterháza in 1771. No other document than Prenner's letter is extant concerning this matter.

The year 1772 is very important in the history of the theatre at Eszterháza. It is in this year that we meet Carl Wahr at Eszterháza for the first time. Wahr is a significant figure in the theatrical history not only of Eszterháza but of Pest, Pozsony and Prague as well. It was also in the same year that one of the most memorable fêtes was celebrated at Eszterháza in honour of Prince de Rohan, the French Envoy Extraordinary.

Born in 1745 in St. Petersburg, Carl Wahr first appeared on the stage in 1764. He had played already with his own company at Sopron in 1770 and in Pest in the years 1771–2; he acted then for five years (1772–7) alternately at Pozsony (in the winter), and Eszterháza (in the summer). Carl Wahr's performances at Pozsony are recorded in theatrical history as the *Glanzperiode* of that theatre, and he is regarded as the pioneer of Shakespearean drama in the German language.

Carl Wahr's first contract with Prince Esterházy was concluded in Vienna on 25th January 1772.[78] Its contents do not differ from those made with his predecessors. The contract was renewed with unchanged clauses for the years 1773 and 1774; it seems that annual contracts were made from the year 1775 but only that concluded for 1776 is now available:[79] it is in no respect different from the 1773 contract. Every contract prescribed 'wenigstens zwölf convenablen gut agirenden Persohnen' although, as a matter of fact, Wahr's company always consisted of more than this number of actors. If Carl Wahr's activity is looked upon as constituting the *Glanzperiode* of the theatre of Pozsony, these five years may with even more justification be regarded as the brightest period in the history of the Esterházy theatre. Beside enjoying the

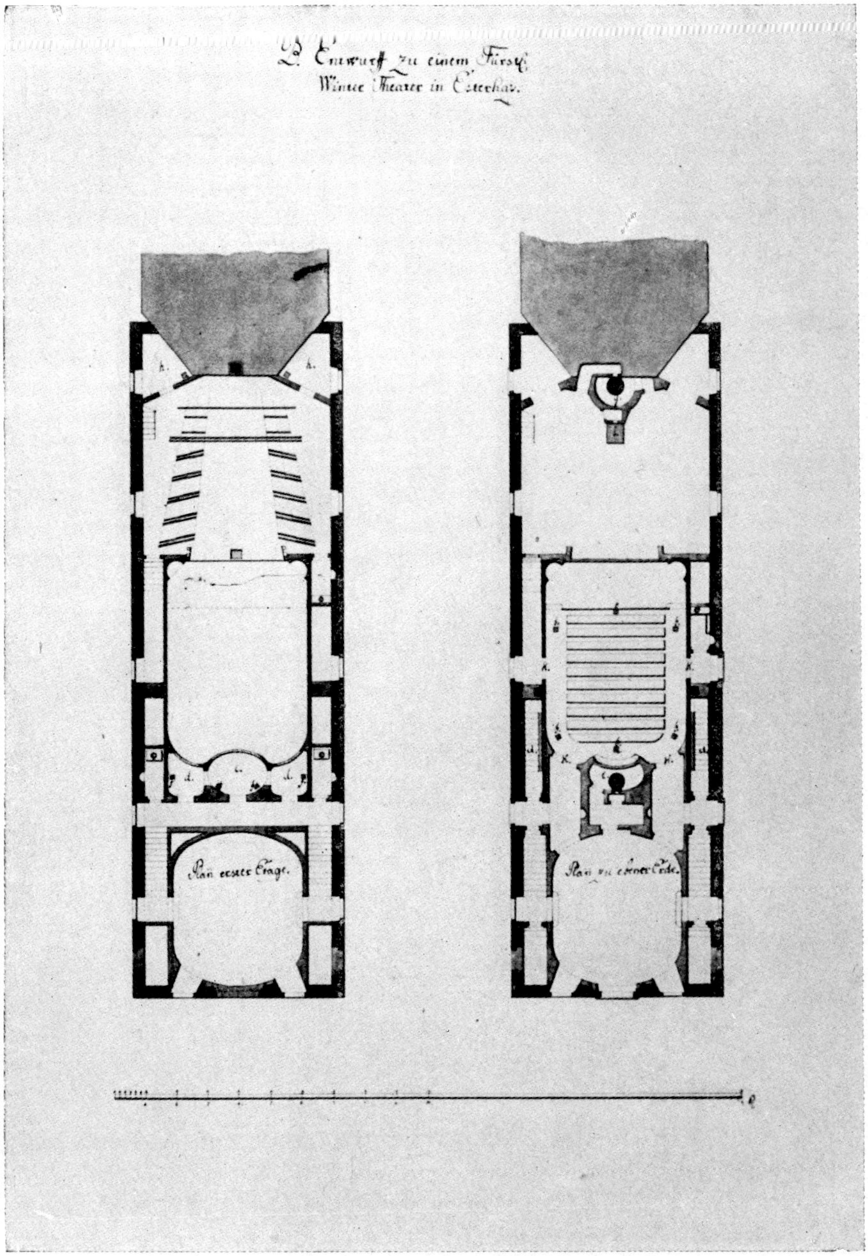


23. Project for a Princely Winter Theatre in Eszterháza

first-rate repertoire and the splendid theatrical achievements of Carl Wahr's company, Eszterháza received during this period the visits of its most distinguished guests as well. These visits afforded the Prince an opportunity of unfolding a pomp excelling all brilliant displays of the past. He employed not only the theatre company and his orchestra but also the singers from Kismarton and artists acquired from Vienna and Sopron. Haydn supplied the theatre with a number of compositions: he wrote at this time four comic operas, a few puppet plays and also incidental music for the theatrical performances. The Prince's puppet theatre was opened in this period.

Carl Wahr's appearance is recorded in the annals of the Pozsony theatre as the consummation of the work begun by Koberwein and Hellmann. This means that Wahr's ensemble performed nothing but 'regular', i.e. written, plays. 'Carl Wahr succeeded to the management of the theatre of Pozsony in November, 1773, and his presence gave the assurance that buffooneries would be suppressed thenceforward'.[80] The only play of the many performed in 1772 whose title is known to us is *Henry IV* as it happens to be mentioned in Bessenyei's poem which describes the reception of Prince de Rohan at Eszterháza.

Students concerned with the literature on Eszterháza have always interpreted the critical passage in Bessenyei's poem as a reference to Shakespeare's *Henry IV* (first so interpreted by Pohl, last by Probst) although another line of the poem makes it evident that we are witnessing a play about the French King performed in honour of the castle's French guests. The error must have been occasioned by Carl Wahr's being known as a pioneer of the Shakespeare cult. It was S.Eckhardt who resolved the problem definitively in an essay,[81] in which it was shown that the play in question was that of Collé, a fashionable playwright of the time, with the title *La partie de chasse du roi Henri IV*. This is clearly evidenced by the winter repertoire of Wahr's company at Pozsony which includes a play with the title *Die Jagdlust Heinrich des Vierten*.

The performance of the play took place in the evening of 12th July 1772, immediately after the arrival of Prince de Rohan and his party; it was, it seems from Bessenyei's poem, not enacted in the theatre but either in the Sala Terrena or the ceremonial hall on the first floor.

Apart from Bessenyei's poem we have two additional descriptions of the succession of feasts arranged in honour of the princely guest: a report published by the *Wiener Diarium* and the memoirs of a French eye-witness. The latter was Zorn de Bulach, a French nobleman, who in his capacity as a member of the French embassy in Vienna accompanied

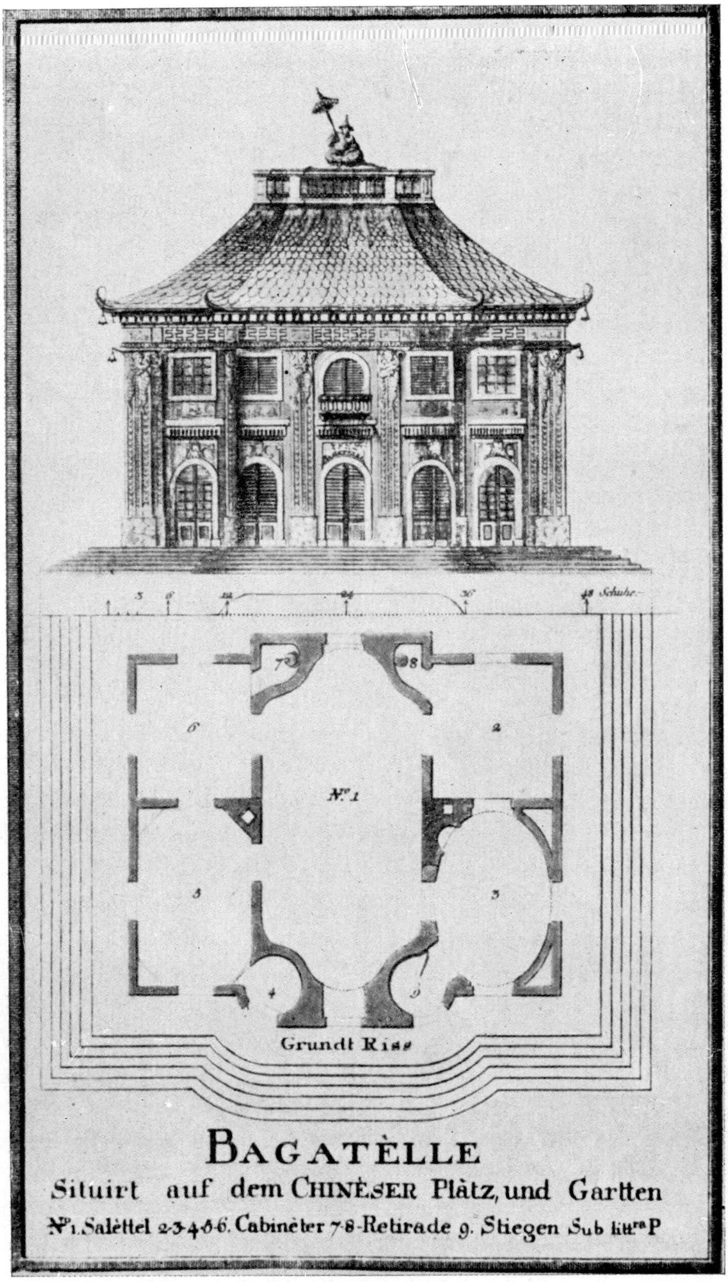


24. The Bagatelle, facing the Chinese square and garden

Prince de Rohan on his trip to Eszterháza. Zorn de Bulach, by the way, travelled over the greater part of Hungary and recorded his impressions[82] (published at Strasbourg in 1901 under the title *L'ambassade du Prince Louis de Rohan)*.

Availing ourselves of these three sources, we are able to reconstruct the celebrations arranged in honour of the foreign prince.

Miklós Esterházy seems to have attached particular importance to the visit of this illustrious guest for two reasons.

Prince de Rohan, a prominent figure of the French aristocracy, Envoy Extraordinary of the French king, subsequently Archbishop of Strasbourg and cardinal, represented in Vienna the happy-go-lucky and extravagant mode of life which was fashionable at that time in all European courts. It was he who was so gravely compromised later in the notorious affair of the Queen's necklace which, because it revealed the depravity of the French aristocracy and discredited the monarchy, helped to pave the way for the French Revolution. Prince de Rohan arranged splendid feasts, balls, fireworks and concerts in Vienna, and succeeded during the three years of his legateship in becoming a central figure of Vienna's aristocratic circles. Miklós Esterházy was, thus, now in a position to present his Gallicised court to a true representative of the original.

Esterházy's other motive was, essentially, of a political nature. Pushed into the background in matters of political leadership, Hungarian aristocrats were ambitious to prove their worth at least in the art of court life against the Austrian aristocracy. Miklós 'the Magnificent,' whose alleged motto was 'What the Emperor can do, I can do,' wished to distinguish himself in the eyes of his illustrious French guest as a prominent Hungarian nobleman.

Miklós Esterházy had been the captain of the Hungarian Bodyguard at the Court of Vienna since 1765. The Prince was fond of his guardsmen and did his best to win their sympathy. He most generously distributed his annual salary among them, and four officers took lunch with him every day. It was thus that György Bessenyei, the poet and pioneer of Hungarian Enlightenment, who joined the Bodyguard in 1765, came into close contact with the Prince. He must have regarded the invitation to Eszterháza as a great honour and was by no means reluctant to become a chronicler of the celebrations there. This was presumably in accordance with the Prince's wishes at whose expense Bessenyei's poem was later published.

Accompanied by a large retinue, Prince de Rohan left for Eszterháza on the afternoon of 12th July. This is known from Bessenyei's poem

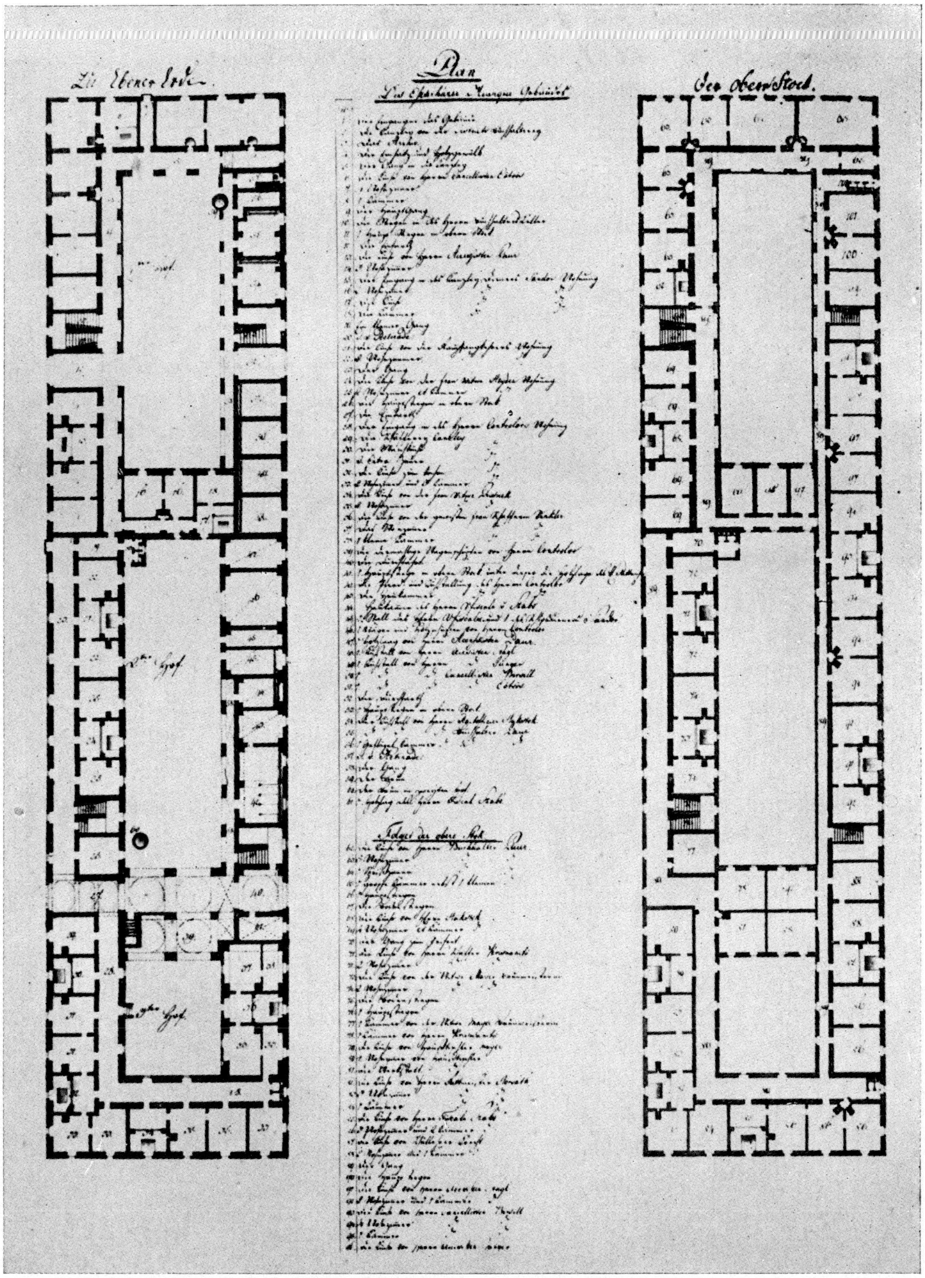


25. Ground plan of the Music House

describing how the princely guest, en route for Eszterháza, was lost in admiration of the country in the evening light. As far as we can judge from Zorn de Bulach's description, it was rather the beauty of the Esterházy Castle which captivated the French guests.

The first item of entertainment was the performance of *Henry IV*, to be followed by a ballet. Miklós Esterházy had engaged for this occasion Noverre, the Frenchman, the ballet master of the Vienna Court Theatre. Noverre, one of the most prominent artists in the history of ballet, performed, together with his own dancers, *The Judgment of Paris*, a ballet that had been presented the year before.[83]

Marguerite Delphine, the most gifted solo dancer of the Imperial Court Theatre of Vienna, was cast in the role of Venus in Noverre's ballet, and her performance at Eszterháza proved to be fatal: she contracted a cold and died a few days after her return to Vienna. The public of the capital was appalled by the untimely death of the young dancer who was only in her fifteenth year. György Bessenyei raised a monument to her memory in his poem *Delfén*. It presents the prodigy in her last role of Venus. There exist very few similar poetical analyses of choreography or such inspired descriptions of a dance performance in the history of ballet as Bessenyei's beautiful poem which, written in archaic Hungarian, cannot be adequately rendered in the English language.

The guests sat down to supper after the performance and then had the pleasure of witnessing a firework display in the park.

Next day, on the 13th, they had a shooting party which was followed by a concert and the performance of a tragedy. Its title is unknown. That the insertion of such 'serious' items in the programme had just the purpose of whetting the appetite of the revellers for the better enjoyment of merrier entertainments is well emphasized in Bessenyei's poem.

Supper was followed by a garden party. A part of the park shone in the light of torch-flames, while booths crowded with sundry bric-à-brac were erected all around. A torch-lit edifice suggested a steeple. A small stage stood in the middle of the place where 'many singers sang of love'.

Extant annual statements concerning the Kismarton period are fragmentory, so that our list is probably incomplete. It is possible that an opera was performed during this period to which reference is contained in a tailor's bill of 18th August. According to it, opera costumes were made for Mad. Friberth and Mad. Dichtler, and also for Mlle Eleonora Jäger; that for Mad. Dichtler was a costume in a burlesque role. Bartha and Somfai assume that an earlier opera was revived, maybe *Lo Speziale* or *La Canterina.*

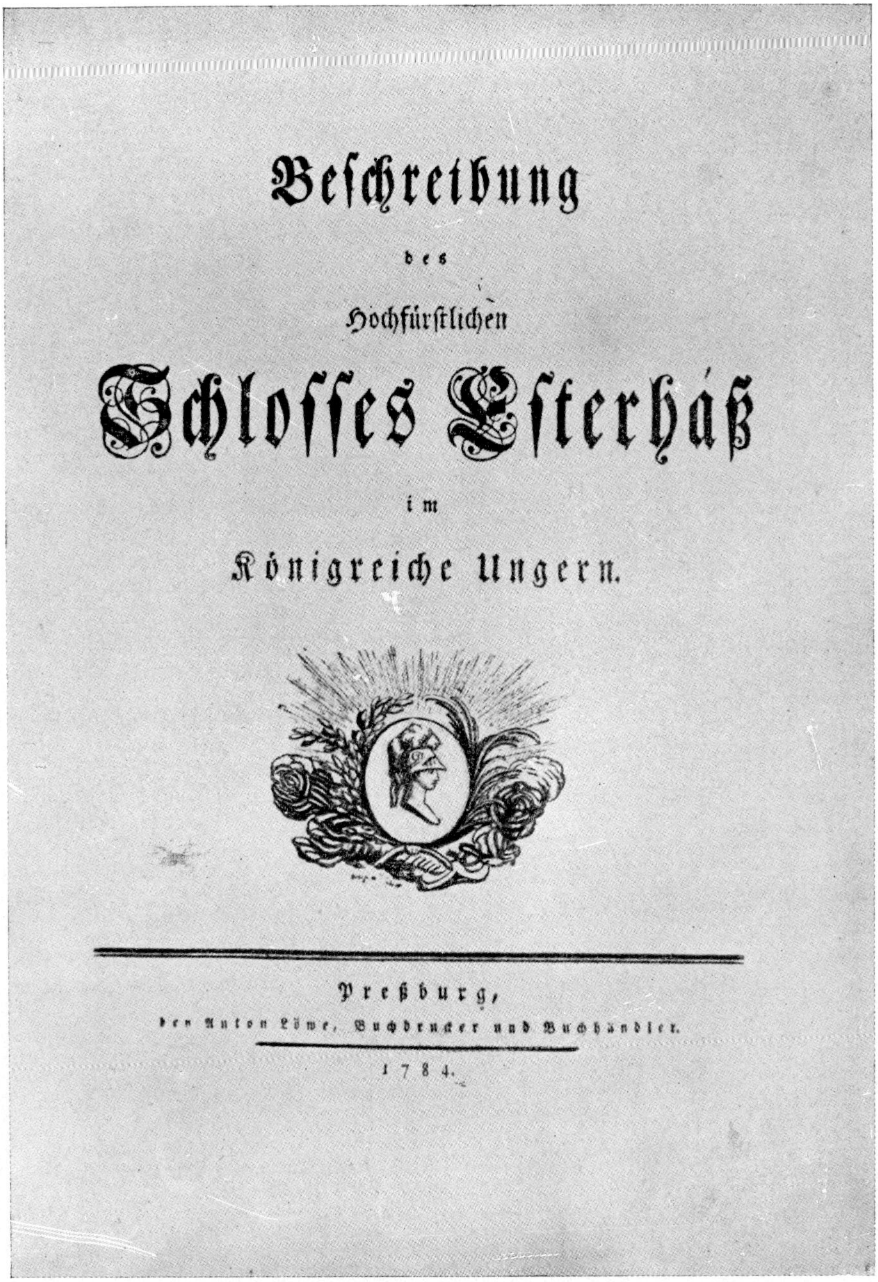

Beschreibung

des

Hochfürstlichen

Schlosses Esterháß

im

Königreiche Ungern.

Preßburg,

bey Anton Löwe, Buchdrucker und Buchhändler.

1784.

26. Title-page of Eszterháza's German 'Description'

27. Portrait of Carl Wahr. Copperplate

A fancy-dress ball in the open concluded the day.

'German Comedians' entertained the guests next afternoon, fireworks and one more fancy-dress ball in the evening. The 'German Comedians', an expression quoted from Bessenyei's poem, must have been the actors and actresses of Carl Wahr's company.

The performance of a tragedy was the order of the day on 12th July after which a popular feast began in the clearing which was illuminated by a special kind of fireworks. After having seen the splendid princely residence, the illustrious guests had to be shown the happiness of the common people also. Bessenyei's poem speaks of some two thousand peasants who, amidst infernal noise, ate, drank and caroused while cheering the Prince. It is difficult to tell whether the popular procession described in Zorn de Bulach's report took place on this or another evening. Giving a summary of the spectacles during his stay at Eszterháza (le Prince donna des fêtes et récréations de toute espèce, bals masqués, feux d'artifice, illumination magnifique, des foires), he makes especial mention of the fact that the Prince assembled more than three hundred couples of peasants: they came from each village under their own flag and accompanied by their own music. Bessenyei tells us that the fourth day, too, concluded with a fancy-dress ball.

The guests stalked deer in the game preserve during the morning of the 16th, the last day of their visit, and went wild-duck shooting on the Lake Fertő in the afternoon. Two performances were held in the evening: a comedy was first played by adult actors, presumably Wahr's people, and then another comedy was presented by child-actors. These may have been the members of Berner's famous children's ensemble which used to appear frequently in Pozsony at that time.

It can be seen that Miklós 'the Magnificent' mobilized his entire household and, not content with his own musicians, singers and actors, engaged Noverre's *corps de ballet* and probably also the children's ensemble of Berner for the celebrations arranged in honour of Prince de Rohan.

Our information about the 1773 repertoire of Carl Wahr's company is somewhat more detailed than that of the preceding year, although the available sources are not fully reliable. Although the repertoire of the season 1773–4 is included both in Karl Benyovszky's book, *Das alte Theater*, and in the *Geschichte der Schaubühne zu Pressburg*,[84] which was published in 1793 and reprinted in 1927, certain data contained in these two sources are contradictory. It is in any case probable that the major part of the facts are correct and may be regarded as applying, to a certain extent, to the previous year as well, as evidently not only newly-

28. Portrait of Sophia Körner. Copperplate

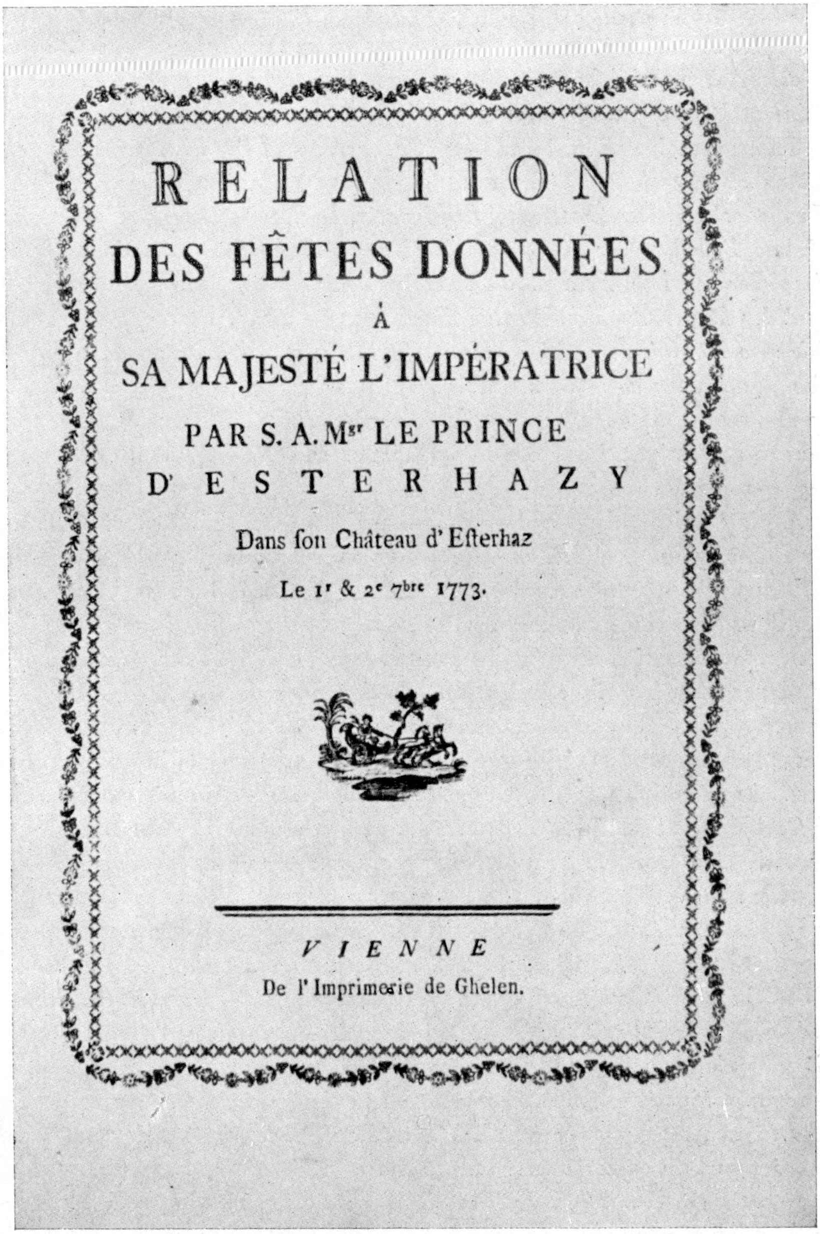

RELATION

DES FÊTES DONNÉES

À

SA MAJESTÉ L'IMPÉRATRICE

PAR S. A. M[gr] LE PRINCE

D' E S T E R H A Z Y

Dans ſon Château d'Eſterhaz

Le 1[r] & 2[e] 7[bre] 1773.

*V I E N N E*

De l'Imprimerie de Ghelen.

29. French description of Maria Theresa's visit to Eszterháza

studied plays were performed. That this is true is shown by the fact that the above-mentioned play about Henry IV, although it had already been presented in June at Eszterháza, figured also in the winter repertoire at Pozsony under the title *Die Jagdlust Heinrich des Vierten.*

The repertoire of 1773 consisted, according to the *Geschichte der Schaubühne zu Pressburg* of the following plays: *Die Hausplage, Die neueste Frauenschule, Der Zerstreute, Semiramis, Die verstorbene Ehefrau, Thamos Yungs Brueder, Der Jurist und der Bauer, Hamlet, Die Jagdlust Heinrich des Vierten, Die Feuersbrunst, Orest und Elektra, Macbeth, Der Jude und der Bauer, Amalie.* To this list should be added Pauersbach's comedy *Die zwo Königinnen* which was performed on 31st August, a day before the Queen's visit to Eszterháza[85] possibly also those plays which were presented at Pozsony during the first months of the winter season and might have been performed at Eszterháza in the preceding summer.

A play written by Gebler, *Thamos König von Egypten,* was presented at Pozsony on the 11th of December and reviewed by the *Pressburger Zeitung.* The performance was attended by Archduchess Christine and her Consort, Prince Albert; according to the report, the scenes and costumes were so rich and the incidental music so excellent that the entire audience was lost in admiration. *Medon oder die Rache des Weisen,* a comedy written by Clodius, was presented on the first day of the new year; the splendid staging of the play was again praised by the *Pressburger Zeitung* which wrote with great appreciation of the histrionic artistry of Carl Wahr and Sophie Körner: '. . . as Medon, Herr Wahr really outdid himself this time . . . Frau Körner was entrancing as always, and both of them moved many of the spectators to tears'.[86]

It was only at the end of 1774 that the *Pressburger Zeitung* devoted a report to the presentation of the *Zerstreute, Hamlet* and *Macbeth* although all of these plays are included in the list given by the *Geschichte der Schaubühne zu Pressburg* so that this information about such early data of these performances should be accepted with some reserve. Such apparent inaccuracy justifies some reserve also in connection with the presentation of *Die Feuersbrunst* for which Haydn composed the music that was to become known as the 59th Symphony.

A notice in No. 43 of the *Pressburger Zeitung,* a newspaper which had previously never given much heed to theatrical matters, throws a sharp light on the rapid success of Carl Wahr's ensemble and shows that this company reached a considerably higher artistic level than any of its predecessors. The notice says that the readers of the newspaper have

Du ſeu de son génie il anima la Danse:
Aux beaux jours de la Grèce il sut la rappeler;
Et recouvrant par lui leur antique éloquence
Les Geſtes et les Pas aprirent à parler.
Noverre.


30. Portrait of Jean Georges Noverre. Copperplate

recently shown great interest in theatrical reports and asked for their continuation.

The composition of the company in the season 1773–4 appears from a list in which the members acknowledge receipt of the bonus distributed at the conclusion of the summer season:

Note of the distribution of 100 ducats presented to the members of the theatre company

| | | | | |
|---|---|---|---|---|
| Mr. Wahr | 20 | florins | 20 | xr |
| Madame Körner | 20 | ,, | 20 | ,, |
| Körner | 20 | ,, | 20 | ,, |
| Seipp | 20 | ,, | 20 | ,, |
| Litter | 20 | ,, | 20 | ,, |
| Mrs. Litter | 20 | ,, | 20 | ,, |
| Lorenzo | 20 | ,, | 20 | ,, |
| Schimon | 20 | ,, | 20 | ,, |
| Mrs. Mauer | 20 | ,, | 20 | ,, |
| Reiner, daughter | 20 | ,, | 20 | ,, |
| Reiner, mother | 20 | ,, | 20 | ,, |
| Schultz, father | 20 | ,, | 20 | ,, |
| Schultz, mother | 20 | ,, | 20 | ,, |
| Schultz, daughter | 16 | ,, | $53^1/_3$ | ,, |
| Zappe | 25 | ,, | 20 | ,, |
| Kessel | 25 | ,, | 20 | ,, |
| Mrs. Kessel | 25 | ,, | 20 | ,, |

By order of His Grace the Prince Total 100 ducats Eszterháza, Oct. 30, 1773. (sgd) Jacob Kaufmann, Secretary.

Carl Wahr's company consisted, therefore, of seventeen members in the autumn of 1773 and included Sophia Körner, the favourite of the public in Pozsony, as also Seipp who was to win fame as the manager of the Pozsony theatre.

The first known musical event of the repertory of Eszterháza in 1773 was the *première* of Haydn's new comic opera, *L'infedeltà delusa.* It was held on the first evening of the celebrations arranged on the 26th and 27th July to honour the name-day of Princess Marie Louise, the widow of Prince Pál Antal. A report written by Rahier, the 'bonorum director', on 7th October[87] informs us that the palace and the park were illuminated after the performance of the opera and that it was followed by a fancy-dress ball at which Archduchess Christine and Prince Albert appeared unexpectedly and incognito. Another ball was held and fireworks were presented next day.

Large-scale celebrations on 1st and 2nd September, 1773, were occasioned by the visit of Maria Theresa to Eszterháza.

It is necessary to call attention here to a frequently-quoted and easily misunderstood utterance the Queen is alleged to have made. Historians of music frequently quote a saying of Maria Theresa to the effect that she made a trip to Eszterháza whenever she wanted to enjoy a good opera.[88] While it is possible that, conscious of the European fame of Haydn's music and also under the influence of her own impressions, the Queen complimented the Prince by telling him that she would henceforth come to Eszterháza whenever in need of good music, the naked historical truth is that her stay at Eszterháza on the first two days of September 1773 was the first and last visit she had ever made or was ever to make there. Her words cannot, therefore, be interpreted to mean that the Queen was a frequent guest at Eszterháza.

The Prince was preparing the Queen's reception with utmost care. Although, by this time, a sort of routine programme had been developed for the celebrations at Eszterháza, special surprises were nevertheless provided for this unusual occasion. One of the sights of the park, the 'Chinese Pleasurehouse', seems to have been finished in that year, for it is first mentioned in the descriptions of the feasts arranged in honour of the Queen. The first day's programme included a banquet, the inspection of the park, the performance of Haydn's *L'infedeltà delusa* and, as the last item, a fancy-dress ball till dawn. It was during an intermission of the ball that the Prince showed his new pleasurehouse to the Sovereign. Its walls were covered with mirrors which reflected the light of innumerable Chinese lanterns and candles and bathed the building in a veritable sea of flames.

The original purpose of the pleasurehouse was to add a specially brilliant sight to the existing ones, and it was here that the princely orchestra, conducted by Haydn, now presented a symphony and selected concert pieces to the Queen.

A special feature of the fancy-dress ball was the site chosen. Bowing to the fashion of *chinoiserie*, the Imperial Palace of Schönbrunn, too, boasted rooms crowded with Chinese works of art. These rooms have been preserved down to our own day, and it can be seen that they were small rooms. Now, according to the *Relation*, (see Ill. 29), the fancydress ball of our splendid Prince took place in a Chinese room which was about one hundred and thirty feet long and received light from eleven chandeliers with a total of six hundred candles; the members of the orchestra were clad in Chinese gala uniform.

The third novelty, namely the puppet theatre, was presented next day, on the 2nd September.

It is the *Relation*, a French description of the Queen's visit to Eszterháza, which offers the most detailed information about the interior of this theatre. The auditorium was flanked on both sides by caves domed with rockery and sea shells in accordance with the *rocaille* style that had become fashionable under Louis XV. Some of the caves were embellished with fresco paintings, others with miniature fountains, and the gurgle of water jets filled the place with a soothing murmur. The walls of the caves were coated with sparkling plasterwork which reflected the light of the chandeliers a thousandfold.

The Prince's chorus and orchestra presented a new puppet opera by Haydn in honour of Maria Theresa, *Philemon und Baucis*, a composition which has recently been revived. The report describes the performance as praiseworthily natural and emphasizes the admirable scenic arrangements. It praises the harmonious proportions of the scenery, the perfect perspective of the scenic tableaux, and goes on to describe the scenes presented on the stage. The first tableau represented a council of the Olympian gods, and it was followed in a rapid sequence by a night scene, a storm, a forest, an open plain, a church, the interior of a luxurious palace and, at last, by the panorama of the park of Eszterháza.

Also the *Pressburger Zeitung* printed reports on the celebrations and the performance of *Philemon und Baucis* in its issues of 11th and 15th September but mentioned quite different scenic tableaux. It is, besides, obvious that the paper must have confounded *Philemon und Baucis* with some other work: the description which fitted the opera appeared as a report on an insignificant musical play, while the true title of Haydn's opera was mentioned in connection with the first day's entertainments.

Both the *Pressburger Zeitung* and the *Relation* give a detailed account of a concluding scene which it would be rather difficult to imagine as forming part of *Philemon und Baucis*: surrounded by a halo, the armorial bearings of the Hapsburg dynasty appeared among the clouds. They were held by Truth, Wisdom and Gentleness, Fame was holding a crown above them and puppets clad in Hungarian costumes and representing Obedience, Devotion and Loyalty were kneeling and singing the praise of the Sovereign.

Considering the uncertainty of the sources which imply that the Hapsburg escutcheon, the tableaux of the park and scenes from *Philemon und Baucis* were presented together, one after the other, it is conceivable that these scenes formed part of a short occasional play which followed the representation, and may have borrowed the fundamental idea, of *Philemon und Baucis.*

Of course, the Empress 'deigned to applaud' the allegorical expression of homage (*Relation*: '... a daigné donner des applaudissements'), and repeatedly assured the Prince of her satisfaction.

Writing of the puppet show we must add that written evidence reveals some uncertainty regarding the beginning of the puppet shows at Eszterháza as also their duration. We give here a number of points which justify our assertion that the puppet theatre was opened in 1773:

1. Reports dealing with feasts at Eszterháza mention the puppet show in connection with the Queen's visit for the first time. It is inconceivable that the comparatively detailed descriptions of earlier entertainments would have only omitted to mention the puppet show which ranked among the most interesting features of Eszterháza.

2. The first known event in the history of this theatre is the production of *Philemon und Baucis* on 2nd September 1773.

3. Michael Ernst, member of the Prince's chorus, made a written petition at Kismarton on 3nd August 1805 in which he asked for a rise in his salary and supported his application by mentioning that he had served the princely family for thirty years and began his service as an alto singer of the puppet theatre at Eszterháza in 1773.[89]

4. Reading the *Pressburger Zeitung* as issued on 11th September, 1773, one finds two perfectly clear allusions to the fact that the puppet theatre was new at that time: 'And then the puppet opera *Philemon und Baucis* or *Jupiters Reise auf die Erd* was performed on a quite new stage.' 'Hereupon, the back part of the newly erected stage began to subside.'

The puppet show on the 2nd September was followed by a festive supper after which the Prince led the Empress through an avenue illuminated with coloured Chinese lanterns to the site of the fireworks. A painted scene was designed for the pyrotechnic performance, and the Sovereign, together with her suite, was seated on a platform facing this scenery. It is mentioned in the *Relation* that the fireworks were prepared by Rabel, the Prince's pyrotechnist.

The Queen herself started the show by igniting a fuse. The first image soaring up from a powerful mass of flames represented Hungary's heraldic bearings against an azure background, flanked on both sides by angels with spread wings and topped by the letters V.M.T. (Probably meaning 'Vivat Maria Theresa'.) The coat-of-arms remained visible a fairly long time, and, before it had disappeared, a great number of spiral and star-shaped figures were let off while a rain of gold fell from above. After a succession of beautiful fireworks the painted scene opposite the royal platform was illuminated as the 'finale' of the performance: the three-windowed façade of a towered castle emerged from the obscurity, with a cascade of flames under each of the arches; meanwhile, fires sprang up right and left, and the show finished amidst the deafening roar of bombs, subterranean mortars and other explosive material.

The company of guests then moved to a wide oval arena-like space which was surrounded by an arcade of regularly trimmed branches. A grandstand adorned with festoons of flowers was erected in the middle. The arches of the arcade were illuminated by a double line of coloured lanterns which followed the outlines of the floral architecture with great precision; each arch was crowned by an illuminated painting with allegorical figures. Transparent tableaux, illuminated from behind and imitating known paintings of van Dyck, were a pleasant novelty for the admiring spectators.

The place, with room for more than eight thousand persons, received light from more than twenty thousand Chinese lanterns. When the Queen and the court were seated on the grandstand, more than a thousand young peasant boys and girls emerged from under the arcades: they came under their own flags and, accompanied by the music of their own orchestra, danced and cheered the Queen. Besides an enumeration of the theatrical performances and other entertainments, the documents concerning the festivities in honour of the Sovereign reveal a number of noteworthy facts in connection with the preparation of these celebrations.

We learn from a bill countersigned by Haydn[90] that a bass from Sopron was engaged for the puppet opera and that he received a total fee of fifteen florins for five days; the bill further shows that Mrs. Griessler, an alto singer, and the tenor Johann Haydn, younger brother of the composer, were ordered from Kismarton to Eszterháza for eight days against a daily fee of a florin.

Two other bills[91] throw some light on the preparation of the bibliographically valuable Esterházy librettos. Two bills were presented on 14th September 1773, by Johann Joseph Siess, a printer of Sopron, who used to print most of the librettos through many decades. The same octavo-sized 'Opera Büchel' of three sheets was produced first in two hundred and then in a hundred and fifty-three copies. One encounters many bills of Siess for printing work performed in the eighties but the number of bills for bookbinding is rather limited, and none of them as detailed as that registered under No. 610/a of the *Acta Musicalia*. This document, a bill made out by Matthias Fischer — a bookbinder of Sopron — refers obviously to the binding of the librettos that had been printed by Siess and formed the subject of his bill. That this is so is borne out by the fact that both bills were paid on the 10th October and that approximately the same lots are mentioned in both cases: firstly Siess with two hundred and Fischer with two hundred and two; secondly Siess with one hundred and fifty-three and Fischer with one hundred and fifty copies. Although neither of the bills contains the title of the libretto, there can be no doubt that it must have been *L'infedeltà delusa*. As a rule, no libretto was reprinted: the opera in question was, however, first performed on 26th July to honour the name-day of the Dowager Princess, and then repeated to honour the Queen's visit on 1st September so that a new set of printed librettos seems to have been issued for this occasion. Matthias Fischer delivered the first batch on 23rd July, the second on 27th August that is, in both cases a few days prior to the beginning of the celebrations.

It emerges from the bookbinder's bill that the printed librettos had three different kinds of cover on both occasions. Six copies were bound in taffeta and fifty in gold brocade paper ('Procat Gold Papier') on both occasions.

Apart from the specimens covered with taffeta and gold brocade respectively, one hundred and forty-six and subsequently ninety copies were bound 'all' ordinaire', i.e. provided with the usual cover of coloured patterns. In addition, four of the librettos printed for the September feasts were bound in damask silk, presumably for the Empress and the most distinguished guests. The price of the ordinary binding was two kreuzer per copy, that of the gold brocade paper seven, of the taffeta thirty-six kreuzers, while each damask-silk cover cost a whole florin.

The costlier copies were probably destined for the use of the Prince, his family and the spectators seated on the first floor, while the librettos bound 'all' ordinaire' were, no doubt, distributed among the audience in the stalls.

In addition to those already mentioned, we can give further facts regarding the repertory at Eszterháza in 1773.

In his report submitted to the Prince from Kismarton,[92] Rahier, the 'bonorum director', writes that 'Georg Habentinger, the manager of the comedians here', claims the reimbursement of certain transport expenses and losses in connection with his appearance at Eszterháza. Habentinger and his company were, according to Rahier, deprived of the proceeds of four performances at Kismarton on account of two puppet shows. We know from F. Probst[93] that Johann Georg Habentinger's reputed 'Hanswurst' company spent nearly the whole year of 1773 at Kismarton.

It is improbable that Habentinger's acting at Eszterháza coincided with Maria Theresa's visit: the detailed report of the *Relation* contains no reference to Habentinger which it would surely have done otherwise. This reveals a continuity in the activities of the puppet theatre of Eszterháza.

Carl Wahr reorganized and enlarged his company in 1774. Only nine members had remained from the previous year. Lorenzo, Schimon, Mrs. Mauer, the three members of the Schultz family and Kessel together with his wife had left the company, but not less than fourteen new members were engaged to fill their places: Elisabetha Pärthl, Johann Prothke, Theresia Klientsch, the Schwarzwald family (husband, wife, daughter), the Schlezer family (also husband, wife and daughter), the Christls (a married couple), Bodingbauer, Starke and Hoffmann.

The names of the members of Wahr's new company are known to us from a list which shows the distribution of a hundred ducats granted by the Prince at the end of the season.[94] In addition to this bonus an extra premium of fifty ducats was handed over by Kaufmann, the Prince's secretary, to Carl Wahr and Sophia Körner.[95] It seems that Sophia Körner, a favourite of the public at Pozsony, had become the pet of Eszterháza as well.

The first report on the summer season at Eszterháza appeared in the *Pressburger Zeitung* on 6th July 1774. Accompanied by the Minister of Modena, 'one of Italy's most distinguished personages' arrived at Eszterháza on 30th June for a visit of two days. Although Miklós 'the Magnificent' was absent, the guest was received with due honour and ceremony. On the day of his arrival, the play *Der Triumph der Freundschaft* was presented by Carl Wahr's ensemble. A concert and a banquet followed the theatrical performance. The following day was filled with sightseeing in the palace and the park, and the guests were entertained in the evening by the performance of *L'infedeltà delusa.* Mentioning in this connection Haydn as the composer of the opera, the reporter of the *Pressburger Zeitung* adds that he has composed a piece of music for Regnard's comedy *Der Zerstreute,* played by Wahr's troupe, and that the composition is regarded by experts as a masterpiece. The music in question was to become known as Haydn's 60th Symphony under the title *Il distratto.*

The year 1774 marked a very important epoch in the theatrical history of Eszterháza: it was in this year that the dramas of Shakespeare appeared there for the first time. There is a notice on the *Geschichte der Schaubühne zu Pressburg*, a publication issued in 1793, to the effect that *Hamlet* and *Macbeth* had been represented by Carl Wahr and his company in 1773 already, while the first performance of *Hamlet* was reported by the *Pressburger Zeitung* 8th January 1774 and the second on 15th November. Among the first performances during the winter season 1774–5 at Pozsony we find *Othello* (19th November) and *Macbeth* (15th December). According to the *Geschichte der Schaubühne zu Pressburg*, *King Lear* was also represented in that same year of 1774. Knowing that Wahr's company spent the winter at Pozsony and the summer at Eszterháza, considering further that their repertoire must have been the same in both places, we can safely conclude that Shakespeare's masterpieces were played at Eszterháza in the course of the year 1774. Repertory representations of Shakespeare's dramas in Pozsony at the beginning of the winter — performances that taxed the company's skill and forces to the utmost — must surely have been preceded by careful preparations during the summer season at Eszterháza. We possess two additional data concerning the cult of Shakespeare at Eszterháza: (i) writing of Eszterháza on 26th July, the reporter of the *Pressburger Zeitung* remarked that Haydn had composed music for *Hamlet;* (ii) Christoph Seipp, a sort of permanently engaged so to speak 'house author' of Wahr's ensemble, when attacked by Wieland in the *Deutscher Merkur* for having altered *King Lear*, defended himself among other things by pointing out that his adaptation had been appreciated by Prince Esterházy himself.[96] True, the dramas *Hamlet* and *Macbeth* had been presented at Pozsony during the winter 1773–4, but it is safe to assume that Eszterháza witnessed the *premières* of both *Othello* and *King Lear*.

These *premières* mark a highly significant event in German theatrical history, since they were the first representations of *Othello* and *King Lear* in the German language. The next performance of *Othello* was that in Berlin in 1775, and *King Lear* was not represented again until the performance at Hamburg in 1778.

Apart from the matter of priority great credit is due to Carl Wahr's performances on account of the fact that the versions played by his actors were much more like Shakespeare's original text than those presented by contemporary theatres. In a period of adaptations tending to dilute Shakespearean tragedies into innocuous plays, it was Wahr who first tried to render Shakespeare's works in faithful translations. Although *Hamlet* was still presented according to the adaptations of Heufeld, a

Viennese playwright, Wahr replaced certain parts of it by passages borrowed from Wieland's translation. Likewise Wieland's translation was probably used for the representation of *Othello.* This is shown by the fact that, while Schröder, to please the audience, felt obliged to allow Desdemona to live,[97] the audience at Pozsony was most impressed by her tragic end.[98] Wahr's tendency in this respect is best illustrated by the performance of *Macbeth* on 9th March 1775, inasmuch as this was the first time when Shakespeare's tragedy was given with the complete German text of Wieland's translation.

Mrs. Körner's Desdemona and Seipp's Iago are noted by the *Pressburger Zeitung* as pre-eminent histrionic accomplishments, while the Almanac of Gotha for 1780 praises Carl Wahr as the best interpreter of Hamlet besides Schröder, Böck and Wäser.

Carl Wahr's initiative proved to be of decisive importance for Shakespeare in Hungary. It was his company which introduced Shakespeare's works to the public of Pest, and it was by actors trained in Wahr's ensemble, in particular by Seipp, who was subsequently to become manager, that Shakespeare's dramas were kept continuously running.

In addition to Shakespeare's dramas two other plays are mentioned by the *Pressburger Zeitung* 23rd November 1774: *Spleen* by Stephanie and *Adelheit von Siegmar* by Gebler, both of which had presumably been taken over from the repertoire of Eszterháza. Both plays scored great successes, and it is noted in the *Pressburger Zeitung* that the role of Siegmar was played by Wahr himself, and that Sophia Körner distinguished herself in the part of Adelheit, especially in the fourth and fifth acts. Pelzel's *Die Hausplage* was given on the 14th and *Die Liebhaber nach der Mode* on the 20th December.

Let us note one more classic play from the repertoire of the winter season of Pozsony in 1774–5, one which seems also to have been brought over from Eszterháza. It was on the 3rd December that *Clavigo,* a tragedy by 'Herr Goethe, a Doctor of Laws from Frankfurt on the Main', was performed. The critic of the *Pressburger Zeitung* again finds special words of praise in connection with the histrionic achievement of Carl Wahr and Sophia Körner: 'The interpretation of Beaumarchais (Herr Wahr) was unforgettable. It was veritably terrible to see him in Act IV when he learns of Clavigo's renewed downfall . . . ; he trembled and foamed with rage, but not stagily: he did it in a natural manner quite as truly to life as the sensitive brother must have begun to rave when seeing his family disgraced in the person of his beloved sister. And how beautifully was our Maria represented, the young girl full of love and noble pride, who, abandoned and dishonoured, sinks to an early grave!'

The statement concerning the distribution of the bonus granted at the end of the season shows the company's repeated reshuffling. It consisted now of twentyone members: Herr Wahr, Mad. Körner, Körner, Christoph Seipp, Friedrich Litter, Elisabetha Pärthl, Josepha Prothke, Johann Prothke, Theres Christl, Franz Christl, Franziska Reiner, Carolina Reiner, Cremeri, Schlezer with wife and child, Charlotte de Ochs, Pauer 'with child', Starke, Spiess.

The year 1775 is the first from which not merely the name of the members but also their parts are known. The *Theater-Almanach* of Gotha also-called *Theater-Kalender* is our source of information: it appeared every year and is now one of the most important sources regarding European theatrical history in general and that of Eszterháza in particular. It published every year the annual history of all theatres and theatrical companies of some importance which were active anywhere between Madrid and St. Petersburg. In 1775, the almanac writes about Carl Wahr's company in the following terms:

*Wahrs Theatre Company*

'It is in Hungary, at Eszterháza and Pozsony. Manager: Herr Wahr. Dramas and musical plays. Actresses: Madam Christel: smaller parts. Madam Körnerin: leading lady; peasant girls. Madam Litterin: second lovers. Madam Mauerin: old women. Mamsel Reinerin: *soubrette*. Mamsel Schlezerin: children. Madam Schwarzwald: mothers, dignified ladies. Mamsel Schwarzwald: first child parts. Actors: Herr Bodingbauer: prompter and smaller parts. Herr Brokhe: amoroso. Herr Christel: tender fathers. Herr Litter: second lovers. Herr Schlezer: insignificant parts. Herr Schwarzwald: pedants and peasants. Herr Seipp: fathers, peevish old people, character parts. Herr Wahr: leading old parts in dramas. Herr Zappe: servant. Musical director, Herr Haydn, conductor to Prince Esterházy.'

The names of Körner, Elisabetha Pärthl, Therese Klientsch, Starke and Hoffmann are not included in this list. This must have been due to insufficient information, for all those whose names figure in the statement concerning the distribution of bonuses must necessarily have played during the summer season. Mrs. Mauer, on the other hand, whose name is included in the list printed by the almanac does not figure among the recipients of premiums, and it is possible that she did not join the company until the beginning of the winter season at Pozsony.

Of the new members it is Madam Prothke who is known to have been a super in Vienna and to have first appeared as member of Wahr's company at the *première* of Stephanie's *Die seltsame Eifersucht* at Pozsony on 2nd April 1775. The *Pressburger Zeitung* praises her on the 3rd May and the critic advises her to follow Sophia Körner.

An interesting letter of Miklós Esterházy has been preserved.[99] It was written in Vienna in March, 1775, and addressed to Rahier, Chief Steward of the Prince's estates. The Prince had learnt that Haydn had a small puppet theatre which, with the co-operation of the orchestra, had given performances during Lent. He informed Rahier that he would need just this kind of entertainment for the eve of his wife's anniversary on 20th March when she was staying at Kismarton. The Prince requested Rahier to discuss with Haydn the details of a performance there.

It is obvious from this letter that theatrical and musical life at Eszterháza did not stagnate even during the Prince's winter sojourn in Vienna. It is quite possible that the reason why Haydn maintained a small puppet show was the possibility of holding rehearsals with a simpler apparatus during winter and so preparing for the puppet operas to be performed during the main (i. e. the summer) season.

The *Pressburger Zeitung*, 6th May 1775, contains the first report regarding the summer season. According to this, the Prince — now visiting his estates in Poland — is expected to return to Eszterháza by the first days of July. The report announces balls, plays, puppet shows and operas as items of the coming summer entertainments at Eszterháza. We encounter the next reference to the great celebrations at the end of August in the reports relating to the preparations for the reception of the Viennese court.

The reporter of the *Pressburger Zeitung* announces from Eszterháza on the 17th August that the Prince is saving no expense in preparing for an adequate reception of the court which is to stay there three days. A new opera has been composed by Haydn to the libretto of Friberth, one of the Prince's singers. The entertainments will include a puppet show written by Pauersbach, the Prince's court poet.

Apart from the preparations for the celebrations, also news concerning the theatrical activities in mid-August are contained in the *Pressburger Zeitung*. Stephanie Sr., a famous actor and playwright of Vienna, stayed at Eszterháza from the 13th to the 17th August. His repertoire consisted of *Der Deserteur aus Kindesliebe*, *Die Leiden des jungen Werthers* and *Zerstreute*, the latter accompanied by Haydn's music.

Meanwhile, preparations for the reception of the Imperial Court in a truly becoming manner were in full progress. A whole floor of twelve rooms was added to the inn and more than a hundred rooms were prepared for the members of the suite in the surrounding villages. A host of merchants, coffee-makers and hawkers arrived from the adjacent towns and from more remote places to cater for the visitors. Headed by Archduke Ferdinand and Beatrice d'Este, the court left Vienna at 3 p.m. on the 28th August and arrived at 8 p.m. at Eszterháza. En route, the party stopped at Sopron, were offered refreshments in the Esterházy palace there and received the homage of the municipal council and the nobility of the county. A courier of the Prince guided the splendid array of guests from Sopron to Eszterháza, where their arrival was heralded by the boom of cannons. Crowding the two sides of the road between Széplak and Eszterháza, the serfs of the Prince, assembled from the neighbourhood, hailed the travellers with flags, the blare of trumpets and loud cheers; arrived in front of the castle, they were welcomed by the music of buglers and drummers seated on a foliage-adorned platform. The two sides of the principal gate were flanked by the Prince's grenadiers and domestic staff: twentyfour footmen in gala dress, six couriers, six heyducks, six guards, the princely orchestra, the chasseurs, the clerical staff, six Hungarian and six German pages.

'A little German play' was performed in the theatre after the festive reception, to be followed by the illumination of the park and the castle, after which a ceremonial dinner was offered to the guests.

They were roused next morning, on the 29th, by the music of a military band; the morning was taken up by an inspection of the ceremonial hall, the Sala Terrena and the puppet theatre, after which a gala-luncheon was served. The guests went for a drive in the afternoon, were shown the sights of the park: the temples of Diana, Sun, Cupid and Fortune, the newly-erected Hermitage and, on their way back, they dropped in to the theatre to enjoy Haydn's new three-act opera *L'incontro improvviso*. Its plot is a guileless seraglio story with a happy ending, a fashionable titbit for the audience, which was addicted in those times to Chinese and Turkish delicacies. The *Pressburger Zeitung* described the libretto as very amusing and the music, only naturally with reference to a composition of Haydn, as magnificent. Since the only remaining picture of a stage scene from Eszterháza displays figures in Turkish garbs, the painting (reproduced on page) can be assumed to represent a scene from the opera in question.

Supper was followed by a fancy-dress ball in the great Chinese hall with one thousand three hundred and eighty participants.

The morning of the third day was given to relaxation. The cannons which had heralded some new surprise every day were silent for once. In the afternoon, the guests went for a drive in the park, and the Prince guided their tour so as to happen upon a road where a village fair was in progress. Twentyfour leafy tents were erected on both sides of the avenue where not only knick-knacks of all sorts but also golden jewels with precious stones were on sale. The avenue led to a glade where a spectacle beating all other popular items of the Eszterháza celebrations greeted the admiring guests: 'Having inspected the various side-shows, they arrived at a large open space which was like a boulevard of Paris. It contained: 1, a Punch and Judy show; 2, the stand of a quack-doctor; 3, a woman displaying broadsheets; 4, the stand of a tooth extractor; 5, a place for dancing to peasant music; 6, a platform for the musicians. Special shows were presented: Harlequin, Pierrot and Pagliaccio, the three known pantomime figures displayed their art as if in Paris; hereupon, a dentist arrived on horseback accompanied by his assistants seated on mechanical horses, and then a quack-doctor sitting in a cart drawn by six oxen; his cart was accompanied by monkeys, lions and tigers. This quack showed all his cures by way of pictures painted on a large sheet of paper, and explained his treatments rather amusingly. Monsieur Bienfait who is actually in the service of the Prince displayed the ingenious movements of his puppets, while a little comedy was enacted by a Parisian cobbler. The barker extolled his own skill, the dentist strutting on stilts eighteen feet high paraded his skill as tooth-drawer, and the woman explained her painted blood-and-thunder stories in French songs.

This whole spectacle in the forest glade is a typical example of how Austrian rococo taste with its penchant for folk idylls was mixed up with the characteristically ostentatious Gallomania of the age. We can be sure that the various groups of market comedians were so skilfully arranged in the foliage-surrounded clearing by Bienfait, the stage director of the puppet theatre, that they must have looked like so many porcelain figures. Only Hanswurst, the most characteristic Austrian popular figure, was absent — lest he might mar the overall picture of the original Théâtre de la Foire.

The forest scene was followed by a performance of *Alceste* in the puppet theatre, an opera-parody of Pauersbach; the evening pro-

31. Opera performance at Eszterháza in 1775

gramme included fireworks, dinner, and was crowned by another fancy-dress ball.

The morning of the next day (the 31st August) was spent with stag hunting, and in the afternoon Carl Wahr's company presented *Der Zerreute*, a comedy by Regnard, with the following cast:

| | |
|---|---|
| Leander ............................ | Herr Wahr |
| Mad. Crognac ....................... | Frau Partl |
| Isabelle, her daughter ................ | Frau Prothke |
| Clarice, Leander's sweetheart ......... | Frau Körner |
| Her brother, the Knight ............. | Herr Litter |
| Valt, Leander's uncle ................. | Herr Christster |
| Karl, Leander's servant............... | Herr Cremeri |
| Johann ............................. | Herr Schlezer |
| Lisette ............................. | Frau Reiner |

After dinner, the guests, accompanied by military music, repaired to a large oval space in the park to witness the festive illumination. 'The place was splendidly illuminated and adorned with large transparent paintings, pot flowers and garlands. A dazzlingly lighted, resplendent gloriette was erected in the middle from which my lords had a good view of the whole area.' A cannon was discharged upon which two thousand Hungarian and Croatian peasants overran the place and who, accompanied by the music of their own popular instruments and flourishing their flags, began dancing 'and filled the air with their merry shouts'. Leaving the popular feast (which lasted well into the morning), the illustrious guests returned to the castle to attend the last ball, while the park reflected the light of innumerable hanging green lamps.

This was the last large-scale festivity during the life of Miklós 'the Magnificent': theatrical life at Eszterháza became more uniform and more intensive thenceforth, and no further gala performances and spectacles involving the mobilization of the entire neighbourhood were to follow.

*

Our source of information regarding the activities of Carl Wahr's company during the year 1776 is the Almanac of Gotha for 1777. This volume of the almanac contains not only the names of the members and their parts but affords information about the more noteworthy histrionic achievements as well, and thus allows us to gain insight into the company's repertoire.

32. Portrait of Christian Gottlob Stephanie Sr. Copperplate

We learn from the almanac that six members left the ensemble in the course of the year: Mr. and Mrs. Christl, Mr. and Mrs. Prothke, the actors Cremeri and Seipp. Wahr not only replaced them by newly engaged members but acquired a number of additional actors and actresses so that, by the end of the season, the total number of the members amounted to twenty. It is impossible to tell whether these changes took place before or during the season at Eszterháza. It is possible that the resignation of old and the engagement of new members occurred only at the end of the summer when the company was leaving for Salzburg and not, as usually, for Pozsony.

The company led by Carl Wahr consisted at the end of 1776 of the following members:

'Actresses: Mamsell Herdlidschka: *soubrettes* and sweethearts. Madam Klimetsch: comic mothers, procuresses, peevish and finicky parts. Madam Körner: leading ladies, heroines, peasant women, *ingénue* parts. Mamsell Matauschin: sweethearts, young and tender parts, *soubrettes.* Madam Riedl: noble, tender mothers. Madam Rosner: initial parts. Mamsell Schlötzer: small parts. *Souffleuse:* Madam Reiner.

Actors: Herr Bauer: secondary parts, he is the scene-painter. Mamsell Bauer: small children. Herr Bulla: violent, nagging old people and other dry parts. Herr Haym: officers, coarse petit-maîtres and villains. Herr Klimetsch: small servants and pedants. Herr Körner: comic servants, jews, caricatures. Herr Litter: lovers, young heroes, knights, sometimes tender fathers. Herr Riedl: comic old men, servants, ribalds. Herr Rossner: kindly old people, soldiers. Herr Schienagl: lovers, young men, cavaliers. Herr Schlötzer: old servants and peasants. Herr Schlötzer jr.: children. Herr Schulz: fathers and servants. Herr Spiess: serious and dry parts. Herr Wahr: amorosos, noble fathers, heroes, passionate and humorous parts, roles requiring good manners. Herr Zappe: chief servants and bumpkins.'

Besides enumerating the names and parts of the members, the almanac also informs us of the roles in which the newly-engaged actors and actresses first appeared on the stage in 1776:

Mamsell Herdlidschka as Julchen in the *Schwiegermutter*
Madam Hulverding as Louise in the same
Mamsell Matauschin as Miss Strange in the *Landmädchen*
Madam Riedl as Frau von Kapellet
Herr Bulla as Katesby in *Richard*
Herr Hulverding as Count Finsterthal jr.

Herr Müller as Karling in the *Minister*
Herr Riedl as Niklas in the *Wölfen unter der Heerde*
Herr Rosner as Präsident in the *Wilhelmine von Blondheim*
Herr Schulz as Paolo in the new *Arria*
Herr Thomas as Wilkin in *Albert I.*

While some of these plays may have first been performed at Salzburg, it is fairly certain that most of them had already formed part of the Eszterháza repertoire. Mrs. Riedl's role of 'Frau von Kapellet' seems to show that even an adaptation of *Romeo and Juliet* must have been played by Wahr's company.

The Almanac of Gotha for 1777 offers information not merely about Wahr's company but also gives details in respect of the Esterházy opera and puppet show. Erroneously, it speaks of Pozsony and not of Eszterháza as their location and makes mistakes in the spelling of the names. The data of the almanac cannot, therefore, be accepted as completely reliable. It says that Pauersbach was the manager of both the opera and puppet theatre. While it is not quite impossible that, besides leading the puppet theatre, Pauersbach was, during the period in question, at the head of the Eszterháza opera also, we possess no other confirmation of this statement. What we know for certain is that later it was Bader, the Prince's librarian, who directed the opera. The almanac enumerates the singers and records the fact that, while singing the part of Belinde in *L'isola d'amore* on 24th September, 1776, Mrs. Dichtler became unwell and fell down dead on the stage immediately after having said that she could hardly stand on her legs ('non posso più sostenermi in pie').

According to the evidence of extant librettos, the Prince's singers rehearsed and performed at least five operas during the season and it now happened for the first time that they were not Haydn's compositions. This means a profound change in musical life at Eszterháza. Considering that henceforth six, seven and even eight librettos were written every year for the opera of the Prince, it must have been in 1776 that he made the decision to have operas continuously performed by his singers at the same time as the theatrical plays and puppet shows. This is substantiated by the fact that the next issue of the Almanac of Gotha contains references to the opera-ensemble of Eszterháza.

This change in the history of the Eszterháza opera is further borne out by the evidence of musical scores that have been preserved. The Esterházy collection of manuscripts is now in the custody of the Musical Department of the National Library; the original stock of this invaluable collection consists of the manuscript operatic material that was systematically assembled from the middle of the eighteenth until the first decade of the nineteenth century. The most precious pieces of the collection are Haydn's autographs, and the manuscript works of the master are now integral parts of musical history. A special interest attaches to those operas which, with a view to being performed at Eszterháza, were transcribed and adapted by Haydn. Those pieces of this collection which date from before 1776 show no trace of Haydn's handwriting, while corrections made with his own hand become more and more frequent thenceforth: we find sometimes whole arias rewritten by the master. Such revealing glimpses of Haydn's activities as opera conductor furnish a further proof that the year 1776 should be regarded as the beginning of regular opera performances at Eszterháza. Up to that time, it was only on exceptional occasions and only to interpret Haydn's works that the singers of the Prince appeared on the stage.

The engagement of seven prominent singers in 1776 is a further proof of the Prince's resolution to give new impetus to his opera. The new singers were Benedetto Bianchi, Pietro Gherardi, Vitus Ungricht, Marianna Puttler, Marie Elisabeth Trever, Marie Elisabeth Prandtner and Katharina Poschwa. (Pohl erroneously quotes the latter as having been engaged in 1777.)

Unlike those in the opera, the performances in the puppet theatre seem to have been continued uninterruptedly since 1773. This is borne out by Michael Ernst's above-mentioned request in which reference is made to his unbroken service in the puppet theatre from 1773 to 1776, and also by the fact that no less than nine plays are quoted from the repertoire by the Almanac of Gotha: *Alceste, Dido, Demophon, Genovefen* (1st, 2nd, 3rd, 4th parts), *Der Hexensabbath, Philemon und Baucis.* A libretto from 1776 enables us to add a tenth play to those performed in that year: *Die Fee Urgele.* It is quite possible that the repertoire of the puppet theatre included more plays: our sources are neither complete nor reliable in this respect. Beside *Dido* and the quadripartite *Genovefen*, one more puppet opera of Haydn is known in musical history: *Die bestrafte Rachgier oder das abgebrannte Haus*, whose score has been recently discovered in the Library of Yale University, USA.

One of the six operas presented in 1776 was Dittersdorf's *Il finto pazzo per amore*, the libretto of which gives only the year without closer indication of the date, while it is known from the respective librettos of the other operas that *L'isola d'amore* (Sacchini) was given during the summer, and that *La buona figliuola* (Piccini), *Il barone di rocca antica* (Dittersdorf) and *Lo sposo burlato* (Dittersdorf) were presented in the autumn. Also the first performance of Gluck's *Orfeo* is referred to by J. Hárich.

It is worthy of note that three out of the six operas were composed by Dittersdorf. We do not know the name of the person who recommended him to the Prince; a letter written by him on 16th December 1776,[100] contains a reference to 'Kammermusicus' Ungricht, one of the newly engaged singers of the Prince's opera, to the effect that these three operas by Dittersdorf are known to the singer: this points to the existence of a closer connection between the composer and the singer. The letter refers also to Pauersbach as the person through whom his compositions were sent to the Prince. This, however, is not necessarily an indication of friendship between Dittersdorf and Pauersbach: if the Almanac of Gotha was right in describing the latter as the manager of both the puppet theatre and the opera, it was natural for all matters regarding opera to pass through his hands.

*

Three documents[101] contain details of a painful episode that occurred during the opera-season at Eszterháza in 1776. While singing an aria during the representation of *Il finto pazzo per amore* on 24th October, Katharina Poschwa 'had to stand in a funny way'. Benedetto Bianchi who was with her on the stage bent down to the floor and twice lifted her skirt with his stick. Katharina Poschwa noticed this tasteless joke at his third attempt only: she was probably warned by the audience, which included her husband. Anton Poschwa and his wife addressed a petition to the Prince next day asking him to obtain satisfaction for them. The Prince sentenced Bianchi to two weeks' imprisonment, a public bastinado of fifty strokes and obliged him to offer his apology before the public during the next performance on 24th October. The words of the apology were in Italian:[102] the singer apologized first for his want of respect toward the Prince, then for his scandalous behaviour to the public and thirdly for his offence against Madam Poschwa.

*

The year 1777 closed an important period in Eszterháza's theatrical life. Carl Wahr's ensemble did not, as in other years, remain there until the end of October but returned to Pozsony as early as July. The company then went to Pest in August, played once more in Pest and Pozsony in 1778, and went to Prague in 1779, never to return to Hungary.

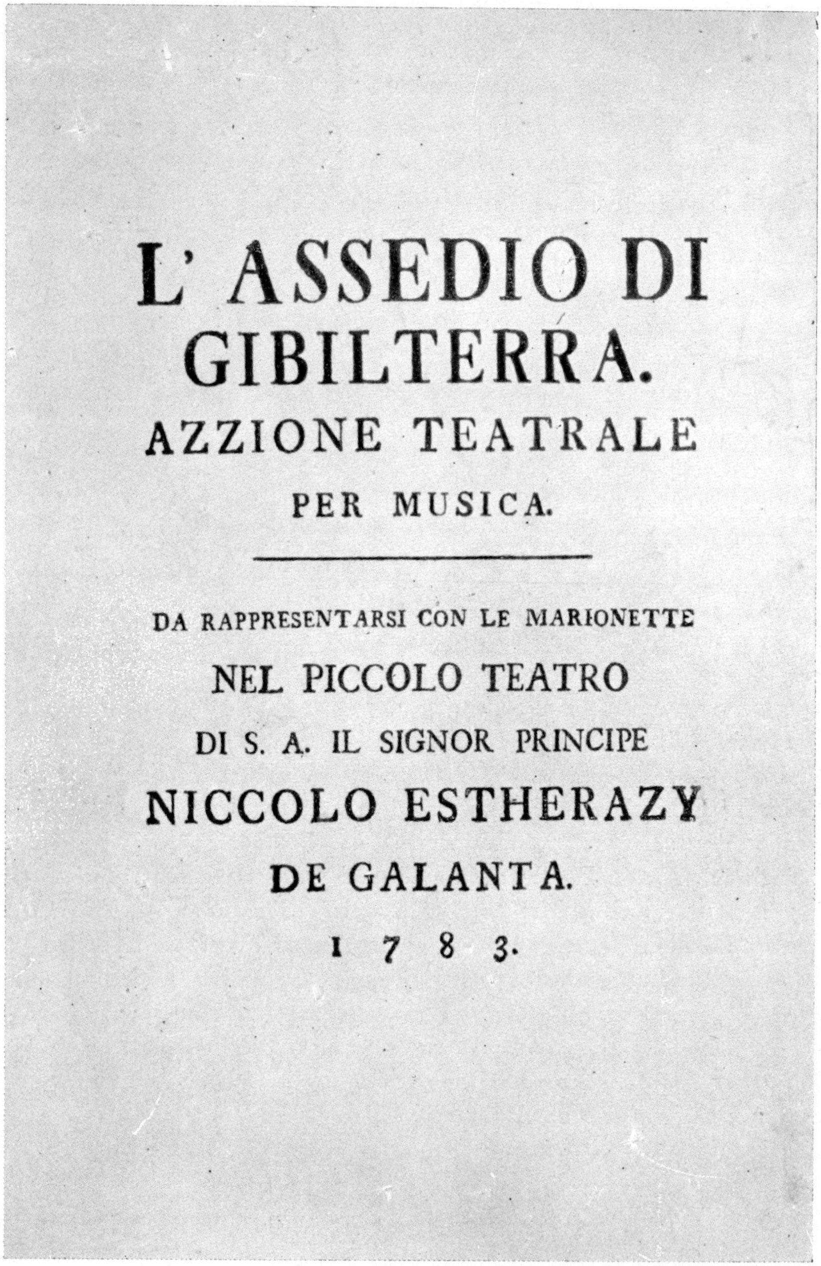
L' ASSEDIO DI
GIBILTERRA.
AZZIONE TEATRALE
PER MUSICA.

DA RAPPRESENTARSI CON LE MARIONETTE
NEL PICCOLO TEATRO
DI S. A. IL SIGNOR PRINCIPE
NICCOLO ESTHERAZY
DE GALANTA.
1 7 8 3.

33a. Title-page of the libretto of the puppet opera, *L'assedio di Gibilterra*

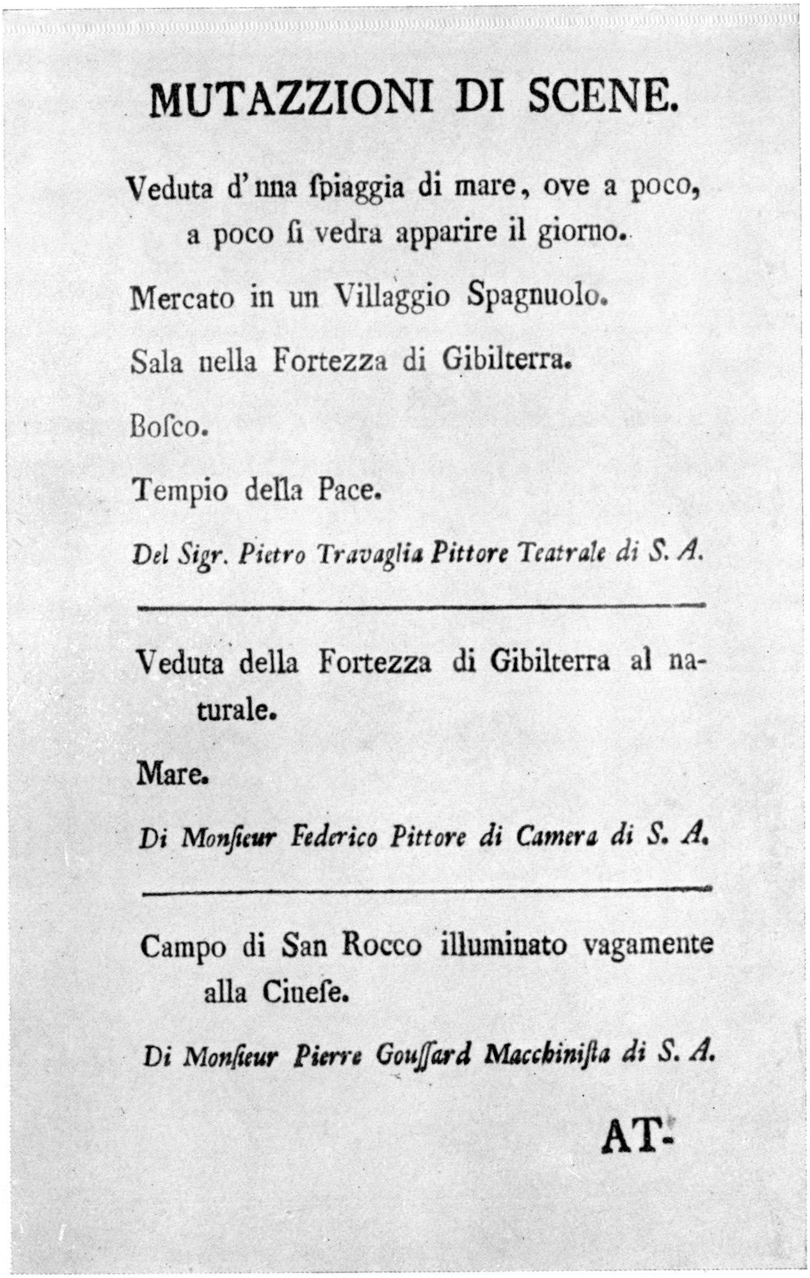

# MUTAZZIONI DI SCENE.

Veduta d' nna ſpiaggia di mare, ove a poco, a poco ſi vedra apparire il giorno.

Mercato in un Villaggio Spagnuolo.

Sala nella Fortezza di Gibilterra.

Boſco.

Tempio della Pace.

*Del Sigr. Pietro Travaglia Pittore Teatrale di S. A.*

---

Veduta della Fortezza di Gibilterra al naturale.

Mare.

*Di Monſieur Federico Pittore di Camera di S. A.*

---

Campo di San Rocco illuminato vagamente alla Cineſe.

*Di Monſieur Pierre Gouſſard Macchiniſta di S. A.*

AT-

33b. A page of the libretto of the puppet opera, *L'assedio di Gibilterra*

# ATTO PRIMO.

## SCENA I.

Veduta d' una ſpiaggia di mare preſſo ad Algheziras.

Diverſi arteſici che lavorano, e riparano de vaſcelli.

## SCENA II.

Mercato in Algheziras, Paeſani, e Paeſane che vendono de comeſtibili. Ufficiali, Soldati che comprano.

*SANDRINA, BERTO, ROSINA, MENICHINO, indi un SERGENTE con Soldati.*

*Meni.* Come è bello il ſol che ſpunta
Dalla placida marina,
Queſt' auretta mattutina
Mi fà proprio giubbilar.

A 3 *Ber.*

33c. First page of the libretto of the puppet opera, *L'assedio di Gibilterra*

While we have no information about the incomplete repertoire of Carl Wahr in 1777, there exist a few facts concerning the activity of the opera-ensemble and the puppet theatre.

Haydn was commissioned by the Imperial Court at the beginning of the year to compose an Italian opera. Although he completed the music of *La vera costanza*, he withdrew his manuscript on account of certain controversies concerning the cast so that the composition was not performed in the Imperial Court Opera but at Eszterháza in 1779.

Accompanied by a number of high personages, Clemens Wenzel, Prince Elector of Trier, arrived in Vienna on 8th July 1777, to see the city. He was entertained by Maria Theresa in the palace of Schönbrunn and, to amuse her guest, the Empress borrowed Miklós Esterházy's opera-company and puppet-ensemble.

Esterházy's 'Bande' presented, according to a report in the *Wiener Diarium*, a 'Spektakel' in the castle-theatre of Schönbrunn on 9th July, played music in the presence of the Empress during the repast on 11th July, and performed a 'prächtiges Schauspiel' on the 14th.

The 'Spektakel' must have been the puppet opera *Dido*, while a work forming part of the Eszterháza repertoire, or a finished opera of Haydn that was to be performed at Eszterháza subsequently, may have been meant by the 'prächtiges Schauspiel'. After giving details regarding the activities of the puppet-theatre, the Almanac of Gotha for 1778 has the following to say of *Dido*: 'A new performance cost 6000 florins last year, and it was so splendid that even the Empress wanted to see it. Therefore, a stage was erected at Schönbrunn, and all the puppets and stage accessories, hangings etc. were brought to Vienna.'

Haydn's comic opera, *Il mondo della luna*, was the chief attraction at the celebrations arranged at Eszterháza on the occasion of the wedding of the Prince's second son, who married Maria Anna Franziska Weissenwolf on 3rd August 1777. It was likewise during these celebrations that Part 4 of *Genovefen*, an interesting puppet show which, as has been mentioned, was commented upon by the Almanac of Gotha, came to be staged. Its performance presented a specially difficult technical problem: it required changes of scene without number, including a hall rigged up for a festive banquet, a library, the infernal regions, an illuminated town, etc. Extant librettos of similar puppet shows as well as descriptions expatiating upon the fabulous expense of the performances, extolling the splendid staging and the precise working of the stage machinery justify the impression that, essentially, puppet shows consisted of a rapid succession of protean and gorgeous scenes which lifted the audience, seated in the extraordinary rocaille-styled auditorium, to the magic realm of fairyland.

The 1777 repertoire of the opera-company included, in addition to *Il mondo della luna*, Gassmann's *L'amore artigiano* in the spring, Paisiello's *La Frascatana* in the summer and Dittersdorf's *Arcifanfano re de' Matti* in the autumn.

Unlike in other years, the Almanac of Gotha has nothing to say of theatrical activities at Eszterháza in 1778, although this was the first year when the Eszterháza season lasted from January to December, and notwithstanding the fact that, in addition to the opera-ensemble, not less than three companies were in charge of the theatrical performances for this year.

A very interesting statement is preserved in the National Archives which enumerates all operas, puppet-plays and prose works — together with the entire programme of the concerts — performed during the year.[103] Pohl published the entire text of the document but — as always — omitted to indicate his source.

Operas were performed twice a week, on Thursday and Sunday, while theatre-plays and concerts filled the programme of the other days. The season opened on the 25th January with the performance of a comedy (*Die Grenadiere*) and a play (*Polyphemus*). Apart from the compositions performed by the opera-company, only three in addition to the said two plays were presented until the 10th March, i.e. the first appearance of the 'Paulische Truppe': two pantomimes of Albert Bienfait and Franz Christl (*Arlequin der Hausdieb* and *Arlequin als Todtengerippe*) and a play with the title *Bellandra*.

Albert Bienfait was, according to the Almanac of Gotha, a former mechanic of the puppet theatre, and Franz Christl a former member of Wahr's company. By a contract, concluded on 23rd January 1778,[104] they bound themselves to perform pantomimes with at least five persons between 24th January and 3rd March as frequently as 'would please His Grace'. The allowance of the little company consisted of lodging, heating, lighting and a weekly salary of five florins and thirty kreuzer. As only pantomimes are mentioned in the contract, it is possible that the two works, referred to without the indication of their respective authors and without defining the genre of the plays, were pantomimes. The little pantomime-company had not too much to do: they held a total of four performances during the term of the contract.

The usual summer season of Eszterháza began in 1778 as early as March. Little is known of the composition and history of the 'Paulische Truppe' which started its performances on 10th March. The statement contains only the names of seven members: Ulrich, Bachmayer, Lamberti and Mayer as actors; Mayer's sister (who was to become Ditelmeyer's wife), Schwarzwald mother and daughter (former members of Wahr's company) as actresses. Johann Mayer, Pauli's co-manager, formed later a company of his own which gave performances at Eszterháza during four seasons in the second half of the eighties. Apart from popular bourgeois comedies — a genre that has since completely fallen into disuse — the repertory of Pauli and Mayer was characterized by the frequent performances of classic works: Lessing's *Emilia Galotti* and *Minna von Barnhelm*, Goethe's *Stella*, Beaumarchais's *Barbier von Sevilien* and Diderot's *Hausvater* were presented. *Julie und Romeo* and *Richard III*, likewise included in the repertory, may have been adaptations of Shakespeare's corresponding dramas, probably those written by Weisse which had been published barely a decade before. A new puppet play, *Das ländliche Hochzeitsfest*, the last one written by Josef Karl von Pauersbach at Eszterháza as court poet and theatre manager, was performed in 1778. He married the singer Maria Anna Tauber in the course of the year and went with his new wife to Russia at the end of it. Pauersbach's departure meant the end of the brightest period of the Esterházy puppet-theatre, a period of five years filled largely by the performance of Pauersbach's plays.

It was only during this single season that Maria Anna Tauber belonged to the opera-ensemble of Eszterháza, and it was she who established a connection between Esterházy's theatre and the opera of the Imperial Court in Vienna. At a concert of the Tonkünstler Societät in March, Joseph II. took a liking to her voice and issued orders to give her the title role in *Lucile*, a one-act opera by Grétry that was to be the next novelty of the Imperial Opera. But she failed to score the expected success at the *première* of 29th June and no permanent engagement resulted. It is quite possible that this lack of success contributed to the decision of Pauersbach and his wife to try their luck abroad.[105]

Pauersbach's subsequent career remains obscure, and there are only a few glimpses in letters he addressed to the Prince between 1784 and 1789. These were written from Regensburg in the years 1784–5 and from Nuremberg between 1787 and 1789. Except the first and the last, all letters merely contain the usual good wishes for new year, birthdays and the like, but all of them show Pauersbach's strong nostalgia for the years he had spent at Eszterháza.

The first letter, written from Regensburg on 8th October 1784,[106] contains important additional information concerning Pauersbach's works

34. Costume design for Haydn's opera, *Armida*

35. Costume design for Haydn's opera, *Armida*

about which our knowledge is rather scanty. To the letter was attached the libretto of *Orpheus* in the German language: Pauersbach offered it to the Prince with the assurance that he had tried to make it as amusing as the Italian original. The libretto must have been an adaptation written for the then still active puppet-theatre of Eszterháza. Nothing is known regarding the fate of the manuscript. It forms no part of the printed Eszterháza librettos, and Bertoni's *Orpheus* was performed in the later course of 1788 with an Italian libretto. Pauersbach presumably received the usual fee for his libretto although it was not staged.

The last letter, written from Nuremberg 27th February 1789,[107] contains Pauersbach's request to the Prince to have some good Hungarian vintage wine sent to him which, according to medical advice, might assuage his illness contracted at Eszterháza sixteen years before.

Contrary to usage, the season of the theatre did not terminate at the end of October. Although the company of Pauli and Mayer presented *Das gerettete Venedig* on the 28th of October as a farewell performance, its departure from Eszterháza did not interrupt theatrical activities even for a day. Piccini's opera *Astratto* was presented by the opera-ensemble on the following day, while, according to the repeatedly mentioned statement, it was on the third day that 'Fing die Diwaldische Truppe an mit *Amalie oder die Leidenschaften*'.

After that of Wahr, Franz Josef Diwald's company was the second to become established for a longer period at Eszterháza. Having previously performed in Pozsony, Baden, Pest and Sopron, it was engaged by the Prince from 1778 to 1785.

The first document dealing with the engagement of Diwald's company for Eszterháza bears the date 4th July 1778.[108] It is a declaration in which Diwald binds himself to give performances with fourteen skilled actors at Eszterháza as from the 1st of November; the declaration contains the customary promise that the ensemble would be considerably superior to its predecessor, i. e. the company of Pauli and Mayer. Diwald further undertakes to bring an imposing wardrobe and — provided he would be allowed to stay at Eszterháza until the beginning of Lent — to replace all actors who might retire in the meantime. Diwald's company began the season on 30th October and gave the last performance on 22nd December (at least, this is the day with which the statement ends).

The variety of the respective repertoires of Pauli-Mayer's and Diwald's companies was really amazing. While the opera-ensemble frequently repeated the same compositions, the two theatrical troupes appeared every day with a new play. The company of Pauli and Mayer presented

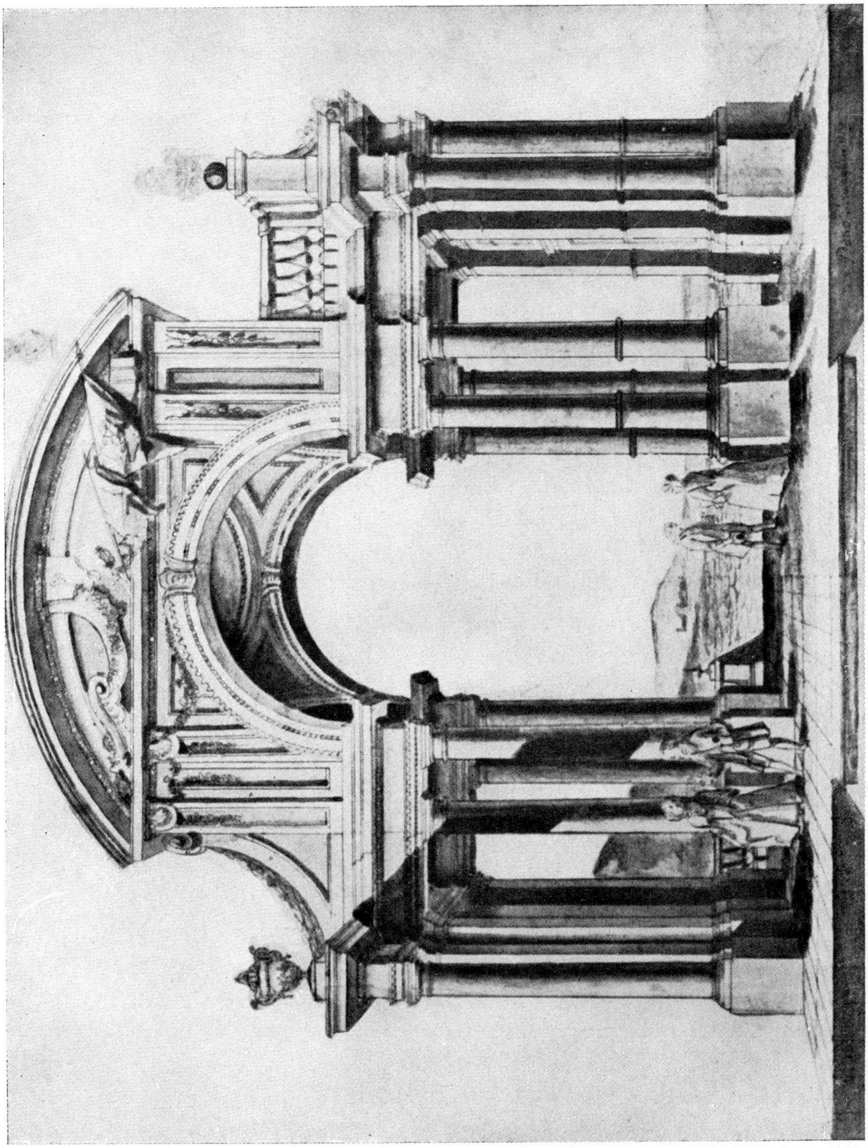

36. Pietro Travaglia's design for an open-air scene

no less than a hundred and thirty *premières* and repeated only eleven plays during eight months, while Diwald and his ensemble held fifty *premières* and repeated only three plays duiing the short time of two months. There were eight plays which figured in the repertoire of both companies which means that if we add the shows presented by Bienfait and Christl, the court of the Prince enjoyed a total of hundred and eighty-two non-musical performances during the year 1778.[109]

The significance of these figures is somewhat lessened by the fact that, comparatively, a great number of one- and two-act plays were presented; yet, even so, to memorize and rehearse so many new plays meant an arduous task for the two small companies. The limited number of the audience explains the necessity of wide-ranged repertoires. It was well-nigh impossible to fill theatres — public or private — for repeated performances of the same play.

The opera-repertoire of 1778 contains four *premières* and five revivals. The newly presented operas were *La sposa fedele* (Guglielmi), *L'astratto* (Piccini), *Il geloso in cimento* (Anfossi) and *La locanda* (Gazzaniga); the revivals were *Il finto pazzo per amore*, *Il barone di rocca antica*, *La buona figliuola*, *La Frascatana* and *Arcifanfano re de' Matti*. The often recurring note, 'at the return of His Grace from Vienna' shows that the continuity of the theatrical season at Eszterháza did not strictly depend on the Prince's presence, in 1778 so that performances were held even if he happened to stay in Vienna.

*

Franz Diwald's company filled the winter months between the Eszterháza seasons with guest performances at Sopron and Wiener Neustadt.[110] It was re-engaged by the Prince for 1779 by a contract concluded in November 1778. The terms of the old contract were left more or less unchanged. Apart from presenting a comedy every day, Diwald had to provide actors for the daily reading of roles in the puppet-theatre. The contract covered the period between Ash Wednesday and the 18th October. It was then renewed unchanged for 1780 and 1781.[111] According to another copy of the contract[112] — which, however, was valid for 1779 only — Diwald's ensemble had to remain at Eszterháza not, as was usual, until the end of October but until the 18th December.

We do not know the complete list of the members of the ensemble that was active in the years 1778–9. The programme for 1778 contains the names of the following eight members who played roles in the performances on 30th and 31st October: Mlle. Knapp, Messrs. Bartly, Schilling, Durst, Weiss, Hr. Menninger, Mad. Soliman, Mlle. Biwald [Diwald].

Four of these actors (Durst, Schilling, Weiss and Diwald) remained members of the troupe during 1780 also so that they, together with the couple Diwald, seem to have formed the permanent stock of the company in 1779. Beside these six members, also the Schwarzwald family — known from the respective ensembles of Wahr and Pauli-Mayer — seem to have belonged to Diwald's company in 1779, since their name figures in every list drawn up by Diwald in and after 1780. It appears that Schwarzwald and his family joined Diwald's troupe at the time when they took the place of the Pauli-Mayer ensemble.

We know only the opera *premières* from 1779. That not less than eight new operas were presented during the season is indicative of the increasing importance of the opera-company of Eszterháza. It was in this year that *La vera costanza*, the opera Haydn had written for the Imperial Opera of Vienna two years before, and Haydn's new opera composed to the libretto of Metastasio, *L'isola disabitata*, were performed. Apart from these two compositions of Haydn, the following operas are authentically known to have been performed: *L'amore soldato* (Sacchini),[113] *Le gelosie villane* (Sarti), *Metilde ritrovata* (Anfossi), *Le due contesse* (Paisiello), *L'isola d'Alcina* (Gazzaniga) and *I visionari* (Astaritta).

There were three smaller festivities at Eszterháza in 1779. Sacchini's opera was presented on the occasion of the wedding of Count Forgách and Countess Ottilia Grassalkovich on the 21st November, while *L'isola disabitata* was performed on the name-day of Miklós 'the Magnificent'. The account given by the *Wiener Diarium* of the celebrations in honour of the Princess on the occasion of her name-day does not mention anything in connection with the theatre but describes a luxurious fancy-dress ball attended by six hundred persons. The guests were particularly impressed by the variety of the many masks and the spectacular entry of Venus and Amor.

No libretto of the opera *I visionari* has been preserved, and only a note of the librarian Bader justifies the conclusion that it was one of the eight operas which had their *premières* in 1779.[114] On the Prince's orders Bader checked the statement of Pietro Travaglia concerning the costumes used in *I visionari*. Bader's notes are of significance not only because they enable us to follow the opera repertoire but also because they afford glimpses into the inner theatrical life and organization of Eszterháza and the preparations that used to precede first nights. It appears that Travaglia acted not only as scenewright but had charge of the costumes also. No indication is contained either in the notes in question or in later documents as to whether Travaglia himself used to design costumes.

Bader's notes are at the same time the first documentary record of that practical work which he — librarian and the administrative manager of the theatre — performed in pursuance of the new organizational statutes regulating theatrical matters at Eszterháza. Hitherto, Bader's name had figured twice in connection with theatrical affairs. The Almanac of Gotha for 1777 and that for 1778 refer to him and Pauersbach as the permanently-engaged authors of the puppet-theatre. We possess no information as to his works. The *Instruction*, i. e. the new organizational statutes of the theatre, drawn up in February 1778 and supplemented in July 1779, contain Bader's promotion to the administrative managership. This important document[115] which presents, so to speak, a cross-section of the theatre's activities, has the following text:

Having entrusted Bader, our librarian, with the direction of our theatre we deem it necessary to issue the following instructions which will have to be complied with and to which both he and all other persons belonging to the theatre will have to conform.

1-mo. Matters regarding the orchestra and the performers as also those in connection with prompting, for which a note-copyist has been engaged, are in the charge of Haydn, our conductor, who has to maintain discipline among the persons concerned.

2-do. Carpenters, the wardrobe attendant, servants, guardsmen and other persons belonging to the theatre will be subordinate to Bader who, while responsible for the administrative management, must not effect changes, make reductions or enlargements without our previous consent.

3-tio. Since, according to Bader, the painter Travaglia is very skilful and able to help him in the management of the theatre, he is to be attached to Bader in order to take care of the scenes and illumination (being versed in painting, the shifting and arrangement of scenery); he will supervise the theatrical staff and report to Bader in all matters so as to avoid possible trouble, without, however, exercising independent authority, for he will continue to be subordinate to our Cabinet Mahler.

4-to. Bader is to keep a precise account of expenses, articles handed over to him and all changes (so that everything can be found surely and promptly); therefore, everybody will have to give him information and account of all articles handed out so as to enable him to render accounts every quarter.

5-to. With a view to fixing future expenses, the wig-maker is to receive a florin, the tailor thirty kreuzer and Mrs. Handl likewise thirty kreuzer for each opera performance.

6-to. All manual stage work is to be done by the following persons: the five theatre carpenters, namely Corbinian, Philipp, Stephan, Johann and the apprentice, also Weber the carpenter and Zimmermann and Andre the grenadiers. They will each receive seven kreuzer for every rehearsal or performance.

7-mo. If necessary, the tailor has to provide two journeymen as gratis supers; the carpenter and tailor, too, have to act as gratis supers.

8-vo. To avoid fire hazards, the chimney-sweep has to stand by during the performances.

9-no. With a view to preventing all possible dangers, the corporal on duty — together with the grenadier Zimmermann and a guardsman — has to inspect the theatre-premises an hour after the termination of every opera, play or concert. Our sub-lieutenant will receive corresponding orders.

10-mo. No guard must leave the theatre during performances without permission from Bader, nor must any guard make frivolous requests. Should any such thing happen, Bader must report it, and the culprit may be punished according to the weight and the circumstances of his misdeed.

11-mo. Mrs. Handl and all persons belonging to the theatre are bound to carry out instructions without contradiction and to avoid all disorder. Contraventions have to be reported and the offenders will receive adequate punishment or, according to circumstances, be dismissed.

12-mo. Except persons whose presence is deemed necessary by Bader nobody must, under any pretext, enter the stage during rehearsals and performances.

13-tio. These instructions are to be made known to all persons belonging to the theatre, and anybody contravening them will without exception be punished or sacked. Given at Eszterháza, on the 14th February 1779.

(sgd.) Prince Miklós Eszterhazy

Pursuant to these instructions, it is forbidden to change, increase or reduce any stage property without our previous knowledge and permission. Therefore, all orders signed by us will have to be registered in our secretariat. Expenses not so authorized will be charged to the person upon whose instruction they were made. Eszterháza, July 26, 1779.

(sgd.) Prince Miklós Esterhazy

37. Title-page of Pietro Travaglia's sketch-book

38. Pietro Travaglia, a room in the house of a Nobleman

Johann Basilius Grundmann was the 'Cabinet Mahler' to whom, according to point 3 of the *Instruction*, Pietro Travaglia was subordinate. Many frescoes of the Esterházy castle were painted by him, and, as borne out by a number of paint-bills. he repeatedly took a hand in the painting of theatre scenery.

The above-quoted appendix of 26th July 1779 has proved to be of great significance in our sources regarding the history of the Esterházy opera. It is due to the new régime of administration introduced in pursuance of the appendix that, thenceforth, daily statements and monthly summaries were prepared concerning the auxiliary staff of the theatre and that we possess detailed descriptions of scenery and costumes needed for first performances. It is from this that our knowledge regarding the repertoire of the following decade is more detailed and more reliable than that of the preceding period. Of course, the *Instruction* only applied to activities regarding opera performances, while all activities connected with non-musical performances remained the concern of the theatre managers.

# THE NEW THEATRE OF ESZTERHÁZA

18th November 1779 saw a great calamity in the annals of Eszterháza. According to the reports of the *Pressburger Zeitung* and the *Wiener Diarium*, tongues of fire leapt up from the roof of the theatre before 4 a.m., and the splendid auditorium was consumed by flames in half an hour. The fire spread very rapidly and destroyed the whole building in a short time. If it had not begun to rain the fire might have spread to the adjacent buildings and even to the castle itself. The loss amounted to more than 100,000 florins.

According to the *Pressburger Zeitung* 24th November 1779, the fire started and spread through the theatre from the world-famous Chinese ballroom. This room, mentioned with great admiration in the *Relation* which had described Maria Theresa's visit in 1773, formed part of that building which — abutting upon and forming a quadrangular block with the theatre — was later used for the accommodation of the clerical staff. There was, according to the *Relation*, a direct communication between the two buildings. They began to heat the ballroom in question a few days before the marriage of Count Antal Forgách with the Countess Grassalkovich, planned for the 21st November. Fires had also been lit in those two Chinese stoves which, otherwise, used to serve decorative purposes only. They were probably overheated and, exploding, must have started the conflagration.

Nothing is more indicative of the great *élan* which had characterized the musical activities of Eszterháza during the last two or three years than the fact that the work of the opera-ensemble was not even temporarily checked by the complete destruction of the theatre building. The marriage celebrations took place three days after the accident, and *L'amore soldato* was performed in the puppet-theatre. Not even three weeks had elapsed before a new opera, *L'isola disabitata*, composed for the name-day of the Prince, was presented, presumably likewise in the puppet-theatre.

The uninterrupted programme of opera performances shows the firm resolution of the Prince to maintain theatrical life at Eszterháza 'à tout prix'. That this was so is best illustrated by the fact that as soon as a month after the catastrophe, on the 18th December, the ceremony of laying the foundation stone of the new theatre, to be built according to the designs of Michael Stöger, was performed.[116] It shows that Miklós, 'the Magnificent' must have issued instructions for the preparation of plans and the beginning of the work of construction almost on the very day of the accident.

Disputes concerning the authorship of the final plans of the new theatre already broke out between Stöger and the 'Hoftischler-meister' Haunold in the course of reconstruction. Stöger, in a letter written to the Prince,[117] emphasized that the foundation stone was laid on 18th December according to his plans, while those of Haunold were finished only by the 26th January 1780. This question was later touched upon by Peter Mollner, 'P.P. Fortifications und burg. Baumeister' in his written report concerning the plans of the new theatre[118] but he did not regard himself as competent to decide the question whether the two architects had or had not borrowed something from each other's work. There is insufficient definite information available to answer this question; it is in any case probable that there was no essential difference between the two designs. Stöger has to be regarded as the principal designer of the new theatre even if he borrowed certain details from Haunold, since it was he who first received the commission and according to whose plans work was begun.

The practical execution of the work of construction devolved upon the master-builder Paul Guba. According to the stipulations of the contract, concluded 28th December 1779, building materials had to be provided by the Prince, while all other tasks were to be the sole concern of Paul Guba. Payments to be made for different kinds of work were precisely fixed by the contract.[119] The masonry of the ornamental gates on the two sides of the theatre was in the hands of Balthasar Emerich, while the group of music-making putti was the work of Johann Heinrich Schroth.[120] The painting of the interior was in charge of Bazalius Grundmann.[121]

The new theatre was not erected on the remnants of the old building but had entirely new foundations. Day labourers needed for excavation are mentioned in the contract of Paul Guba, and Peter Mollner's abovementioned report contains the objection that the foundations were not thicker than the walls erected on them. This was his sole objection to

39. Pietro Travaglia, Royal Hall

the new building which was praised by him in all other respects: 'generally speaking, the whole arrangement is very pleasing and has been made with great artistic skill, much industry and strict accuracy, a great credit to the designer'. It was with similar appreciation that the Almanac of Gotha for 1781 commented on the erection of the new theatre that had been completed in barely ten months: 'Prince Esterhazy, the friend and patron of arts, has replaced the destroyed theatre by a considerably more sumptuous and costly new building. It was opened on the name-day of Her Majesty the Empress with the performance of a tragedy, *Julius von Tarent*, which was introduced by a prologue written for this special occasion'. This passage from the almanac was contained in the report on Diwald's company. The ensemble also spent the season of 1780, i.e. that from Ash Wednesday to 18th December which covered the reconstruction of the theatre, at Eszterháza. Performances were held in the puppet theatre or in the park until the 15th October, the day when the new theatre was inaugurated. That the season of this year was, like that of the preceding one, prolonged by two months seems to be proved by the existence of a protocol drawn up on 13th November, 1780. It records the fact that Johann Schilling, the amoroso of the company, tried, with the assistance of the prompter Jacob Münzenberger, to elope in the night of 12th November with Diwald's wife, the company's heroine. This shows that the ensemble was still at Eszterháza in November. The attempted elopement cost Johann Schilling two weeks in the prison of Kapuvár with a diet of dry bread and cold water on every alternate day and a prohibition to return to Eszterháza as long as Mrs. Diwald was to stay there. The prompter, as accomplice, had to spend three days in prison on a diet of bread and water.[122]

The document containing the extension of the original contract with Diwald for 1780 included a clause in which it was stipulated by the Prince that the company was to be improved and the wardrobe of the actresses to be more beautiful than in the last season. While we possess no further information regarding the enrichment of the wardrobe, the Almanac of Gotha for 1781 contained the complete list of the members of the company, whose number had been raised to nineteen, and it also described the parts to be played by each member. We encounter the name of Pärtl among the new members: as an actor of Passer's ensemble, he had already performed at Eszterháza in 1771 together with his present manager.

'Place of abode: Eszterháza. Manager: Mr. Diwald. Actresses: Mrs. Diwald: leading ladies in comedies and tragedies, young and *ingénue* parts. Mrs. Kettner: second ladies in comedies and tragedies. Miss Diwald: secondary parts. Mrs Schwarzwald: sentimental mothers, comic women. Miss Schwarzwald: young, sentimental *ingénue* parts. Actors: Mr. Diwald: nimble old men in tragedies, funny disgruntled old men in comedies, servants, peasants and parts of low comedy. Mr. Durst: second sentimental lovers and young heroes. Mr. König Sr.: tender lovers and young heroes. Mr. König Jr.: small lovers' parts and servants. Mr. Kirschmayer: sometimes secondary parts. Mr. Morocz: older sedate persons. Mr. Münzenberg: prompter, but plays sometimes pedant parts. Mr. Partl: first tender fathers and sedate parts. Mr. Schilling: first *amoroso*, young heroes, comic parts. Mr. Schwarzwald: pedants, sober servants. Messrs. Suttor and Hipfel: secondary parts. Mr. Weiss: impulsive lovers and servants. Mr. Walter: impulsive old men and sedate lovers. Musical director: Mr. Haydn, conductor of Prince Esterházy.'

Of the repertoire, only *Julius von Tarent* is known with which, according to the Almanac of Gotha, the new theatre was opened. It was in favour and often performed at that time; the Almanac of Gotha for 1778 even presented a picture showing a scene from the play. Different prologues had been written for *Julius von Tarent*; that presented at Eszterháza is contained in the almanac of 1781: '*Prolog zum Julius von Tarent, im Character des Julius: für ein gesellschaftliches Theater.*'

This information about the performance of *Julius von Tarent* raises an interesting problem of opera-history. The front page of the Italian and German libretto of Haydn's new opera *La fedeltà premiata* announces that it was presented at the opening of the new theatre. No other notice regarding the presentation of this opera has been preserved. J. Hárich suggests that the *première* of the opera was postponed until February 1781 since the new theatre was not yet suitable for the performance of operas in the autumn of the year 1780.

The following four operas are kown to have been presented in 1780: *La forza delle donne* (Anfossi) on 17th February; *La vendemmia* (Gazzaniga) on 27th April; *La scuola de' gelosi* (Salieri) on 27th July; and *La finta giardiniera* (Anfossi) on 29th October.

The lists of supernumeraries are our most reliable sources from which we can reconstruct the complete repertoire. Those available in Budapest are, unfortunately, very incomplete. This can be remedied only by a complete exploration of the princely archives of Kismarton which contain a full series of protocols with the statements in question. With a view to reconstructing the whole repertoire of the 1780s, such exploratory work has now been performed, and its results will shortly be published in J. Hárich's next monograph.* Yet, the statements concerning supers give not only chronological data but furnish also reliable information about the auxiliary staff which was employed at the rehearsals and performances. It was *La forza delle donne* which required the greatest apparatus in 1780: two scene shifters, sixteen grenadiers, two boys and four girls as supernumeraries. Apart from the carpenters who were permanently engaged in the manipulation of scenery, as a rule, the auxiliary staff numbered twenty, but Haydn's *L'isola disabitata*, for example, required only three grenadiers and a boy as super. The number of the auxiliary staff reached its peak in the middle of the eighties in connection with the performances of *Giulio Sabino* and *Armida* when they amounted to no less than fifty persons. A higher number of auxiliaries could not have been employed on the comparatively small stage of Eszterháza.

*

Beside Diwald's company and the opera-ensemble a troupe of children was also engaged for Eszterháza in 1780, and remained there until the end of the year.

According to the contract of 15th March 1780, made between the Prince and Franz Merschy, the manager of the company, the latter undertook to add two new members to his ensemble of seven children and to perform with his little troupe comedies and tragedies, musical plays and a pantomime or ballet for the amusement of the Prince. He also undertook to provide for the musical accompaniment of the performances and to see that his wardrobe was pleasing; he, moreover, promised to write a pantomime. Merschy was entitled to a weekly salary of 25 florins.

*

The year of 1785 was the last in which Franz Diwald's company appeared at Eszterháza. According to a report of the Almanac of Gotha dealing with the theatrical season of 1784, only the couple Diwald, the family Schwarzwald and the actor Weiss had remained of the original ensemble.

* Hárich, J., Das Repertoire des Opernkapellmeisters Joseph Haydn in Eszterháza (1780—1790). Haydn-Jahrbuch. Universal Edition, Wien.

40. Pietro Travaglia, a room decorated with pictures

Three undated letters of Diwald contain information about the members who had resigned and the new ones who had been engaged in the course of time.

One of the letters[123] contains Diwald's promise — presumably exacted by the Prince — to engage Ditelmeyer for tragic parts and to replace Mrs. Schwarzwald by another actress playing mother parts. Ditelmeyer used to be a member of the Pauli-Mayer ensemble in 1778. Another letter[124] seems to be of later date, for the list of members contained therein includes Ditelmeyer and also Mrs. Schwarzwald, who appears to have remained with the company. It had fourteen members at this time, of whom eight had belonged to the old stock of 1780. It is, therefore, probable that this letter could not have been written after 1782. The company thus included at this time Mr. and Mrs. Diwald, the family Schwarzwald, Ditelmeyer, König, Schilling, Münzenberg, Olperl and the two married couples Heigel and Rindel.

Diwald's third undated letter[125] speaks likewise of a company of fourteen members: Franciscus Nuth, Carolina Nuth, Theresia Schwarzwald, Josepha Schwarzwald, Anna Alram, Franz Alram, Joseph Alram, Theresia Ulam, Gottlieb Pärtl, Johann König, Jacob Münzenberg, Joseph Sartorius, Emilia Diwald and Franz Diwald. A comparison with the earlier list shows that Schilling and Ditelmeyer were no longer members of the ensemble. After presenting this list, Diwald adds that he will enlarge both the female and the male wardrobe.

It was in 1785 that the Almanac of Gotha referred to Diwald's company for the last time. The ensemble seems to have consisted of eighteen members in 1784, and only three actors and three actresses belonged to the original group:

*Diwald's company*

'Place of abode: Eszterháza, Hungary. Leader and manager: Mr. Diwald. Actresses: Mrs. Diwald, first ladies in comedies and tragedies, young and *ingênue* parts. Mrs. Kopp: *soubrettes*, lovers, sings and is the *prima ballerina*. Mrs. Klimetsch (formerly Wanner): old, comic women and jewesses. Mrs. Schwarzwald: tender mothers in tragedies, comic women in comedies. Miss Schwarzwald: second lovers in comedies and tragedies. Mrs. Pfeil: secondary parts. Actors: Mr. Diwald: impetuous old people in tragedies, comic and disgruntled old men in comedies, chief servants, peasants and parts of low comedy. Mr. Dahmen: first and second *amorosos* in comedies and tragedies. Mr. Kopp: sedate heroes, tender or comic old people in tragedies, mature lovers in comedies; first dancer. Mr. König: tender fathers and soldiers. Mr. Prandt: *amorosos*, young heroes in tragedies, also second *amorosos* in comedies; dancer. Mr. Prillmayer: lovers in comedies and tragedies. Mr. Schwarzwald: pedants, old people, sober servants. Mr. Schletter (poet of the company): plays sometimes smaller parts and acts as prompter. Mr. Weiss: second lovers in acts as prompter. Mr. Weiss: second lovers in comedies and tragedies, jews. Mr. Pfeil: secondary parts. Children's parts played by Nicolaus Diwaldt, Eleonora ielin (*sic!*) and Stephan Klimetsch.'

Of the company's repertoire during four years it is only that of 1784 that is recorded. According to the Almanac of Gotha for 1785, the first two *premières* of Schiller's dramas (*Fiesco* and *Kabale und Liebe*) were held in 1784 at Eszterháza. Schiller had written *Fiesco* only two, *Kabale und Liebe* only a year before these *premières*. Also a play about *Maria Stuart* was enacted in this year, but Schiller's tragedy had not been composed yet. The play *Das stumme Mädchen* was performed as adapted by Schletter, the 'poet' of the company, and also others of his comedies and one-act plays were played during the season, such as *Irrtum in allen Ecken*; *Der argwöhnische Liebhaber*; *Liebrecht und Hörwald*; *Hannibal, Gerechtigkeit und Rache*; *Die Neugierigen*; *Das vermeinte Kammermädchen*. The authors of the plays quoted by the Almanac of Gotha are unknown: *Verbrechen aus Ehrsucht*; *Kommst du mir so, so komm ich dir so*; *Die Weltweise*; *Karl von Freystein*; *Der Besuch nach dem Tode*; *Die reiche Freyerin*. This list has, on the evidence of the statement of supernumeraries, to be completed with the addition of *Macbeth* and *Hamlet*.[126]

*

The seven years' period of Diwald concluded at the end of 1785. Diwald's company constituted a strong link between Eszterháza and Hungary's German theatrical art. Diwald entered into an engagement in Pest in 1786, at Temesvár and Nagyszeben in 1787, at Kolozsvár, Arad, Temesvár and Szeged in 1788, at Temesvár, Ujvidék, Pétervárad, Zimony, Nagyvárad and Kolozsvár in 1790, at Győr in 1791. The years spent at Eszterháza must have influenced his further histrionic activities, and it is certain that, in his wanderings from town to town, he was able to repeat the repertoire of Eszterháza for many years.

The contract made with his successor at Eszterháza bears the date 23rd May 1785.[127] According to this, Johann Mayer and his company undertook (with the traditional stipulations) to perform plays, ballets, German operettas and a puppet opera between Easter and the end of the year 1786. It appears from a long letter of Mayer that his enemies made some unsuccessful attack against him.[128] This enemy may have been Diwald who would have liked to remain at Eszterháza.

Mayer informed the Prince in this letter of the composition of his company and his plans for the next season. He wrote that, besides himself, the company contained seventeen members and emphasized that the ensemble, led by him, was a well-united and reliable troupe. Writing of the various parts, he points to the dancers of the company who formed a special *corps de ballet* of eight members. The existence of this little *corps de ballet* may have made the Prince decide in favour of Mayer's company rather than that of Diwald which included only three dancers. The letter presents the following description of the new company:

'Male comedians: I: first fathers, first heroes, character parts. Mr. Anton Hornung: first *amorosos*, young character and comic parts. Mr. Matthias Mayer: second lovers. Mr. Lang: second fathers, second character parts. Mr. Paul Hornung: secondary parts, especially those of low comedy. Mr. Harr: jews, secondary parts. Mr. Lorenz: prompter. A boy actor.

'Actresses: my wife: first mothers in tragedies and comedies. My sister, Mrs. Ditelmeyer: leading ladies. Mrs. Therese Mayer: first *soubrettes*. Nanette Hornung: second *soubrettes*. My daughter: performs.

'In the ballet: Mr. Anton Hornung: first dancer, master of ballet. Matthias Mayer: comic dancer, master of ballet. Both are good and dance after their own fashion. Paul Hornung and Lange act as supernumeraries. The boy dances. Mrs. Therese Mayer: *prima ballerina*. Miss Nanette Hornung: second dancer. My daughter: dances.'

Mayer adds that four members of the company are singers as well, while without being consummate artists, the others can sing also. He promises to add one more heroine to Mrs. Ditelmeyer, to engage an actor for pedant parts and those of chief servants, further, to engage a good dancer and a good *danseuse*, as also a few actors for secondary roles. As was usual in letters of this kind, that of Mayer contains a self-satisfied comparison with the wardrobe of the preceding company and finishes with a reference to an annexed declaration written by General Count Saaro (?) concerning the company's activities at Temesvár. The General praises Mayer's wardrobe and declares that the performances of the ensemble had met with the approval of the local nobility, the army and the general public.[129] It further appears from the document, written on 3rd October 1785, that Mayer's company, together with a group of actors from the ensemble of Bulla and Schmallögger, theatre managers in Buda, remained at Temesvár until the end of the Carnival.

Mayer's role in the history of German acting in Hungary was similar in importance to that of Diwald. The two couples Mayer and Ditelmeyer,

41. Pietro Travaglia, Apartment leading to a gallery

together with Anton Hornung and a few others, separated from the German ensemble of Pest on 4th April 1783, and became the founders of a regular German theatre in Buda. The two married couples were kinsfolk: Ditelmeyer's wife was the sister of Mayer, and they had all stayed at Eszterháza in the seventies.

Mayer's company played in the theatre of Pozsony during the season of 1787 but returned to Eszterháza in the following year to remain there till the death of Miklós 'the Magnificent' at the end of September 1790.

Johann Lasser, the manager of the theatre at Linz, wrote a letter and offered his services to the Prince as soon as the news of Mayer's Pozsony engagement reached him.[130] It was followed by a second letter, dated the 4th January,[131] in which Lasser informed the Prince of his activities regarding the formation of his company and his plans for the future. The letter also contained a provisional list of the members of his ensemble. It appears from the latter that the Prince insisted on the engagement of the actor Nuth and the actress Mrs. Teller, and that it was not yet certain whether it would be possible to get hold of Miss Repke as solo dancer.

A contract was concluded four days later with the usual clauses.[132] It, too, contains a list of the members which does not seem to have been the final one, since the names therein are not quite in agreement with those published by the next year's issue of the Almanac of Gotha. The only new stipulation in the contract binds the company to perform ballets in operas. According to the Almanac, Lasser's company included the following members in 1787:

'Contractor: Mr. Lasser. Stage manager: Mr. Nuth. Actresses: Mrs. König: lovers, *ingénue* parts, sings. Mrs. Mayer: first *soubrettes*, first dancer. Mrs. Müller: first lovers in comedies and tragedies, *soubrettes*, sings, dances. Miss Repke: *prima ballerina*. Mrs. Schulze: secondary parts. Mrs. Teller: any part requiring decorum and solemnity. Orsinas, Bardonias and Mrs. Unger: all first tender and comic mothers, character parts. Actors: Mr. Breda: second old men, tender fathers, pedants. Mr. Giesecke: all *amorosos* in comedies and tragedies, gallicizing Germans, character lovers. Mr. König: second *amoroso*, comic peasants, dances. Mr. Löffler: prompter, plays also pedants and old men. Mr. Mayer: comic servants, easy-going fellows, master of ballet. Mr. Müllner: secondary parts, jews. Mr. Nuth: all parts requiring decorum, and dignity, kings, noble fathers, old people, brisk veterans, heroes. Mr. Schulze: comic servants, knights, pedants, sings, dances. Mr. Unger: comic old men, pedants, confidants.

While no information regarding the repertoire of Mayer's company is available, the Almanac of Gotha mentions the following new plays presented by Lasser's ensemble: *Der vernünftige Narr* (com.), *Räuschchen* (com.), *Heyrath durch Irrthum* (com.), *Verstand und Leichtsinn* (com.), *Liebreiche Stiefmutter* (com.), *Stille Wasser sind betrüglich* (com.), *Nachschrift* (com.), *Johann von Schwaben* (trag.), *Adelheid von Salisbury* (trag.), *Schwarze Mann* (trag.), *Schauspielenschule* (com.), *Mädchen und den ganzen Kram* (com.), *Verlobung* (com.), *Neue Emma* (com.), *Jeder reitet sein Steckenpferd* (com.), *Wind für Wind* (com.), *Was ists?* (com.), *Der Schreiner* (com.), *Die Drossel* (com.), *Liebhaber ohne Namen* (com.), *Die eingebildeten Philosophen* (musical play), *Die Feldmühle* (com.), *Liebe von Ungefähr* (com.), *Armuth und Liebe* (com.), *Athelston* (trag.), *Die Brille* (com.), *So zieht man dem Betrüger die Larve ab* (com.), *Muttersöhnchen auf der Galeere* (com.), *Dagobert* (*trag.*).

It appears from the Almanac that the season of 1787 finished at the beginning of December on account of the Prince's departure for Vienna when — save a few members — Lasser's company went to Passau. Of those who had resigned from the company, Nuth and Mrs. Teller landed at Pest, while the young couple Mayer returned to Eszterháza next year as members of the ensemble of Mayer Sr.

Lasser renounced the managership of the company at Passau on Ash Wednesday of the year 1788 and entered, together with a few of his colleagues, into engagement at Graz. It was from here that he wrote his last extant letter to the Prince on 23rd July, 1790, in which he suggested a sweeping reorganization of the theatrical life of Eszterháza.[133]

He submitted three alternatives to the Prince so as not to lose much time with correspondence.

The first is a proposal to assemble a good theatrical company which would also perform ballets, for the usual fee of a hundred florins and a supplement of twenty-five florins. The more prominent members of this company which he undertook to collect from a number of different towns would have been the following:

'Mr. and Mrs. Schotz are playing here now, in Graz, and all visitors from Vienna are full of their praise.

'Mrs. Rolland: is now playing the part of first lovers in Brünn, Princess Maria knows her qualities.

'Mr. Prandt: is playing first lovers at Brünn; his acting has improved since his departure from Eszterháza.

'Mr. Korndorffer: is playing leading parts at Innsbruck.

'Mrs. Vigano: she is very strong here in Graz.

'Her daughter: a good dancer.

'Mr. and Mrs. Mayer, Mr. Schulze: well-known.'

Madam Vigano who was to become famous as a dancer, did not appear at Eszterháza, but was engaged for Kismarton a few years later.

The reasons adduced by Lasser to justify his request for an extra weekly allowance of 25 florins are very interesting. He writes that prices have soared and the number of theatres has risen more rapidly than that of available actors. Being more in demand, actors claim higher salaries. Should the Prince find this sum too high, the alternative solution proposed by Lasser was that he and his wife, as members of the Italian opera-ensemble of Eszterháza, should receive the same salary as would be paid to them if they were first singers of the German opera ensemble at Graz, or, else, he could run two companies simultaneously in which case he would come to Eszterháza only once a week to see to the casting, and the company might be managed in his absence by Scholtz and Prandt.

Lasser's second proposition was that — for a weekly salary of 200 florins — he would engage a company which would include a good German opera-ensemble and a *corps de ballet* of twelve dancers. The following pieces are mentioned by him as forming part of the intended opera repertoire: *Grotta di Trofonio, L'arbore di Diana, Cosa rara, Doctor und Apotheker, Das wütende Heer, Der Fagottmeister, Hieronymus Kniker, Dorfdegutirte, Unruhige Nacht.* Should this project be accepted, Lasser and his wife would become members of the Prince's Italian opera ensemble, and, provided that no more than two Italian operas per week were to be performed, the Prince would only have to engage five more Italian singers.

The third suggestion is based on a weekly salary of 300 florins. If the Prince saw his way to allow a salary of this magnitude, Lasser would undertake to assemble a company which could perform every kind of play; he would, moreover, maintain a *corps de ballet* and such a German opera as would be not inferior in quality, and superior in number, to Schikaneder's ensemble in Vienna.

We do not know how Miklós 'the Magnificent' received Lasser's proposals since he died before the next theatrical season.

While Lasser was making plans in Graz for the reorganization of the theatrical life of Eszterháza, Mayer's company was once more engaged by the Prince and stayed there during the last three seasons. Mayer's success at Pozsony was but moderate in 1787 because of the keen competition of Count Erdődy's Opera there. Mayer's contract obliged his company to perform at Eszterháza from Easter to the end of 1788[134] and from the 1st January 1789,[135] so that there was no interruption in the

42. Pietro Travaglia, Chinese Apartment

performances. We possess no reliable data concerning the end of the 1789 season and the beginning of the season in 1790.[136] The clause that the company has to perform the ballets occurring in operas appeared first in Lasser's contract for 1787 and was then included in Mayer's contracts concerning the last three seasons.

There were many changes in the composition of Mayer's company during these last three years. It included the following members at the beginning of the season in 1788.[137]

| 'Names of actors: | Parts: |
|---|---|
| Johann Mayer, manager: | fathers and character parts |
| Hornung: | lovers; dancer |
| Math. Mayer: | servants and peasants; dancer |
| Kunst: | lovers; dancer |
| Ferrary: | servants, character parts; dancer |
| Hart: | friends, second lovers; dancer |
| Horschfeld: | fathers |
| Hübner: | secondary parts; acts as supernumerary |
| Löfler or another: | announcing wardrobe-attendant |
| Actresses: | |
| Mayer or Titelmayer: | mothers and other leading parts |
| Mad. Kunst: | first lovers |
| Mad. Mayer: | young girls; dances |
| Mad. Hornung: | lover; dances |
| Josepha Mayer: | young girls; dances |
| Mad. Hart: | secondary parts; dances |
| Heiline: | auxiliary parts; acts as supernumerary' |

By the end of 1790 only Mayer, Mrs. Ditelmeyer, Hornung and Hart had remained from this company. The last list of the company dates from 5th October, 1790, when Anton Hornung, Leopold Hart, Karl Augenstein, Heinrich and Josepha Zunger, Karl Medastini, Franz Bürger, Leopold and Julianna Haim, Josepha Bittam and Xaverius Max received, between them, a sum of 200 florins which was granted by Prince Antal, the successor of Miklós 'the Magnificent', as 'a special gratuity' to indemnify them for being dismissed without notice. It was on 30th September that Mayer and Mrs. Ditelmeyer cashed the last 100 florins for the last week of the season,[138] Mayer — at that time already member of the Imperial Court Theatre in Vienna — asked in 1795 to be paid 1300 florins as salary for the last three months of 1790 due to him under his contract with Miklós 'the Magnificent'.[139]

# THE OPERA REPERTOIRE OF THE NEW THEATRE

As regards life in the new theatre of Eszterháza, our information about the activities of Diwald's, Mayer's and Lasser's companies is rather incomplete. Much more detailed, on the other hand, is our knowledge regarding the repertoire and the whole activity of the opera ensemble of Eszterháza.[140] Two features which had already characterized the last two or three years of the old theatre became dominant in the life of the new one: the theatrical season covered almost the whole calendar year, and the production of operas received more emphasis. It was especially since Mayer's engagement that, side by side with operas, ballets also came into the foreground. Except perhaps the months of December and January which Miklós 'the Magnificent' was in the habit of spending in Vienna, the Prince remained at Eszterháza practically throughout the year. While previously only two operas had been performed every week, their weekly number was raised to three during the eighties. About three fourths of all operas presented at Eszterháza were produced in the new theatre.

In addition, the administration of the theatre was reorganized. Estimates for the cost of the theatrical wardrobe as also the bills of the Sopron printer Joseph Siess were signed by Pietro Travaglia. It was on his representation that the Prince approved the wardrobe estimates so that Bader's supervision came to an end in this field. In his bill of 20th June 1781, Siess refers to Travaglia as 'Hochfürstl. Theater-Directeur in Esterház.'[141] This might be regarded as the sole proof that Travaglia ranked as theatre-manager if this title, applied by Siess, had not been used by him for courtesy's sake rather than as one actually due to Travaglia. In any case, even if Travaglia had not the official title of manager, his sphere of authority was no narrower than that of Bader, the earlier, and Porta, the later manager: the musical leadership was always in the hands of Haydn, while costumes, illumination and all practical problems of the stage always belonged to the sphere of Travaglia's authority. This is clear from the administrative statutes of 1778–9 already referred to. 'Nunziato Porta was engaged as manager of the opera and as inspector of the theatre wardrobe for an annual salary of 150 florins and the necessary firewood...'[142] Therefore, the next bill of Joseph Siess, made out on 26th July 1781, refers no longer to Travaglia but Nunziato Porta who figures as manager in the entire subsequent history of the Eszterháza operas. Of course, he was also responsible for the printing of the librettos, the supervision of the wardrobe estimates and, generally, for all administrative matters connected with the theatre. Beyond being an exemplary and consciencíously accurate administrator — for which theatrical and opera history is deeply indebted to him — Porta excelled as a permanent playwright of the Eszterháza theatre. It was immediately after his engagement that Righini's *Il convitato di pietra* was performed with Porta's libretto in the summer of 1781. He was the librettist of Haydn's puppet operas *Orlando Paladino* and *L'assedio di Gibilterra* in 1783, and it was he who wrote the libretto of *L'isola di Calipso* and *I contratempi* in 1784, and that of the opera *L'incontro inaspettato* in 1786.

*

Seven opera premières were held in 1781; *La fedeltà premiata* (Haydn) on 25th February; *Isabella e Rodrigo* (Anfossi) in April; *L'avaro deluso* (Paisiello) in May; *La contadina in corte* (Piccini) in June; *Il francese bizzarro* (Astaritta) in July; *Il convitato di pietra o sia il dissoluto* (Righini) likewise in July; *La schiava riconosciuta* (Piccini) in August. Except *La contadina in corte*, librettos had — according to our sources — been prepared for all these operas; and two hundred copies were issued, 175 of which were printed on common and 25 on a special paper. Although no librettos of the operas *Il francese bizzarro* and *La schiava riconosciuta* have been preserved, there can be no doubt that they existed since bills of their printing and delivery are still extant.[143]

Eight new operas were presented in 1782; *Zemira ed Azor* (Grétry) and *La fiera di Venezia* (Salieri) in February; *Il cavaliere errante* (Traetta) in March; *L'innocente fortunata* (Paisiello) in April; *Lo sposo disperato* (Anfossi) in August; *Il curioso indiscreto* (Anfossi) in September; *I filosofi immaginari* (Paisiello) in October, and *Orlando Paladino* (Haydn) in December. The librettos were printed in editions of 200 copies in this year also, and only Haydn's operas and *Zemira ed Azor* were exceptions: the librettos of *La fedeltà premiata* and of *Zemira ed Azor* were issued in 400 and that of *Orlando paladino* in 500 copies.

43. Pietro Travaglia, Atrium leading to the temple

It is stated in the libretto of *La fedeltà premiata* that the ballet in the opera was danced according to Luigi Rossi's choreographic instructions. Rossi entered the service of the Prince on 19th March 1779,[144] and distinguished himself even as *ad hoc* playwright in 1780. His poem, glorifying the Prince, appeared in 1780 at Sopron in the Italian and German languages.[145]

We know of seven new operas that were presented in 1783: *Il ratto della sposa* (Guglielmi) and *La vedova scaltra* (Righini)) in March; *L'italiana in Londra* (Cimarosa) on 4th May; *Giulio Sabino* (Sarti) on 21st May; *Fra i due litiganti il terzo gode* (Sarti) on 10th August; and *Il Falegname* (Cimarosa) at the end of November. Besides, the première of the puppet-opera *L'assedio di Gibilterra* took place on 20th August.

We know the precise dates of six first performances and a revival regarding the year 1784: *Armida* (Haydn), 26th February; *I viaggiatori felici* (Anfossi), 21st March; *L'amor costante* (Cimarosa), 27th April; *La Didone abbandonata* (Sarti), 26th or 29th July; *La villanella rapita* (Bianchi), 29th August; *L'isola di Calypso abbandonata* (Bologna), 11th November — *Le gelosie villane* (Sarti) which had already been performed in 1779 was revived on the 6th July. With the exception of *Le gelosie villane* and *L'isola di Calypso abbandonata*, there existed librettos to all these operas.

Two more operas were to be presented in 1784: Pietro Travaglia submitted on 8th June the estimates regarding the scenery of *L'incontro improvviso* and Porta submitted on 1st June the estimates regarding the costumes of *I contratempi* (Sarti).[146]

Yet, neither of them is included in the complete list of the repertoire from 18th February to 5th December. The first must have been identical with Righini's opera *L'incontro inaspettato* the libretto of which was produced in 1786. The opera was performed in the latter course of the same year. Neither does the list of Johann Schilling, a music copyist, which contains an account of all musical compositions presented in 1784, include the opera in question.[147] *I contratempi*, on the other hand, is mentioned in Schilling's list and it figures also in the bill of Siess, the printer, according to which a hundred copies of its libretto were issued in September 1784.[148]

There were four premières in 1785: *I contratempi* (Sarti) in April (its libretto had been printed in the year before); *Montezuma* (Zingarelli) on 5th June, *Il matrimonio per inganno* (Anfossi) on 3rd July; *Le astuzie di Bettina* (Stabingher) at the beginning of October.

The repertoire of 1786 contained eight new operas: *Alsinda* (Zingarelli) in March; *La ballerina amante* (Cimarosa) on 2nd April; *Chi dell' altrui si veste presto si spoglia* (Cimarosa) on 2nd May; *Ifigenia in Tauride* (Traetta) on 4th July; *L'albergatrice vivace* (Caruso) on 6th August; *L'incontro inaspettato* (Righini) on 1st October; *Idalide* (Sarti) on 24th October and *I due baroni di rocca azzurra* (Cimarosa) on 6th December.

A schedule, prepared by Director Porta for the year 1786, has been preserved. It contains the roles in which the ten members of the opera-ensemble are to be cast, and shows the singers who may step in for each of them if necessary. The estimates for the cost of the costumes amount to 1,627 florins, and that of the scenes to 1,386 florins for the whole season.

That librettos for the operas *Alsinda, La ballerina amante, L'albergatrice, Chi dell'altrui si veste, Ifigenia* and *Idalide* were printed is evident from the printer's bills, and we actually possess those of the three last-named operas.[149] In addition, a copy of the libretto for the opera *L'incontro inaspettato* has likewise been preserved.

According to available data, the following new operas were staged in 1787: *Il sordo e l'avaro* (Anfossi) in February; *Il disertore* (Bianchi) in April; *La quaquera spiritosa* (Guglielmi) on 3rd June; *Alessandro nell'Indie* on 26th July, and *Le gare generose* (Paisiello) on 18th September. No libretto of the last-named opera has been preserved but a bill from the printer, dated the 20th August 1787, proves that this libretto had also been prepared.[150]

The year 1788 witnessed seven premières: *Giunio Bruto* (Cimarosa) on 2nd February (its libretto had been printed in the year before); *I finti eredi* (Sarti) on 9th March; *I due castellani burlati* (Fabrizi) on the 6th, 6th July; *La vendetta di Nino* (Prati) on 1st August; *Orfeo ed Euridice* (Bertoni) in September; *Il marito disperato* (Cimarosa) in October, and *Il tamburo notturno* (Paisiello) in December.

Six news operas were presented in 1789: *I due supposti conti* (Cimarosa) at the end of February; *La gelosie fortunate* (Anfossi) in mid-May; *Il pittore parigino* (Cimarosa) at the beginning of June; *La Circe ossia l'isola incantata* (Cimarosa) at the end of July; *Le vicende d'amore* (Guglielmi) in October and *L'arbore di Diana* (Martin) in the middle of November.

The company presented four new operas during the last season at Eszterháza: *Il barbiere di Seviglia* (Paisiello) on 9th May; *L'impressario in angustie* (Cimarosa) and *Il credulo* (Cimarosa) on 6th June; *L'amor contrastato* (Paisiello) on 13th July. In addition, the statements refer to three more operas, the titles of which are unknown to us.

September, 1790, was the last month in which performances were held at Eszterháza. It was on the 18th of this month that Prince Miklós 'the Magnificent' died. His decease finished musical life at Eszterháza.

According to J. Hárich, more than a thousand opera performances were given in the newly erected theatre of Eszterháza during ten years, and a good many of the premières preceded those in Vienna. The best part of the Italian operas composed in the 18th century were staged at Eszterháza during more than two decades.

44. Pietro Travaglia, a room in the house of a Burgher

# THE STAGE OF THE OPERA AT ESZTERHÁZA

While we are able to reconstruct the history and the repertoire of the theatre without many gaps, it is considerably more difficult to reconstruct a picture of the actual stage, i.e. the visual aspect of the performances. So far, historians of operatic art have known but a single picture from which they could form an idea of the stage at Eszterháza as it appeared to contemporary spectators (see p. 99). The recent discovery of Pietro Travaglia's sketchbook provides a great step forward in this respect. The conclusions we can draw from his sketches are supplemented by statements concerning scenery and costumes preserved in various archives.

Separately, neither the sketches nor the statements offer full information. There is no permanent picture of the stage; it was constantly changing and fluctuating by the incessant comings and goings of the actors, by the increase or decrease in their number, by the variations of the stage illumination, and even by the moving scenery. Sketches which have been preserved are, therefore, but a skeleton which only a knowledge of the operation of the whole theatrical apparatus can transform into a living organism.

Pietro Travaglia's activities as a scenewright, begun in 1773, were of decisive importance for the entire history of the theatre of Eszterháza. His name is mentioned in practically all opera librettos, and it is only in one or two cases that the names of Basilius Grundmann and 'Federico' appear in the capacity of 'Cabinet Mahlers'. The '*Instruction*' of 1778–9 makes it quite clear that Travaglia was the master stage-designer: 'he is versed in painting as also in the shifting and arrangement of scenes'. His advantage over the usual court painters was that, besides being a master of pictorial art, he was familiar with the tricks of the theatrical 'trade' without which no stage setting could be designed.

Travaglia was, according to the librettos of *La vera costanza* (1779) and *La fedeltà premiata* (1782), a disciple of the brothers Galliari ('Jüngling der berühmten Gebrüder Galeari') so that he had learnt his art in Milan at one of the best schools of the time.

The family Galliari belonged to a famous dynasty of stage-designers in the eighteenth century. They worked at Milan and Turin through three generations, and practically all European theatres of some importance belonged to their *clientèle*. We know from his petitions addressed to Prince Esterházy and a letter preserved among his sketches, that Travaglia's family lived at Milan and that he was presumably a disciple of the two most famous members of the Galliari family, Bernardino and Fabrizio, during the 1760s. The two brothers are looked upon by historians of the theatre as having contributed, in the spirit of free picturesqueness and a peculiar eclecticism, to the liberation of scenic fine arts from Baroque convention. On the other hand, the two brothers insisted on sweeping lines and the well-balanced structure of the stage designs in contrast to the minute details of the Rococo which was superseding the Baroque in many places.

The sketches contained in Pietro Travaglia's extant collection were made in the second half of the eighties. They show that Travaglia had remained loyal to the principles of the Galliari school; the sketchbook is, therefore, a relic of great importance which throws light upon the hardly-known classicist art of stage-designing towards the end of the eighteenth century.

With the exception of *Fiesco*, *Maria Stuart* and *Armuth und Edelsinn*, all of Travaglia's estimates for scenery apply to operas, so that the sketches of his collection should be regarded as representing scenes from operas. It is probable that already-used scenes from operas were employed for the dramatic performances of the theatrical company.

The architectural scenes represented in Travaglia's book reveal quiet and distinctly outlined plans which are in sober harmony with the dimensions of the theatre. They were executed by means of a linen sheet attached to one or two wooden frames on the forestage and a back curtain which closed the space or opened up to a further perspective. Architectural scenes as used in the time of the Eszterháza theatre had two advantages: the artificiality of the soffits was not as conspicuous as in the representation of open landscapes (high perspective drop curtains were unknown as yet); besides, they offered wide possibilities for scenic designs. Although Travaglia made good use of these possibilities which enabled him to give width and depth to the available space, his designs never lost sight of the requirements of the smallness of the stage and invariably revealed a certain discipline. One feels this tranquil balance in looking

45. Pietro Travaglia, design for scenery

at his only extant landscape design,[151] a snowbound scene for the *Orlando Paladino* which, with its romantic-dramatic atmosphere, must have been quite a novelty in his time.

However, much more animated and colourful than the picture revealed by the sketches must have been the reality of the actual stage: scenery and stage-designs were but a frame for the costumes, and both had to be adapted to the plays (or operas) enacted. The comic operas, especially, needed nicely varied scenery and colourful — often exotic — costumes. A painting from 1775 (see p. 99) shows a typically Rococo scene: we see garlands, a placid rural landscape, Turkish costumes, and angels peeping through clouds. In the middle of the eighties, the airy colourfulness of the comic operas was followed by the crowded bustle of a few '*dramme per musica*' which made excessive demands on the entire theatrical equipment. According to the estimates for the scenery and costumes of the opera *Didone abbandonata*,[152] not less than sixty performers and supers filled the stage, whom the libretto describes as having been garbed in Roman, Turkish, Moorish and Trojan dresses and accompanied by sham elephants, tigers and lions. Nor were the setpieces in this work less spectacular: the city of Carthage, set on fire at the behest of Iarba in the concluding scene, collapsed amidst a blaze of flames at the end of each performance.

With the exception of the snowy landscape for *Orlando Paladino*, it is very difficult to determine for which pieces the designs contained in Travaglia's sketchbook were intended. Investigations are hindered by the fact that the same scenery was usually employed for the performance of several different plays, dramas and operas. This was especially true in the case of such scenes as are sketched in Travaglia's book, e.g. 'Sala Nobile', 'Gran Salone Reale', 'Stanza Nobile' and the like, which could be used for nearly all kinds of pieces; it applies even to the 'Appartamento Chinese' which could be found in all up-to-date scene docks.

Travaglia's estimates for the costs of scenery for the entire year of 1786 contain a precise enumeration of those existing sets which were to be employed for the performance of new operas. For example, with certain modifications, the scenery of *La Didone abbandonata* was to be used for the first and that of *Montezuma* for the last-but-one scene of the *Alsinda*. 'Servirà la decorazione fatta per la *Didone* però con rincangiamento.'[153]

That a set could be put to manifold uses was partly due to the requirements of economy but partly also to a lack of a sense of historical nuance, to a want of susceptibility to *couleur locale* on the part of the public

46. Pietro Travaglia, design for scenery

of those times. With only a few alterations, pieces with classical themes were performed quite as much among Baroque surroundings and in Rococo costumes as plays with modern stories.

Apart from scenery and costumes, lighting is the most important factor in stage presentation. From Travaglia's regularly recurring demands for '*Spiritus*' and from a bill concerning repairs,[154] we know that lead-lined alcohol lamps were used for stage illumination. Beside '*Spiritus*', Travaglia often required flashlight powder ('*Plitz Pulver*') from the pharmacy of Eszterháza, presumably for the representation of lightning and fires.

Apart from the interior lighting of the theatre, Pietro Travaglia also had the task of seeing that the castle or the park was specially illuminated in honour of illustrious guests or for family celebrations. Thousands of tallow-filled jars, placed on the palace, the adjacent buildings and along the paths were employed for this purpose. An account, drawn up by Travaglia, shows that no less than 4,268 such tallow lamps were used for such an illumination on 12th September 1784. Of these jars, 2,600 had to be refilled, which alone required no less than seven hundredweight of black tallow.[155]

The illuminated castle in front of the park, sparkling with Chinese lamps and fireworks must have offered an impressive sight indeed. A courtier of the eighteenth century — whose whole life was passed in a stagelike milieu — must have really felt at Eszterháza as Goethe did in the city-park of Frankfurt, decorated with radiant globes, pyramids and Chinese lamps, which he described as the '*Esterhazysches Feenreich*': a land of dreams come true, an artificial fairyland.

# DECLINE OF ESZTERHÁZA

The successor of Miklós 'the Magnificent', Antal Esterházy, dissolved the opera-ensemble in October 1790, dismissed the actors whose contract would otherwise not have expired until the end of the year, and — apart from the so-called 'field' (i.e. a sort of military) band — retained only Haydn and Tommasini out of the musicians.

There was, during the three and a half years' princehood of Antal Esterházy, only a single celebration which recalled the old days of splendour, namely between the 3rd and 6th August 1791, on the occasion of the Prince's installation as lord-lieutenant of the county of Sopron. It is rather difficult to explain why Prince Antal put an end to Eszterháza's flourishing musical and theatrical life with one stroke. The cessation of gaieties could by no means have been due to economy, since those 300,000 florins which the Prince spent for the celebration of his installation would have sufficed to cover the musical and theatrical expenses of Miklós 'the Magnificent' for a whole decade. Neither could the change have been occasioned by a feeling that the style and forms of court life at Eszterháza had become obsolete (as they were later regarded by Prince Antal's successor, Miklós II), since the celebrations on the occasion of the installation were held in the spirit and style of Miklós 'the Magnificent' and also because Prince Antal did not transfer his seat to Kismarton. We have to accept the explanation of music-historians that, in contrast to Prince Miklós I, himself a gifted musician who sometimes played Haydn's barytone concertos before his guests, Prince Antal had absolutely no taste for music and perhaps none for the arts in general. Unlike his forefathers and descendants, he did not increase the family's scientific or art collections, and rather seemed to display a penchant for a military and political career: he took part in several military campaigns both before and after 1790.

It was in connection with these exceedingly sumptuous installation celebrations that the theatre of Eszterháza came into its own for the last time. Prince Antal commanded Haydn, who happened to be in London, to return; since Haydn was unable to come, the Prince commissioned Joseph Weigl, conductor of the Imperial Court Theatre of Vienna, to compose a new musical work. The cantata *Venere e Adonis*, composed for Abbate Casti's libretto, was then performed by the singers of the Vienna Court Opera: Mlle Giuliani, Mme Busani, Calvesi and Adamberger. The *première* must have been outstandingly splendid if we can rely on the descriptions published many decades later in the journals of the capital[156] according to which it had cost 40,000 florins. Opera *premières* did not cost, as a rule, more than some 3,000 florins during the reign of Miklós 'the Magnificent', although it must be borne in mind that, in this particular case, the composer as also the performers (the latter brought from Vienna) had to be paid extra.

Apart from the theatrical performance, a splendid ball, fireworks and hunts were arranged for the entertainment of the illustrious guests: the heir to the crown, the Palatine, the Prince-primate of Hungary, the diplomats and the representatives of the counties. The fireworks were prepared by a pyrotechnist of the name of Stuwer, who illuminated the palace and the park by means of 80,000 floating wicks. A contemporary engraving showing the military parade in the courtyard of the palace (see p. 157) is the only existing illustration which conveys a true idea of the large-scale celebrations arranged for the installation.

When the celebrations were over, Prince Antal had his guests accompanied by a cortège of musicians all the way to Buda.

Thereafter, Eszterháza became increasingly quiet and lonely. The Prince visited it rarely, and there were no more performances in the theatres. One solitary member of the old theatrical staff remained: Mrs. Handl, the wardrobe attendant, who fulfilled the functions of a sort of stock-keeper. It seems that even the ageing Travaglia had to look out for a new job, for — having been pensioned off in 1798 -- he asked for and received a certificate from Prince Antal's widow[157] in which she attested that Travaglia had been called back from state-service and promised a lifelong pension by her deceased husband. This suggests that Travaglia found a temporary job at the Court Theatre of Vienna.

Travaglia submitted several requests in connexion with his pension because in 1798 he had been awarded a pension of only two hundred instead of the expected three hundred florins. The last document, dated 8th January 1809,[158] refers — by way of refusing his claim to a higher pension — to a decree of the Prince from 1796 according to which he would be entitled to a pension of 300 florins only as long as he was

47. Pietro Travaglia, Snow-covered mountains for Haydn's opera, *Orlando Paladino*

jobless; since, meantime, he had become a *Hausinspektor* of the Grassalkovich family, he forfeited his right to receive more than two hundred florins.

Worthy of note is the fate of an Italian painter who happened to have arrived in the court of Eszterháza. It seems that right to the end of his life he had failed to get assimilated to his milieu, for he was repeatedly reproached by the Prince's officials for not having learnt to speak a good German despite a long service of from twenty to twenty-five years. The painter in question appears to have definitively opted for Hungary: he took the oath of naturalization at Kismarton in 1791 and tried to find his thirteen year-old lost son by means of an advertisement in the *Pressburger Zeitung* which stated that the boy spoke Hungarian and German as well as Italian.

After Prince Antal's death in 1794, Travaglia and Mrs. Handl again had more work in connection with the wardrobe and the stage properties of the Eszterháza theatre.

A written instruction, issued by Prince Miklós II, 8th July 1794[159] ordered Travaglia to supervise the work of reconstruction on the theatre at Kismarton for the festivities planned for the Prince's coming installation. He had also to concern himself with the festive illumination and the fireworks. As soon as the celebrations ended, the Prince issued an order for a precise inventory to be made of the wardrobe that had remained in the theatre of Eszterháza, including those costumes which for some reason had been retained by Travaglia.[160] Prince Miklós II issued instructions in July, 1796, according to which the old and worn-out scenery had to be transported in carts to the Lake Fertő and washed there so as to make them serviceable again.[161] It was likewise at that time that he gave orders to tidy up and air the scene dock and wardrobe at Eszterháza, and commanded Travaglia to advise Holzer, the machine-operator of the Kismarton theatre, and the carpenters, which of the theatrical hangings could still be used, and to see to their being transferred to Kismarton.[162] The serviceable costumes, too, were packed and carried away,[163] and Holzer dismantled all the stage fittings at Eszterháza together with the curtains and soffits.[164]

Countess Klutsewsky purchased those costumes of the Eszterháza stock which were not needed by the Prince's theatre at Kismarton and paid a price of 1,000 florins for them: it was Travaglia — already on the retired list at that time — who took delivery of the discarded pieces on behalf of the countess, and this was the last stage in the liquidation of the theatrical wardrobe of Eszterháza.

*

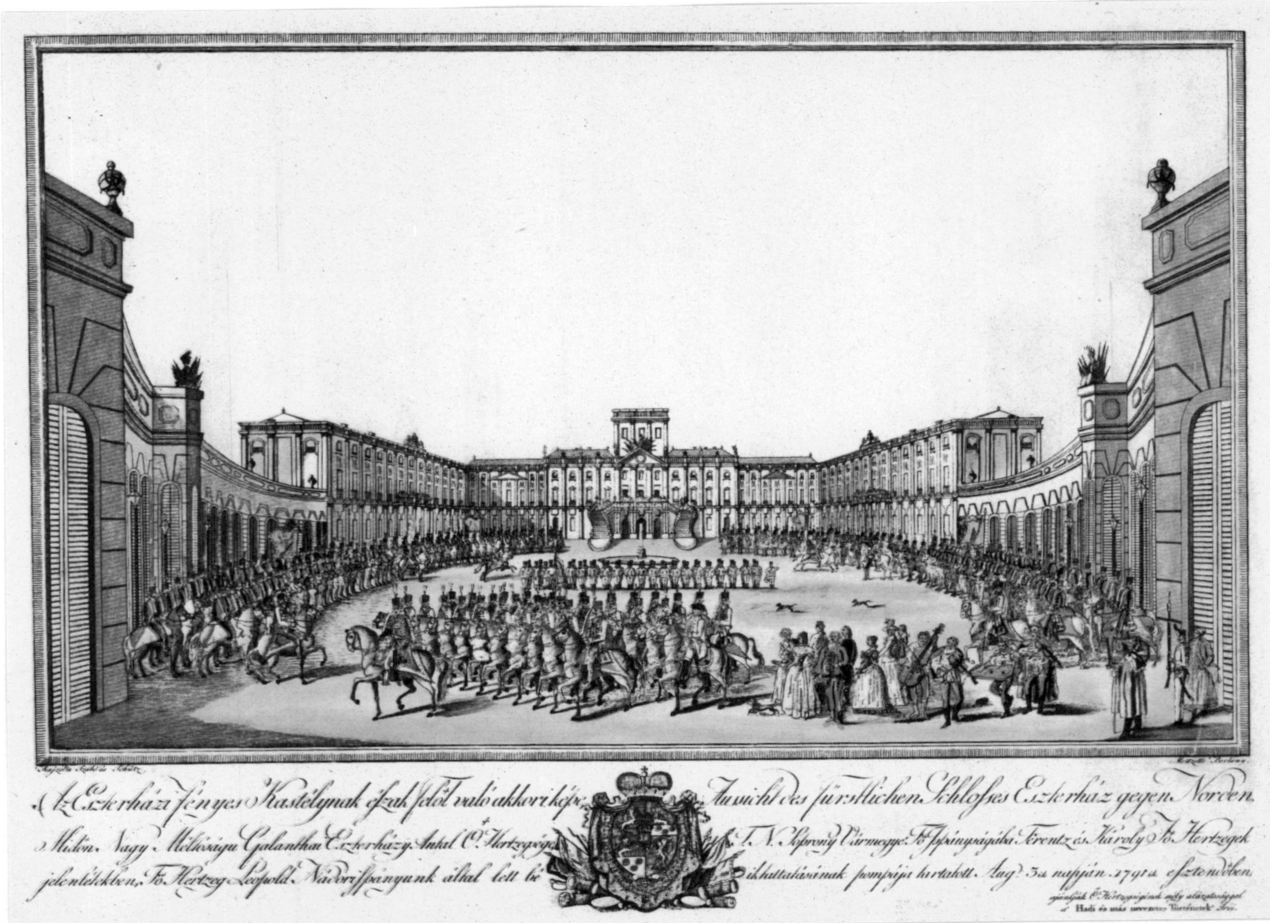


48. Feast at the installation of Antal Esterházy as Governor of the County, on 3rd August 1791

The fairyland of Eszterháza reflected the last rays of the sun that was setting upon the great lordly Baroque courts of the eighteenth century. That the splendour displayed at Eszterháza had come to be regarded as out of date is best illustrated by the fact that the grandson of Miklós 'the Magnificent' turned his back on Eszterháza as if its court life — vigorous, pulsating, sumptuous and dazzling but a few years before — had been completely alien to him. The fashion of Versailles had become obsolete and the Rococo a thing of the past. The era of a new classicism had begun, and French parks were being rearranged in the English style.

By 1803, the puppet theatre of Eszterháza had been turned into a mere storehouse for hunting gear,[165] while — according to a description in the *Tudományos Gyüjtemény*[166] — straw was being stored in the theatre buildings in 1824. According to the '*Inventarium* über die in dem Esterhazer Schlosse, Bagatelle und Theater vorhandenen Mobilien und Effecten', prepared in 1832, the large theatre building was used as a woodyard where the old sceneries lay about higgledy-piggledy, one on top of the other. The puppet theatre was likewise used as a timber storehouse by the joiner. All pieces of value were transferred from the palace to Kismarton by Miklós II in the 1790s who left the buildings and park of Eszterháza to their fate. When the work of restoration was started at the turn of the next century, only ruins marked the place of the operahouse. As the *Tudományos Gyüjtemény* remarked, 'autumn melancholy reigned supreme' at Eszterháza.

# BACK TO KISMARTON

Though looking upon Eszterháza as anachronistic and in spite of having transferred his seat to the family's ancient castle at Kismarton, Miklós Esterházy II had nevertheless remained loyal to the traditions of Miklós 'the Magnificent' inasmuch as he was a munificent patron of arts in general and the theatre in particular.

His orchestra and chorus were even bigger than those of his grandfather; he not only maintained his own theatre but was at the same time one of the most significant leaders of the Vienna Court Theatre. By purchasing Count Neuperg's library in 1795, he greatly enriched the ancient library of the Esterházy family; he established a cabinet of medals and a collection of snail shells; last but not least, he was the real founder of the famous Esterházy picture gallery. The gallery inherited from Miklós 'the Magnificent' contained, apart from Raphael's Esterházy Madonna, very few really valuable masterpieces. Prince Miklós II, gifted with a taste considerably superior to that of his forefathers, showed great wisdom in choosing Joseph Fischer as his collaborator: with his assistance, he succeeded in creating one of the most beautiful and comprehensive collections of paintings and engravings in the entire Monarchy. This is the collection which was to serve as the basis of the Museum of Fine Arts in Budapest.

The celebrations arranged for the Prince's installation at Kismarton in 1794 and his earliest activities made it clear that the Esterházy theatre had found a new patron in the person of Miklós II. While, at first, the Prince engaged only *ad hoc* theatrical companies, he subsequently organized a new opera-ensemble when the development of the orchestra had made good progress: this ensemble was continuously active from 1804 to 1812. So far, theatrical history has recorded the activities of the Prince's theatre up to 1807 only, although the most prominent singers were engaged after this date and despite the fact that the cult of Mozart, the most memorable achievement of the Esterházy theatre at Kismarton, was developed after 1807.

At the celebrations provided for the installation on the 24th—25th June 1794, the ensemble of the Leopoldstädter Theater — led by Marinelli and also including Salvatore and Maria Vigano, the famous ballet dancers — gave a guest performance at Kismarton.[167] The two Viganos had toured all over Europe, and Salvatore Vigano afterwards became the ballet master of the Scala of Milan. A few costumes, taken from Eszterháza, were used for the performance at Kismarton.[168] Music for the ball, held during the festivities, was supplied by an orchestra composed of thirty-six musicians.[169] According to Travaglia's statement, 177 pounds of tallow were used for the festive illumination.[170]

Very little is known about the repertoire of the following year. It is certain that there were fireworks and theatrical performances during September and October. We know that Travaglia drew a sum of 300 florins on 17th September for the expenses of a pyrotechnic show arranged on the feast day of Our Lady,[171] while the plays *Armuth und Edelsinn* and *Skizze der rauchen Sitten unserer guten Vorältern* (performed on 16th September and 8th October 1795, respectively) are referred to in the notes of the accounts department commenting upon Travaglia's statement concerning theatrical expenses for the year 1795. Travaglia's statement and the notes of the accounts department refer to other significant works as well. For example, the notes comment upon the excessive amounts paid for joiners and carpenters. They admit that these extra expenses were justified by the urgency of the works involved but say that works of this kind would have to be performed by permanently employed tradesmen in the future.

An estimate for the costs of scenery representing a Gothic castle, a peasant's room and the hell[172] reveals the fact that the soffits had a length of twenty-four feet, from which it follows that the width of the stage must have been the same. The perspective picture of the Gothic castle had a height of sixteen feet. This goes to show that the stage of Kismarton was smaller than that of Eszterháza, but we cannot tell where it was actually situated. The descriptions always refer to the theatre in general without information regarding its site. A record according to which the theatre of Kismarton was reconstructed for the installation festivities suggests that it must be dealing with the conservatory theatre erected in the sixties. It is, on the other hand, clearly stated in the memoirs of Heinrich Schmidt, who became the manager of the Kismarton theatre a decade later, that theatrical performances were held in the great ceremonial hall of the palace. These two sources are not necessarily contradictory. It is quite possible that performances were held on the con-

49. Portrait of Miklós Esterházy II

servatory stage at the beginning, and in the palace itself at a later date. The ceremonial hall was reconstructed and enlarged according to Moreau's plans and the wall adjacent to the garden was pulled down at the beginning of the new century: it can be supposed that the theatre was transferred there only after its reconstruction.

We have no information regarding the name of the company that was staying at Kismarton during autumn 1795, but it is possible that it was the same ensemble of Marinelli which had already played in the preceding season and was to be re-engaged a couple of years later.

Preparations for the autumn season started in June 1796. Works of repair in the theatre were taken in hand and scenery was designed by Travaglia;[173] costumes were sent over from Eszterháza by the wardrobe attendant there.[174] A contract for the engagement of Karl Stadler's company, which was to start performances in the autumn, was already concluded on the 1st of July.

Johann Karl Stadler was an excellent young actor and, at that time, the manager of a company at Wiener Neustadt. Born in 1768 in Vienna, he started his acting career at Graz. He was a handsome young man who had scored his first successes as *amoroso* in Laibach and Trieste. He joined the Theater an der Wien in 1787 and became a member of the Hofburgtheater during the season 1789—90. He appeared in Pest in 1791—2, and in Prague in 1792—3. He grew rather fat at that time so that, thenceforth, he appeared only in father parts. He emerged later at Kassel and Frankfurt, to become thereafter manager of the Municipal Theatre of Bremen. Stadler died at Hannover in 1812. He was a dramatic actor in the first place but, having a good voice, appeared also in operas.

Stadler addressed a desperate letter to the Prince, 4th March 1796, requesting the latter to engage him, even if for only a short time, since he was in a tight corner on account of the conditions arising out of the war.[175] He enclosed with the letter a list in which sixty-three dramas and twenty-three operas were enumerated, any of which his company was able to enact. Let us note that the list of operas included three operas by Haydn (*Armida, Orlando Paladino, La fedeltà premiata*). In contradiction to Pohl's statement, it is evident from the still extant printed repertoire that none of them were staged.[176]

It seems that Stadler's urgent solicitation was received favourably by the Prince, since it was presumably on the latter's behest that Stadler forwarded a statement to the Prince at the end of March. The statement had been drawn up by the Municipal Council of Wiener Neustadt to the effect that Stadler's company had given full satisfaction by its musical

50. Mad. Vigano, Josepha Maria Medina

and dramatic performances and that the ensemble had been leading a respectable life during their stay in the town.[177]

The contract, concluded on 1st July, bound the company to hold performances in the German language every Tuesday, Thursday, Saturday and Sunday between the 1st September and the 15th October. Stadler undertook to amplify his repertoire by additional popular plays, to provide all costumes except those of the supers, and to engage carefully selected singers. The company was to draw a weekly salary of 110 florins.[178] The final list of the members and the actual repertoire were as follows.

'Staff of theatre company assembled for Kismarton:

Actors:

Peterka: first lovers, heroes; comic parts in operas. Schmidtmann: first lovers in operas, lovers in dramas and plays. Normann: basso; character parts in dramas and plays. Horst: intriguants, pedants. Stadler: tender fathers, quarrelsome old people, decorous parts. Berke: baritone; dignified parts. Hanold: second tenor; subordinate parts in plays. Koch: secondary parts; prompter.

Actresses:

Eiersperg: comic parts in operas, heroines; decorous parts in plays. Horst: mature lovers, young women, decorous parts. Normann: coquettish women, termagants. Stadler: young lovers, *ingénue* parts. Kunfeld: first singer. Willmers: comic parts, *soubrettes*. Kreutzer: *dilettantes*, first lovers, heroines, decorous parts.[179]

| | | |
|---|---|---|
| September | 1. | *Das rothe Käppchen*. Opera |
| | 3. | *Johanna von Neapel*. Drama |
| | 4. | *Impressar in der Klemme ; Der Dorfbarbier*. Two comedies. |
| | 6. | *Die unmögliche Sache*. Comedy. |
| | 8. | *Die Waldmänner*. Opera. |
| | 9. | *Huldane, König der Düren*. Drama. |
| | 10. | An occasional play. |
| | 11. | *Der Neffe*. Play. |
| | 13. | *Rings 1ter Theil*. Comedy. |
| | 15. | *Rings 2ter Theil*. Comedy. |
| | 17. | *Graf Benyovsky*. Drama. |
| | 18. | *Hieronymus Kniker*. Opera. |
| | 20. | *Bettelstudent ; Schadenfreude*. Two comedies. |
| | 22. | *Die drillings Brüder*. Comedy. |

51. Rearrangement of the Kismarton park in the English style, plan from the beginning of the nineteenth century

24. *Klara von Hofmeichen.* Drama.
25. *Die Zauber Zither.* Opera.
27. *Die Hiader* (Fiacher?). Comedy.
29. *Der Hochzeit-Tag.* Comedy.

October 1. *Kusper der Thoringer.* Drama.
2. *Der Gutsherin.* Opera.
4. *Die verschlossene Thür.* Comedy.
6. *Der Taubstumme.* Comedy.
8. *Otto von Wittelsbach.* Drama.
9. *Die Zauberflöte* (*The Magic Flute*). Opera.
11. *Der Fremde.* Comedy.
13. *Das Ehrmarrt.* Comedy.
15. An occasional play at the termination of the spectacles performed.'

The most interesting item of the repertoire is the representation of *The Magic Flute.* While the Hummel biography of Karl Benyovszky and the diary of Karl Rosenbaum say Mozart's opera was first represented in the year 1804, the above repertoire shows that its *première* took place eight years earlier at Kismarton.

A noteworthy feature of this first Kismarton repertoire is that, in marked contrast to the repertoires of Eszterháza, it contains only plays and operas in the German language. Instead of the proposed three operas by Haydn, the actual repertory included *The Magic Flute, Die Waldmänner*, an opera likewise composed for Schikaneder's libretto, as also three spectacular new German operas: *Hieronymus Kniker, Die Zauber Zither* and *Der Gutsherin.* Italian opera buffa seems to have been definitively superseded by the advance of German operas on the stage of the Esterházys.

*

Life in autumn, 1797, was again full of activities in the castle of Kismarton. The Empress paid a visit to Eszterháza and Kismarton on 19th August. The palace and the park of Kismarton were festively illuminated, and fireworks were arranged in the evening on the 9th and 10th September in honour of Princess Maria. Karl Rosenbaum's diary[180] informs us that, on the 17th, the officials of the Prince's court and the guests participated in the first rehearsal of Iffland's play *Die Aussteuer.* The rehearsal was repeated on the following two days, and the *première*

52. Charles Moreau, reconstruction of the Esterházy Palace at Kismarton

took place on the 20th September. Marinelli's company appeared on the stage on the 21st.

A shooting party in honour of the guests who had arrived in the suite of Palatine Archduke Joseph was arranged on 26th September, while, according to Rosenbaum's diary, Marinelli's ensemble presented the comedy *Der reisende Student* in the evening. The performance was followed by Vigano's ballet *Pygmalion* with the participation of the author himself.[181] The day concluded with a fancy-dress ball and a splendid illumination attended by 1,200 guests.[182]

Hunting, balls, festive illuminations and concerts were arranged for the entertainment of the guests on 27th and 28th. Female singers were brought from Pozsony for the concert on the 28th (Rosenbaum).

The presentation of a comedy (*Stadt und Land*), written by Spiess, was one of the most noteworthy events of the autumn season. The play, the cost of which is recorded in Rosenbaum's diary, was performed by the inhabitants and the guests of the palace as a piece of amateur theatricals. Together with the notabilities, Rosenbaum and his son, as also Grundmann, the old court painter, appeared on the stage:

'Cast:

| | |
|---|---|
| Countess Albingen, a rich widow ... | Countess Charlotte Weissenwolf |
| Baroness von Halber, her sister-in-law ........................... | Countess Charlotte Hohenfeld |
| Miss Lottchen .................. | Princess Grassalkovich |
| Miss Beata, the baroness's daughter | Countess Fanny Weissenwolf |
| General von Hilsenburg ........... | Kühnel, cavalry-officer |
| Major Count of Wieden ........... | v. Kárner, secretary |
| Baron von Schildberg ............. | Lieutenant Seitz |
| von Wattsdorf .................. | Count Johann Weissenwolf |
| Nanette, chambermaid of the Countess | Countess Julia Esterházy |
| Michel, servant of the Baroness .... | Rosenbaum Jr. |
| Servants ........................ | Rosenbaum, Grundmann' |

According to Rosenbaum's comments, this amateur performance, though not very good was, of course, received with good-natured applause.

We have no information about the further repertoire of the month of October but it can be taken for granted that Marinelli's ensemble continued to give performances without interruption during the whole month.

The Palatine's second visit to Kismarton, reported in detail by the *Magyar Hirmondó*,[183] was the season's last outstanding event. 'The Pala-

53. Charles Moreau, reconstruction of the Esterházy Palace at Kismarton

tine and, together with him, the illustrious guests were received and honoured here yesterday and the day before. His Royal Highness, arriving from Laxenburg, began hunting on Prince Esterházy's estates near the border. When the chase was over, he betook himself amidst the boom of cannons to Kismarton. Soon after his arrival, almost a hundred guests took their seats at richly decorated tables. The palace, together with the opposite building and the park, were lit up in the evening by green, red and gold-coloured lamps, and the illumination was so splendid that its like has seldom been seen anywhere in the world. Artificial fires conjured up the picture of the King and Queen as also their names. Comedians, brought from Vienna, performed a merry play in the Prince's theatre ; and a new ballet, with the title *Pygmalion*, was then presented by the famous Vigano, his wife and young daughter. This was followed by a fancy-dress ball and an opulent banquet in the great hall of the palace. The Palatine rose early the next morning, the 27th October, in order to inspect the coal mines of Wandorf where he was received by Count Saurau, Councillor Ruprecht and other gentlemen. He returned to Kismarton at midday to consume a light meal, then he participated in a shooting party at which a thousand hares and nearly as many pheasants were brought down. Dinner began at 6 o'clock followed by the performance of Haydn's splendid composition "The Seven Words" for which many musicians and singers had been engaged from Vienna. Before this, when the Palatine entered the theatre, Haydn's well-known composition "God Save Francis the Emperor" was sung. After these delightful musical performances Vigano and his family danced again. The same evening the castle and the opposite building were illuminated, and a ball was held in the smaller dancing room of the palace.'

*

Available information is considerably less complete regarding theatrical life at Kismarton between 1798 and 1804. We know nothing of regularly engaged and continuously performing companies which, however, need not necessarily mean that there were no performances during the autumn season. We find the following report in the *Magyar Hirmondó*[184] in connection with Mary's Day in 1801: '. . . the name-day of Princess Esterházy was celebrated the day before yesterday. There arrived many guests even from Vienna, among them Cardinal Prince Albani, Muravief-Apostol the Russian Envoy Extraordinary, as also Prince Carl Schwarzenberg who had returned from St. Petersburg. I do not feel competent enough to describe all the splendour, such as the

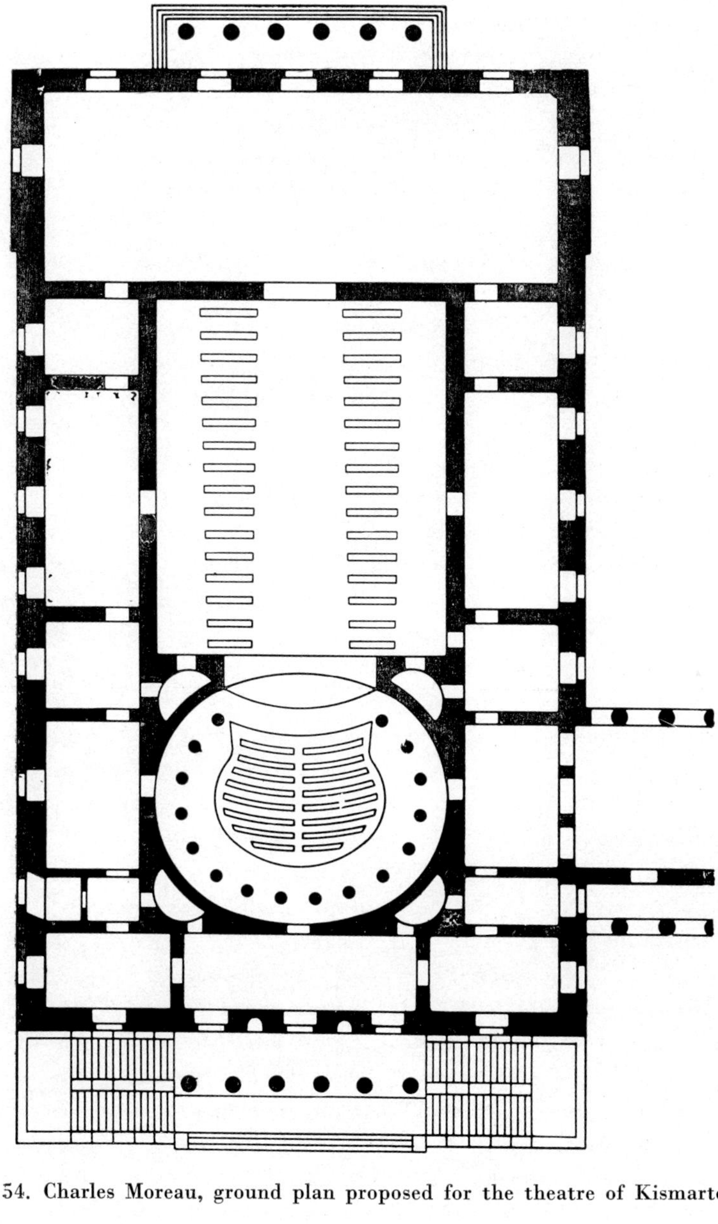

54. Charles Moreau, ground plan proposed for the theatre of Kismarton

dancing, the illumination of the ceremonial hall with eight hundred candles, the opulent dinners and suppers, the deafening roar of the cannons and the wonderful music in the evening.'

So there was no theatrical performance on this day. On 29th August of the following year Rosenbaum noted in his diary that 'Haydn, Elsler and Mayer came after the meal'. This may have referred to the appearance of Mayer's company at Kismarton.

Although our ideas of theatrical life at Kismarton in these years are hazy, we know that the Esterházy orchestra was reborn at this time, that the new choral ensemble was gradually taking shape during this period and that — as part of his sweeping architectural plans — the idea of a new theatre at Kismarton was maturing in the mind of Prince Miklós II.

At the request of the Prince, the ageing Haydn was pleased to shoulder the task of organizing and directing the new orchestra, while somebody else had to be entrusted with the actual task of conducting. Therefore, the Prince engaged Johann Nepomuk Fuchs in 1802 to conduct the church orchestra and chorus, while Luigi Tommasini became the head of the chamber-music ensemble. The latter had been engaged by Prince Pál Antal already, and used to play first violin in the orchestra of Miklós 'the Magnificent'. The engagement of Johann Nepomuk Hummel, made on the recommendation of Haydn on the 1st of April, 1804, was the most important step in connection with the revival of the Esterházy opera. Hummel came from a *milieu* that was out-and-out theatrical. His father had been conductor of the Municipal Theatre of Pozsony till 1780 and later held the same position at the Theater an der Wien; Johann Nepomuk, ten years of age at that time, an infant prodigy, disciple of Mozart, accompanied his father on a three-year concert-tour through Europe. It was during this tour that he made the acquaintance of Haydn in London in the year 1791. He later moved from Kismarton to Weimar where he became a prominent figure of musical life by the side of Liszt.

Along with the development of the orchestra the castle and park of Kismarton underwent considerable transformation. The park was greatly enlarged in the first years of the century and remodelled after the English fashion according to the design of Moreau. Pumps run with the aid of animals used to ensure the water supply of the lake and fountains of the park until the visit of Miklós II to London in 1803 where he purchased a steam engine manufactured by David Matson.[185] The new engine-house, together with other new buildings of the park, was then inaugurated amidst splendid festivities in 1805; to commemorate the event, a piece

55. Portrait of Johann Nepomuk Hummel

of each coin then in circulation was immured in the basement wall. After France and Germany, Hungary was the third country to possess a steam engine.

Simultaneously with the remodelling of the park, Moreau prepared plans for a classical reconstruction and a considerable enlargement of the palace. According to Moreau's design, the palace was to be extended toward the park, and two new wings, right and left, were to be annexed to it for the accommodation of the theatre and the library. The plan of the new theatre shows a conspicuously large stage. The ground plan of the auditorium shows a transversely arranged oval figure surrounded by columns (p. 171).

The two annexes were never been built, but certain reconstructions and the enlargement of the palace toward the park were carried out nevertheless, and also a splendid colonnade, envisaged in the plan, was erected. The ceremonial hall, scene of the opera performances at Kismarton, was likewise amplified.

*

The performance of *The Magic Flute*, presented on 10th August 1804, was the first event of significance, a sort of introduction to the opera repertoire of 1805. We learn from Karl Rosenbaum's diary that the performance was held at his expense at the Engel-Gasthaus in the town. Hummel undertook its musical direction, while the scenery was the work of Carl Maurer.

Maurer, a man of mediocre talent but a very lively person, was engaged by Prince Miklós II in 1802 as 'Hofkammermaler'. It was he who suggested on 29th August 1803, that the Prince should transform the empty palace of Pottendorf into a picture gallery and entrust its supervision to an inspector. Maurer can, therefore, be regarded as having first conceived the idea of the subsequently famous Esterházy picture gallery.

The representation of *The Magic Flute* offered a good opportunity for Maurer to rise above the rank of a simple house-painter. That the scenery was actually designed by Maurer is best illustrated by the fact that, on the verso of page 11 of his sketchbook,[186] he registered the scenery under the following heading: 'Decorationen zur Zauberflöte. 1804 für Eisenstadt. Inv. Maurer'. The sketchbook contains the designs of eight scenes for *The Magic Flute* and a drawing of Sarastro's state carriage. Both these and Maurer's later scenic designs reveal little independence and a strong influence of the Vienna scenewright Anton de Pian. This influence is most striking in the designs contained on pages 124 and

56. Title-page of Carl Maurer's sketch-book

129 of the sketchbook. The first is a scene for the drama *Don Gutierre*, the second that for the opera *Lodoiska*. Apart from slight simplifications, these designs are the same as the corresponding ones of Anton de Pian.[187]

Hummel seems to have been engaged by the Prince in spring, 1804, with the express purpose of producing opera performances in the autumn season. The new conductor submitted invoices in August and September concerning the copying expenses of a great number of musical stage compositions. Overtures and parts of Mozart's and Cherubini's operas had chiefly been copied obviously for the purposes of concerts.[188] Apart from invoices of this kind, we find also others which make it evident that entire operas must also have been staged, e.g. 'Copiatur aller Stimmen der Oper *Die beiden Füchse* nebst Soufleurs auszug; 15 Büchel verschiedener Opern à 20 xr; 12 Detto von *Neusonntagskind*'. This note is accompanied by the account for various dresses for men, women and children, for hats and other stage property, further '2 Klavier ins Theater, und wieder weg tragen 2 fl.'[189] Another note refers to expenses arising out of the vocal scores and the libretto of the operas *Neusonntagskind* and *Doctor und Apotheker*, as also for the repeated transport of a piano to and from the theatre.[190] All these documents, referring to administrative theatrical work, go to prove that opera performances in the palace of Kismarton had become continuous by the autumn of 1804.

We are much better acquainted with the repertoire of the following year. The imposing array of Esterházy opera librettos was restarted in this year. Leopold Stolz, who had been a member of Anton Polkas's theatrical company in the town of Kismarton in 1802, left the ensemble, organized a children's troupe and established a printing-shop in which the libretto of Haydn's *Creation* was printed in 1804. He printed eighteen librettos for the reorganized opera company of the Prince between 1805 and 1810. These librettos constitute the most important documents regarding the opera repertoire of the castle of Kismarton. Beside facilitating the compilation of a list of the operas performed, they contain data regarding the artists who took part in them.

Eight librettos were issued by Stotz's printing-office in 1805: *The Elopement from the Harem* (Mozart); *Der Dorfbarbier, Der Fassbinder, Arien aus dem Fassbinder* (Schenk); *Das Findelkind* (Benda). The others were 'domestic' compositions, i.e. pieces written by local authors. Heinrich Schmidt's two one-act comedies: *Der Junker in der Mühle* and *Die Stutzperücke*. The first was enacted with Antonio Polzelli's accompanying music on the name-day of the Princess. Worthy of note among the items

57. Carl Maurer's design for scenery for the performance of Mozart's opera, *The Magic Flute*, at Kismarton

of the repertoire is the musical comedy *Die beyden Genies* with libretto by Georg von Gaal, the Prince's librarian, and the music of Hummel. The protagonists of the play are the playwright and the composer themselves, staged as the poet Lindenhain and the composer Stork. These two parts were performed by the two authors in person. The comedy in question belongs, therefore, to the most valuable documents bearing on amateur theatricals at Kismarton.

Other sources enabling us to reconstruct the repertoire of 1805 are the notes of the hairdresser Anton Elsler regarding his services for the theatre between the 13th of September and the 12th October. We learn from them that, apart from the pieces quoted above, the following works were also staged: *Der Bettelstudent, Neusonntagskind, Haus Tochter, Beidefügs, Wochenblatt, Unglücklichen.*[191]

A person who played an important role in the vigorously revived theatrical life of Kismarton was the new theatrical manager Heinrich Schmidt who had been trained in theatrical art by Goethe in Weimar. A thorough knowledge of the stage and a wide circle of acquaintances enabled the new manager to maintain a steady contact between the princely opera and the centres of German culture. It is in his memoirs that we find the most authentic description of the Esterházy theatre:

'So I have now become the leader of Prince Esterházy's theatre at Kismarton and, in my capacity as a secretary of all matters concerning art, I am responsible also for the Prince's musical and art collections. The theatre in which nothing but operas were performed was far from being a simple and common one. Joseph Haydn, Hummel, Fuchs and — later — Henneberg were the conductors of a prominent orchestra whose manager was Tommasini, the reputed violonist; an institute where young boys were trained in choral songs and also musically well-trained large male and female choruses; male and female singers such as Wild and Forti in the heyday of their youth and fame, Mlle Cornega, the disciple of Salieri (who went subsequently to Paris and London in quest of glory), Frau von Vadász, Mme Froll, Demoiselle Stotz, Messrs Grell and Schuster were, all and sundry, eminent artists. Performances were always held in September, October, November and December, together with splendid hunting parties and other celebrations, the costs of which truly expressed the splendour of the princely house. The guests belonged to the highest *élite*, and usually almost the entire aristocracy and the *corps diplomatique* of Vienna were present. The singers and, in bad weather, the greater part of the audience were brought in closed carriages to the theatre which

58. Carl Maurer's design for scenery for the performance of Mozart's opera, *The Magic Flute*, at Kismarton

was situated in a huge hall of the palace. The charging of entrance fees was unknown: on the contrary, gratis refreshments of all kinds were offered to singers and audience alike.'[192]

*

We know six printed librettos from the year 1806. Two of them are Hummel's works: *Die vereitelten Raenke* which was a new version of *Le vicende d'amore*, further *Endimione e Diana* which was written for the wedding of Leopoldina Esterházy; two other librettos were written by D'Alayrac: *Die beyden Savoyarden* and *Gulistan oder der Hulla von Samarkanda*; the fifth was the libretto of Le Brun's opera *Pächter Robert* and the sixth that of Umlauf's opera *Das Fest der Liebe und der Freude.*

The author of the libretto written for the last named opera was Joachim Perinet, the permanently engaged playwright of the Leopoldstädter Theatre, who — accompanied by six of his colleagues from Vienna — took part in the performance at Kismarton on 12th April together with the members of the Prince's ensemble. The guest performers from Vienna were the author and his wife, as also Ignaz Schuster, members of the Leopoldstädter Theater; Hasenhut from the Theater an der Wien; Weidmann and Baumann from the Burgtheater; another guest performer was a certain Demoiselle Neumann. Heinrich Schmidt's memoirs describe the performance as more or less a failure. The courtly audience had a fastidious taste and made a wry face at the coarse jokes of the popular Viennese comedians and their saucy Esterházy-etymologies, which seem to have satirised Miklós 'the Magnificent'. We find the following passage in Schmidt's notes: 'Perinet, the "domestic" playwright of the Leopoldstädter Theater, who had already written a number of musical plays (e.g. the *Neusonntagskind* and *Die zwei Schwestern von Prag*) produced the libretto of a new opera for this occasion under the title *Das Fest der Liebe und Freude.* The three most popular and best comic actors of Vienna, namely Weidmann, Hasenhut and Beckmann, further Perinet himself and his wife, as also a number of male and female dancers arrived from Vienna to take part in the *première* at Kismarton. Unfortunately, the libretto contained so many scurrilous and scabrous passages that I felt induced to warn the Prince. Authorized by him, I blue-pencilled the most offensive parts and altered the text. The author did not like it, for, in his experience, just such tasteless passages could be expected to produce the greatest effect. At the performance, the guest actors from Vienna did not pay much attention to my alterations, recited most of the deleted passages and shocked all the audience. For instance, an old and deaf school-

59. Carl Maurer's design for scenery for the performance of Mozart's opera, *The Magic Flute*, at Kismarton

master, a sort of old monkey from the *Findelkind*, splendidly represented by Weidmann, explained the origin of the name Esterházy in something like the following terms: 'The ancestor of the princely family, a great conoisseur in matters feminine, lost his way during a chase in the forest. Looking round in his embarrassment, he beheld a pretty young girl, he ran to her, embraced her and wanted to know her name: — "Tell me your name, beautiful child" — "Ester has i" (They call me Ester) — said the maid, and — turning into a fairy — led him out of the wood.'[193]

In 1807, J. N. Fuchs too became a 'domestic' composer of the Kismarton theatre. Using the libretto of Gewey, he composed the comic opera *Der hölzerne Liebesbothe oder: die Neuigkeitswuth.* Extant librettos show that also Cimarosa's adaptation of Mozart's *The Impresario*, the *Theatralische Abenteuer*, further a comic opera that had scored a great success at the Theater an der Wien, namely Méhul's *Der Schatzgräber*, were staged at Kismarton. We possess information also about another item of the 1807 repertoire, the appearance of a ballet ensemble.[194] Domenico Strain, 'k.k. Hoff Theatral Garderobbe Inspektor', submitted a statement on 12th August 1807, regarding costumes, diadems, garlands etc. supplied for the 'festivity of Kismarton' on the order of the ballet master F. Taglioni. Apart from the latter, the statement mentions also the name of Mme Corally, Mlle Neumann and Bandini.

Correspondences between the respective repertoires of 1804 and 1805 show that, beside new pieces, also compositions that had already been represented in previous years formed part of the current repertoire. The Prince's opera company had, by this time, presented three compositions of Mozart, and their number was to increase in the years to come. We find, on page 40 of Maurer's sketchbook, a design of the Capitol with the note that it had been drawn for the *Titus*, and the intensive cult of Mozart's music at Kismarton justifies the conclusion that this formed part of the scenery planned for the *première* in the Esterházy theatre. Although the sketchbook contains a number of Maurer's later sketches not drawn at or intended for Kismarton, the greater part of the drawings can, nevertheless, be regarded as having been made at and intended for the Kismarton theatre. The sketchbook contains 130 pages: the first drawings bear the date 1804, the scenery for *Don Giovanni* on page 118 was probably made for the Kismarton representation of 1808, while the year 1812 is noted on the title page. Apart from a short interruption at Pozsony, Maurer worked during the whole time at Kismarton. The scenery for *La clemenza di Tito* (The Clemency of Titus) seen on page 40 was, thus, made for Mozart's fourth opera which was represented presum-

60. Carl Maurer's design for scenery for the performance of Mozart's opera, *The Magic Flute*, at Kismarton

ably in 1807, for neither the repertoires of the preceding nor those of the subsequent years include *La clemenza di Tito.*

Only a single repertoire from the years subsequent to 1807 is extant, that of the opera *Cendrillon* from 1810 — although the development of the theatre in those years was still on the upswing. Miklós Esterházy established a close contact with Vienna's theatrical life in 1807. It was in that year that the so-called *Gesellschaft der Cavaliere*, composed of the Princes Joseph Schwarzenberg, Josef Lobkowitz and Miklós Esterházy, the Counts Hieronymus of Lodron, Miklós Esterházy, the two Counts Ferenc Esterházy, further the Counts Ferenc Zichy and Ferdinand Pálffy, took over the lease of the two Court Theatres and the Theater an der Wien from Baron Braun for a payment of 1,200,000 florins. These theatres were then run by the syndicate in the form of a joint-stock company till 1813. Prince Miklós II, who paid 200,000 florins towards the venture, took an active part in the management of the three theatres and concerned himself especially with the staging of Shakespeare's, Schiller's and Goethe's works.

From 1808 a *Rapport* was daily printed for the members of the theatre and the orchestra indicating the persons who had to appear that day at rehearsals or performances. The *Rapport* contained the names of all singers and musicians, and indicated in every case the title of the composition in the performance of which this or that member had to take part.

According to the *Rapports*, the following operas were presented between the 27th August and the 27th October 1808: *Der Barbier von Sevilien, Don Giovanni, Die verehlichte Freyer, Das Haus zu verkaufen, Pächter Robert, Gulistan oder der Hulla von Samarkanda* and *Die drey Sultaninnen.* A note by J. N. Hummel from 23rd October[195] enables us to add to this list the following operas: *Agnes Sorel, Tage der Gefahr, Uniform, Die beyden Füchse, Der Telegraph, Neusonntagskind, Zwey Worte, Die beyden Savoyarden, Der Dorfbarbier, Der Schatzgräber.* These compositions are referred to by Hummel as having already been performed but presentable at any time.

Many of the casts include the name of Anton Forti, pride of the theatre mentioned repeatedly also by Schmidt. This excellent singer had been born in 1790 in Vienna so that he was only eighteen years of age at his first appearance. He played the viola in the orchestra of the Theater an der Wien when the Prince engaged him. Forti's career as a singer thus began at Kismarton. He soon returned to Vienna there to remain the favourite of the opera-going public till the end of his life. Opera-history knows him as one of the best interpreters of Sarastro and Don Giovanni.

61. Carl Maurer's design for scenery for the performance of Mozart's opera, *The Magic Flute*, at Kismarton

It is probable that he first sang the part of Don Giovanni at Kismarton, for his name appears in all rehearsals of *Don Giovanni.* How attractive his voice must have been is illustrated by a romantic episode recorded in Schmidt's memoirs: 'Forti, in the prime of youth at that time, was helped by one of the Hungarian noblemen who were directing the theatre of Pozsony to run away from us in the dead of night. I lost no time in following him next day with a view to bringing him back, but failed to get hold of him at Pozsony because one of the noblemen had taken him to his castle near Pozsony to keep him in a safe place. Arriving at the castle, I found myself in a difficult position seeing that in those times a Hungarian nobleman was entitled to many privileges on his own estates. However, after repeated attempts I succeeded in bringing Forti back to Kismarton where he continued to sing his parts until the termination of the festivities.'[196]

Two further documents enable us to complete the repertoire, as reconstructed on the evidence of the *Rapports*, by the operas *Schatzgräber* and *Agnes Sorel.*[197] These documents reveal some controversy between Schmidt's wife, Elise Schneider, and Madame Vadász which induced the former to give up to the latter the part for which she was cast in the *Schatzgräber*, under the pretext that her, i.e. Mme Schmidt's, whole time was taken up memorizing the part of Elvira in *Don Giovanni* and the title role in *Agnes Sorel.*

Our next information regarding the activities of the Esterházy theatre dates from 1810. A statement of Schmidt accounts for the expenses laid out for two performances of the *Schweitzer Familie* held on 30th April,[198] while a letter of Hummel, addressed to the Prince on 6th April contains the news that he succeeded in engaging Franz Wild, the prominent tenor of the Imperial Court Theatre, for the theatre of Kismarton.[199] Franz Wild, eighteen years of age at that time, 'quite a young boy, sang diffidently and charmingly like a nightingale. He was not yet conscious of his great talent and the sweeping effect of his miraculous voice. This was the secret of his being so attractive and moving.'[200]

Although we do not know their full repertoire, it is safe to assume that these one or two years constituted the brightest period of the Esterházy theatre at Kismarton. The number of the musical staff had risen to fifty and, led by Fuchs, Hummel and the newly-engaged Henneberg, it gave concerts of fine quality and presented operas with a high artistic skill. Even the incompletely known repertoire makes it clear that the performance of the musical works, represented during the preceding years, was continued with unabated vigour. Rosenbaum records the per-

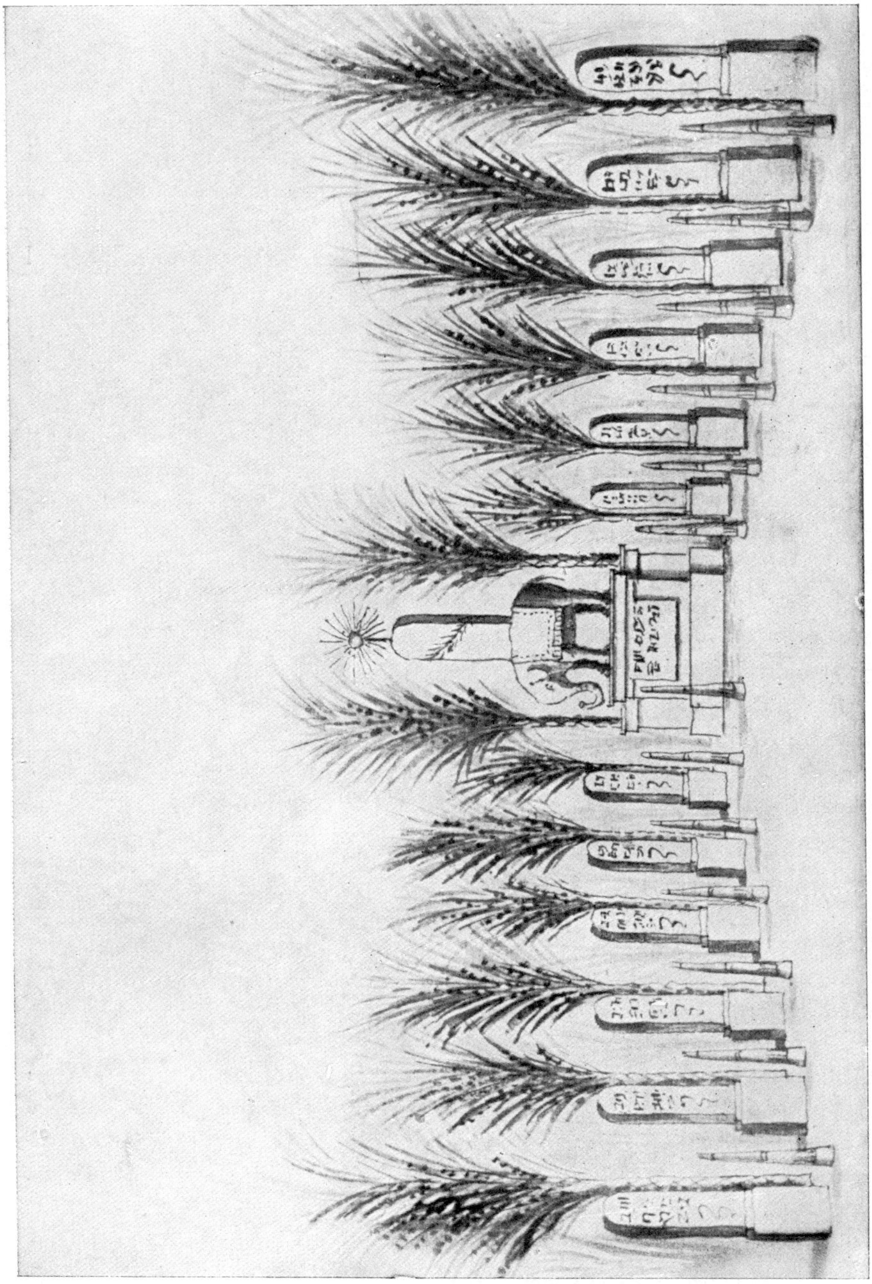

62. Carl Maurer's design for scenery for the performance of Mozart's opera, *The Magic Flute*, at Kismarton

formances of the operas *Schweitzer Familie*, *The Elopement from the Harem* and *Agnes Sorel* in September 1810. In addition, the *première* of Isouard's three-act opera *Cinderella* was held during the season; Schmidt's memoirs contain the following passage in this connection: 'It was on this stage that the opera *Aschenbrödel* was first represented in Germany with an unprecedented staging. Prince Esterházy saw the opera in Paris when it was new, got hold of the libretto and the score for a princely fee, brought them to Kismarton where he desired the opera to be performed for the fête of the Princess, the 9th of September. Although the time available for preparation was less than four weeks, everything had been finished by the evening of the performance. I began the work of translation without delay. Hummel was keeping pace with the progress of the translation by inserting the translated passages in their proper place and by holding continuous rehearsals with the singers, so that it was possible to present the *Aschenbrödel* on the desired day. Dummies were brought by the Prince from Paris, and all dresses and costumes were then made after these models. It was here that velvet gowns interlaced with gold and silver threads appeared for the first time on a German stage. Wild represented the prince, Forti was cast in the part of Dandini, Schuster interpreted the part of Baron Montefiascone, Mlle Cornega played the role of Clorinde, Mme Vadász that of Thispe, while Mlle Stotz appeared as Aschenbrödel. All were excellent. The Prince was so pleased with the splendid and rapidly prepared performance that he gave me the score and the libretto as a present. I sold them subsequently to all theatres of Vienna after having amplified the opera with a few poignant episodes for its performance in Vienna, e.g. with the magic scene at the end of Act I or the trumpet march at that of Act II, the latter composed by Fuchs in Vienna. Neither of these supplements can be found in the French original.'[201]

The estimates drawn up by Schmidt for the year 1812 refer to expenses connected with the representation of nine opera *premières*. The nine operas were these: *Der Kaliph von Bagdad*, *Das Lotterielos*, *Mädchenrache*, *Theatralische Abenteuer*, *Der Augenarzt*, *Das Waisenhaus*, *Das Hausgesinde*, *Der Zauber Spiele* and *Der lustige Schuster*. The old operas mentioned in the statement as included in the current repertoire were *Aschenbrödel*, *Die Schweitzer Familie*, *Gulistan*, *Agnes Sorel* and *Die beyden Füchse*.

The Theater an der Wien presented the *Cinderella* on 2nd April 1811: it held the boards until the end of June 1823, and had run by that time into 107 performances. Its libretto reached three editions in 1812. The *première* at Kismarton proved, thus, to be the beginning of an unprece-

63. Carl Maurer's design for scenery for the performance of Mozart's opera, *The Magic Flute*, at Kismarton

dented stage career. Schmidt's aforementioned statement shows that the opera, under the title of *Cendrillon*, formed a recurrent item of the Kismarton repertoire.[202] An *entrée* was inserted into the opera for the teaching of which a dancing master was engaged from Vienna who trained Mlle Stotz and the child-performers.

The warning signs of the approaching economic crisis could already be felt at this time. Costs were rising every day and the price of seats was raised by the theatres of Vienna as from 1st April 1811. Prince Miklós II had to put a stop to his lavish extravagance and to curtail his budget in which his theatre was but one, and not even the most costly, item. Though theatrical activities still continued as before, we find repeated traces of economy measures in the documents. It was presumably due to increasing financial difficulties that the Prince had to abandon the engagement of Cherubini although it had been agreed in Paris during the winter season 1810—11 that Cherubini would enter the Prince's service. Existing letters exchanged in this connection[203] constitute an important source of Cherubini's biography, and show the great composer to be turning at this time more and more towards church music. All that even the most recent music literature can tell us about the relationships between Prince Miklós Esterházy and Cherubini[204] is that the Prince showed great sympathy towards the composer during the former's stay in Paris in 1810. Their cordial relations are well illustrated by the fact that Cherubini dedicated his compositions *Canto funebre sulla morte di Haydn* and *Litania della Vergine* to the Prince and that the latter, when leaving Paris, presented the composer with a valuable ring studded with precious stones. Had Cherubini taken the place of Haydn in the court of the Prince he would undoubtedly have composed a number of works for the Esterházy orchestra. The unfulfilled engagement meant, because of preparations that he had already made for his departure and also because of the refusal of important offers, a heavy financial loss for Cherubini who asked the Prince for indemnification in 1813.[205]

The final act of the history of the Esterházy theatre is a decree, issued by Prince Miklós II on 14th March 1813, which — referring to economic difficulties — dismissed thirty-five members of the musical staff and instituted severe economy measures in other branches of the household. This meant the cessation of a theatrical life in the court of the Esterházys which had been maintained for nearly six decades, and meant at the same time the termination of a period in Hungary's theatrical history which, though having produced much of importance, has hitherto been scarcely known.

64. Carl Maurer's design for scenery for the performance of Mozart's opera, *The Magic Flute*, at Kismarton

Appendix

# THE ESTERHÁZY LIBRETTOS

Apart from scores and archival documents, our chief sources for the study of musical and theatrical life at the court of the Esterházys are the extant librettos. Prior to the staging of every musical work performed at the court theatre, a few hundred copies of its libretto were printed. The total of these librettos constitutes a veritable storehouse of important data regarding theatrical and music history, but no complete collection can be found in any library. Thirty-two librettos are in the custody of the National Library, Budapest and a few further copies are preserved in the Budapest University Library as also in the respective libraries of the 'Berzsenyi' High School at Sopron, the Music-Lovers' Society and the National Library in Vienna. The major part of the German librettos printed after 1800 can be found in the National Library, Budapest, and also in the National Library, Vienna, and the Burgenländische Landesbibliothek. Comparatively the most complete collection before the Second World War was that kept in the Budapest archive of the Esterházy family. As far as we know, the librettos were preserved in or together with the fascicles labelled *Acta Musicalia.* Although the latter were transferred to the Department for Theatrical History of the National Library, Budapest after the war, the librettos disappeared without a trace. It is possible that they were destroyed, together with the Buda archives of the Esterházys and a part of their library there, during the battles fought for the liberation of the Fortress of Buda.[206] The Esterházy librettos figure in many a bibliography, the most detailed among them being those written by E. Csatkai, J. Hárich, C.F. Pohl, K. Zolnai and M. Horányi resp. the Haydn monograph by Bartha—Somfai.

As far as possible, we give the full text of the title-page of every libretto. Data regarding librettos known only from the printer's invoices are supplemented by the archival classification. The names of the composer and the librettist are usually indicated on the second or third page

65. Carl Maurer's design for scenery for the performance of Mozart's opera, *The Magic Flute*, at Kismarton

only. They are placed above the text of the title-page in our following list. Data not contained in the librettos, collected from various bibliographies, are in brackets. Names and titles are given in the language and orthography of the original sources, while the texts of the title-pages are given in English.

1715

1. *Das wahre Ebenbild Eines Vollkommenen Fürsten*
(The True Image of a Perfect Prince.) At the glorious name-day celebration of His Most Serene Highness the Prince Michael Esterhasi of Galanta, hereditary Count of Forchtenstein. At the behest and order of Her Most Serene Highness the Princess Anna Margaret Esterhasi of Galanta, born Marchioness of Desana. Performed and sung at their princely residence at Eysenstadt. Words by J.B.H. Set to music by Wenzeslao Francisco Zivilhofer, conductor to His Serene Highness. Printed in Vienna, Austria by Andreas Heyinger Univ. Press.

1749

2. *Oratorium* (Oratorio). Justice provoked to great wrath by Adam's fall, considering temporal and eternal doom. But at last happily defeated by charity contriving all means of help imaginable. Composed as a musical mourning-scene and sung by a princely Esterhasi court choir in the local seignorial hospital church of the Saint Sepulchre at Eisenstadt, April 4 A.D. 1749, under Gregorium Josephum Werner, the then conductor of His Serene Highness. Printed by Samuel Müller, Vienna, Univ. Press.

1751

3. Conforti, Niccolo
*Gli orti Esperidi* (The Gardens of the Hesperides), cantata for four voices. Presented in Naples, May 13, 1751, the day on which falls the birthday of Her Majesty the Empress Maria Theresa, Queen of Hungary and Bohemia, etc. By Her Ambassador Extraordinary to His Majesty the King of the two Sicilies. In Naples MDCCLI. At the printing press of Giovanni di Simone, printer of the Royal Palace.

1752

4. Conforti, Niccolo
*L'Endimione* (Endymion) cantata for five voices. Presented in Naples the 26th day of June, 1752 by the Imperial Royal Ambassador to his

66. Carl Maurer's design for scenery for the performance of Mozart's opera, *The Magic Flute*, at Kismarton

Majesty the King of the two Sicilies, at the occasion of his public entry. In Naples MDCCLII. Printed by Giovanni di Simone with the licence of the authorities.

1755

5. *Ecloga Pastorale* (Pastoral Eclogue). To be sung at the occasion of the birthday of His Highness the Prince Esterhasi. (Poetry by Signor Abe Giovanni Claudio Pasquini. Music by Signor Francesco Maggiore).

1759

6. *Die drey Pilgräme* (The Three Pilgrims), going on pilgrimage to the Holy Sepulchre in Jerusalem. Subsequently accompanied homeward by an anchoress to (her) and all zealous Christians' wholesome remembrance of the bitter and painful sufferings of our blessed Saviour Jesus Christ. Presented in oratorial dirges. Sung by a chapel choir of His Highness Prince Esterhasi at the local castle parish-church of the Holy Sepulchre, April 13 A. D. 1759. Under Gregorium Josephum Werner, the Prince's conductor at the castle of Eisenstadt. — Neustadt, printed by Joseph Adam Fritsch.

1762

7. *Oratorium. Antiochus der wütende Tyrann* (Antiochus the Raging Tyrant), and prototype of the future Antichrist, lays siege to the sacred Temple of God, strangles a great part of the Israelites. Judas Maccabaeus, the heroic warrior-prince, nevertheless, defeats him by the mighty hand of the Lord. As a warning example to all such flaunting foes. Sung at the palace of Prince Estorhasi at the Holy Sepulchre by his court-chapel at Eysensttadt, April 9, 1762. Under Gregorium Josephum Werner, conductor to His Serene Highness. Neustadt, printed by Joseph Fritsch.

1763

8. Haydn, Joseph
*Acide*, Theatrical Festival, performed at Eisenstadt, at the occasion of the happy wedding of Their Highnesses Count Anthony Esterhasy of Galantha ... and the Countess Theresa Erdődi of N... January 11, 1763. Vienna, at the printing press of Ghelen. MLSV. (Copy by Pohl.)

1767

9. Haydn, Joseph
*La canterina* (The Singer). Opera buffa performed during the Carnival for the entertainment of Their Royal Highnesses. Pressburg, at the printing press of Giov. Michele Landerer 1767. MLSV. VLB.

67. Carl Maurer, design for scenery

1768

10. Haydn, Joseph — (Goldoni, Carlo)
*Lo speziale* (The Apothecary). Comic opera to be performed at Esterház, at the theatre of H.H. the Prince Esterhazy of Galantha in the autumn of the year 1768. MLSV.

1770

11. Haydn, Joseph — (Goldoni, Carlo?)
*Le pescatrici* (The Fisherwomen). Comic opera to be performed in the autumn of the year 1770. At the theatre of H.H. the Prince Esterhazy of Galantha ... at Esterhaz. Printed by Giuseppe Siess at Sopron. MLSV. (Copy by Pohl.)

1773

12. Haydn, Joseph
*L'infedeltà delusa* (Unfaithfulness Deceived). Musical drollery in two acts to be performed at Esterház at the occasion of the most glorious name-day of H. H. the Dowager Princess Esterházy, born Lunati Visconti, at the theatre of H.H. the Prince Nicholas Esterházy of Galantha, July 26, 1773 Oedenburg, Joseph Siess. Sopron Berzsenyi Grammar School.

13. Haydn, Joseph
*L'infedeltà delusa* (Unfaithfulness Deceived). Musical drollery in two acts to be performed at Esterház. At the occasion of the most glorious arrival there of Her Majesty the Empress Maria Theresa. At the theatre of H.H. the Prince Nicholas Esterházy of Galantha. In the month of September of the year 1773. At Oedenburg at the printing press of Joseph Siess. NLB.

14. Haydn, Joseph
*Philemon und Baucis oder Jupiters Reise auf die Erde* (Philemon and Baucis or Jupiter's Journey to the Earth). At the occasion of the most joyful presence of Her Imperial and Royal Apostolic Majesty and Her Most Serene Dynasty. A puppet operetta performed for the first time at Esterház on the princely puppet stage in the year 1773. Vienna, with Ghelen's characters. MLSV. (Copy by Pohl.)

1775

15. Haydn, Joseph — Frieberth, Carlo
*L'incontro improvviso* (The Unexpected Meeting). Comic drama for music translated from the French and performed at Esterház. At the occasion of the most happy arrival of His Most Serene Highness the Archduke

68. Carl Maurer, design for scenery for Mozart's opera, *La clemenza di Tito*

Ferdinand of Austria and of Her Most Serene Highness the Archduchess Beatrice d'Este. At the theatre of H. H. the Prince Nicholas Esterházy of Galantha. In the month of August of the year 1775. At Oedenburg, at the printing press of Joseph Siess. MLSV.

1776

16. Ditters de Dittersdorf, Carlo
*Il barone de rocca antica* (The Lord of the Old Castle). Intermezzo for four voices. To be performed at the theatre of Esterhaz. In the autumn of the year 1776. At Oedenburg at the printing press of Joseph Siess.

17. Piccini, Niccolo — Goldoni, Carlo
*La buona figliuola* (The Good Daughter). Comic opera in 3 acts. To be performed at the theatre of Esterhaz. In the autumn of the year 1776. At Oedenburg, at the printing press of Joseph Siess.

18. *Die Fee Urgele. Oder was den Damen gefällt* (The Fairy Urgele or What the Ladies Like). A puppet operetta in four acts. From the French of M. Favart. At Esterhaz, on the princely puppet stage. Performed in the winter month 1776. Oedenburg, printed by Johann Joseph Siess.

19. Ditters de Dittersdorf, Carlo
*Il finto pazzo per amore* (Feigned Madness for Love). Operetta for four voices. Performed at the theatre of Esterhaz in the year 1776. Oedenburg, Jos. Siess NLB.

20. Sacchini, Antonio
*L'isola d'amore* (The Island of Love). Comic operetta for music. To be performed at the theatre of Esterhaz in the summer of the year 1776. At Oedenburg, at the printing press of Joseph Siess.

21. Ditters de Dittersdorf, Carlo
*Lo sposo burlato* (The Tricked Husband.) Intermezzo for four voices. To be performed at the theatre of Esterhaz. In the autumn of the year 1776. In Oedenburg, at the printing press of Joseph Siess.

1777

22. Gassmann, Florian Leopold
*L'amore artigiano* (Craftsman Love). A gay play in three acts. To be performed in the theatre of Esterhaz in the spring of the year 1777. Printed in Vienna by Giuseppe nobleman of Kurzbeck, NLB.

69. Carl Maurer's design for scenery

23. Ditters de Dittersdorf, Carlo
*Arcifanfano re de' Matti* (Arcifanfano, King of the Fools). Gay and satirical play in three acts. Performed at the theatre of Esterhaz in the autumn of the year 1777. Printed in Vienna by Giuseppe noble of Kurzbeck, oriental printer of H.I.M.R.A.
24. *Genovefens.* A puppet operetta in three acts. First performed on the princely puppet stage at Esterhaz in the summer of 1777. MLSV. (Copy by Pohl.)

25. Paisiello, Giovanni — (Livigni, Pietro)
*La Frascatana* (The Woman of Frascati). Comic opera in three acts. Performed at the theatre of Esterhaz in the summer of the year 1777. Printed in Vienna by Giuseppe noble of Kurzbeck, oriental printer of H.I.M.R.A.

26. Haydn, Joseph
*Il mondo della luna* (The World of the Moon). A comedy in three acts. Performed at the theatre of Esterhaz, at the occasion of the happy wedding of Nicholas, Count Esterházy of Galantha and the Countess Maria Anna Weissenwolf. In the summer of the year 1777. Printed in Vienna by Giuseppe noble of Kurzbeck, oriental printer of H. I. M. R. A. NLB. MLSV. (Copy by Pohl.)

1778

27. Anfossi, Pasquale
*Il geloso in cimento* (The Jealous Man on Trial). Comic opera by Giovanni Bertati. To be performed at the theatre of Esterhaz in the summer of 1778. Printed by Giuseppe noble of Kurzböck.

28. Gazzaniga, Giuseppe — (Bertati, Giovanni)
*La locanda* (The Inn). Comic opera to be performed at the theatre of Esterhaz in the autumn of the year 1778.

29. Guglielmi, Pietro
*La sposa fedele* (The Faithful Wife). Comic opera. To be performed at the theatre of Esterhaz in the year 1778. Oedenburg, Siess. NLB.

1779

30. Sacchini, Antonio (Felici, Alessandro — Tassi, Niccolò)
*L'amore soldato* (Soldier Love). Comic opera. To be performed at the occasion of the wedding of Count Forgács, Countess Ottila Grassal-

70. Carl Maurer's design for scenery

kovich. At the theatre of Esterház, in the year 1779. Oedenburg, at the printing press of Giuseppe Siess. NLB.

31. Paisiello, Giovanni
*Le due contesse* (The Two Countesses). Musical intermezzo. To be performed at the theatre of Esterház in the spring 1779. Vienna, printed by Giuseppe noble of Kurzböck.

32. Sarti, Giusseppe — (Grandi, Tommaso)
*Le gelosie villane* (Country Jealousies). Comic opera. To be performed at the theatre of Esterhaz in the year 1779. Oedenburg, at the printing press of Giuseppe Siess.

33. Gazzaniga, Giuseppe — (Bertati, Giovanni)
*L'isola d'Alcina* (The Island of Alcina). Comic opera. To be performed at the theatre of Esterhaz. In the year 1779.

34. Haydn, Joseph
*L'isola disabitata* (The Uninhabited Island). Musical play in two parts by the famous Abbot Pietro Metastasio, imperial poet, to be performed at the occasion of the glorious name-day of H. H. the Prince Nicholas Esterhazi of Galantha. In the year 1779. Oedenburg, at the printing press of Giuseppe Siess. MLSV.

35. Anfossi, Pasquale — (Petrosellini,Giuseppe)
*Metilde ritrovata* (Mathilda Recovered). Musical comedy. To be performed at the theatre of Esterhaz in the year 1779. Oedenburg, at the printing press of Giuseppe Siess. NLB.

36. Haydn, Joseph —Puttini, Francesco
*La vera costanza* (True Constancy). Comic opera to be performed at the theatre of Esterhaz in the spring of 1779. Vienna, printed by Giuseppe noble of Kurzböck. MLSV.

1780

37. Haydn, Joseph
*La fedeltà premiata* (Faithfulness Rewarded). Comic opera to be performed at the opening of the new theatre of H. H. the Prince Nicholas Esterhazy of Galantha. In the autumn of the year 1780 MLSV. (Copy by Pohl.)
*Die Belohnte Treue* (Faithfulness Rewarded). Comic opera. Performed at the opening of the new theatre at Esterház, in the year 1780.

71. Carl Maurer's design for scenery

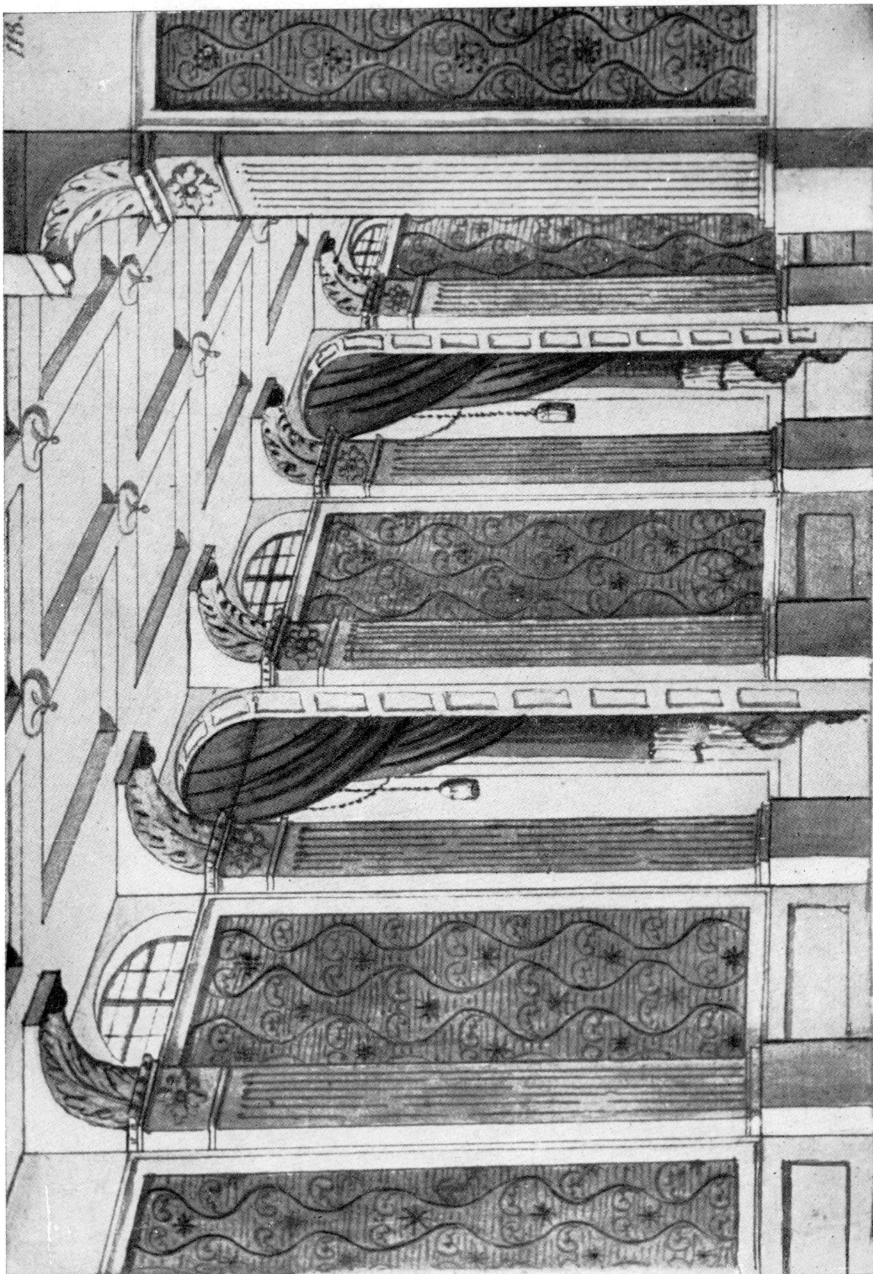

72. Carl Maurer's design for scenery for Mozart's opera, *Don Giovanni*

38. Anfossi, Pasquale
*La finta giardiniera* (The Disguised Gardener). Comedy set to music. To be performed at the theatre of Esterhaz. In the autumn of the year 1780. NLB.

39. Anfossi, Pasquale — (Bertati, Giovanni)
*La forza delle donne* (The Power of Women). Comedy set to music. To be performed at the theatre of Esterhaz. In the spring of the year 1780. Oedenburg, at the printing press of Giuseppe Siess.

40. Salieri, Antonio — (Mazzola, Caterino)
*La scuola de'gelosi* (The School for Jealous Men). Comedy set to music to be performed at the theatre of Esterhaz in the summer of the year 1780.

41. Gazzaniga, Giuseppe — (Bertati, Giovanni)
*La vendemmia* (Vintage). Comedy set to music. To be performed at the theatre of Esterhaz. In the spring of the year 1780. Oedenburg, at the printing press of Giuseppe Siess.

1781

42. Paisiello, Giovanni
*L'avaro deluso* (The Ridiculed Miser). Comedy set to music. To be performed at theatre of Esterhaz on the year 1781.
*Der verspottete Geizige* (The Ridiculed Miser). A comedy set to music, performed at the princely theatre at Esterház. In the year 1781 (Joseph Siess, Ödenburg.) NLV.

43. Righini, Vincenzo — Porta, Nunziato
*Il convitato di pietra o sia Il dissoluto* (The Stone Guest or The Rake) Tragicomedy set to music. To be performed at the theatre of Esterhaz in the summer of the year 1781. (Joseph Siess, Ödenburg.) NLB.

44. (Astaritta, Gennaro)
*Il francese bizzarro* (The Queer Frenchman). (Joseph Siess, Ödenburg) (A.M. 4008.)

45. Anfossi, Pasquale — (Bertati, Giovanni)
*Isabella e Rodrigo o sia La costanza in amore* (Isabella and Rodrigo or Constancy in Love). Comedy set to music. To be represented at the theatre of Esterhazy in the spring of the year 1781. (Joseph Siess, Ödenburg.)

46. (Piccini, Niccolo)
*La schiava riconosciuta* (The Identified Slave-girl) (or under the title: *Gli Stravaganti* (The Eccentrics), (Joseph Siess, Ödenburg.) (A.M. 4007.)

1782

47. Traetta, Tommaso — (Bertati, Giovanni)
*Il cavaliere errante nell'isola incantata* (The Knight Errant on the Enchanted Island). Heroi-comic drama set to music. To be performed at the Esterházy theatre in the year 1782. (Joseph Siess, Ödenburg.)

48. Haydn, Joseph
*La fedeltà premiata* (Faithfulness Rewarded). Pastoral comedy... to be performed at Esterház in the year 1782. NLB.

49. *La fiera di Venezia* (The Fair of Venice). Comedy set to music by Giovanni Gastone Bocherini Lucchese. To be performed at the theatre of Esterház in the year 1782. (Siess, Ödenburg.)

50. (Paisiello, Giovanni — Livigni Filippo)
*L'innocente fortunata* (The Fortunate Innocent). (Joseph Siess, Ödenburg.) (A.M. 4007.)

51. Haydn, Joseph — Porta, Nunziato
*Orlando Paladino* (Orlando Paladin). Heroi-comic drama in three acts to be performed at the Esterhazy theatre in the year 1782, NLB. MLSV.

52. (Anfossi, Pasquale — Bertati, Giovanni)
*Lo sposo disperato* (The Desperate Husband). (Joseph Siess, Ödenburg.) (A.M. 4001.)

1783

53. *L'assedio di Gibilterra* (The Siege of Gibraltar). Play set to music. To be performed with puppets at the little theatre of H.H. the Prince Nicholas Esterházy of Galantha. 1783. NLB.

54. Cimarosa, Domenico
*Il Falegname* (The Carpenter). Comedy set to music to be performed at the theatre of His Highness the Prince of Esterhazi. In the year 1783. Printed in Vienna by Giuseppe noble of Kurzbeck.
*Der Zimmermann* (The Carpenter) Comedy set to music. Vienna, by Joseph nobleman of Kurzbeck.

73. Carl Maurer's design for scenery for Mozart's opera, *Don Giovanni*

74. Anton de Pian's design for scenery for the tragedy, *Don Gutierre*

75. Carl Maurer's design for scenery for the tragedy, *Don Gutierre*

76. Anton de Pian's design for scenery for the opera, *Lodoiska*

77. Carl Maurer's design for scenery for the opera, *Lodoiska*

55. Sarti, Giuseppe
*Giulio Sabino*. Musical drama. To be performed at the theatre of H.H. the Prince Esterházy of Galantha. 1782. NLB.

1784

56. Cimarosa, Domenico
*L'amor costante* (Constant Love). Comedy in two acts. To be performed at the theatre of H.H. the Sovereign Prince Nicholas Esterhasi of Galantha. In the year 1784. Printed in Vienna by Giuseppe noble of Kurzbeck.

57. Haydn, Giuseppe (Joseph)
*Armida*. Heroic drama to be performed at the theatre of H.H. the Sovereign Prince Nicholas Esterasi of Galantha. Set to music by Maestro Haydn in the year 1784, At Oedenburg, at the printing press of G. Siess.

58. (Sarti, Giuseppe — Porta, Nunziato)
*I contratempi* (Unexpected Difficulties). (A.M. 4021.)

59. Sarti, Giuseppe
*La Didone abbandonata* (Dido Forsaken). Musical drama by the famous Abbot Pietro Metastasio, to be performed at the theatre of H.H. the Sovereign Prince Nicholas Esterhasi of Galantha. In the year 1784. Oedenburg, Gius. Siess. NLB.

60. Anfossi, Pasquale
*Die glücklichen Reisenden* (The Happy Travellers). A musical comedy. Performed at the princely theatre at Esterhaz. Vienna, by Joseph Nobleman of Kurzbeck. 1784.
*I viaggiatori felici* (The Happy Travellers). Comedy set to music to be performed at the theatre of His Highness the Prince of Esterhasi. In the year 1784. Printed by Giuseppe noble of Kurzbeck.

61. Bianchi, Francesco
*La villanella rapita* (The Abducted Country Girl). Comedy by Giovanni Bertati set to music, to be performed at the theatre of His Highness the Prince Esterhasy of Galantha. In the year 1784. At Oedenburg, at the printing press of Giuseppe Siess.

1785

62. Stabingher, Mattia
*Le astuzie die Bettina* (The Artfulness of Bettina). Comedy set to music to be performed at the theatre of H.H. the Prince Sovereign of Esterhasi.

In the autumn of the year 1785. Oedenburg, Gius. Siess. NLB.

63. Anfossi, Pasquale — Diodati, Giovanni
*Il matrimonio per inganno* (Marriage through Deception). Comedy set to music to be performed at the theatre of H.H. the Sovereign Prince Esterhasi. In the summer of the year 1785. Oedenburg, at the printing press of Giuseppe Siess. NLB.

64. Zingarelli, Niccolo
*Montezuma.* Musical drama. To be performed at the theatre of H.H. the Sovereign Prince Esterhasi. In the summer of the year 1785. Oedenburg, at the printing press of Giuseppe Siess.

1786

65. (Zingarelli, Niccolo — Moretti, Ferdinando)
*Alsinda.* (Joseph Siess, Ödenburg) [A.M. 4019] NLV.

66. (Cimarosa, Domenico — Palomba, Giuseppe)
*La ballerina amante* (The Loving Ballerina). [Joseph Siess, Ödenburg A.M. 4018)] NLV.

67. Cimarosa, Domenico
*Chi dell'altrui si veste presto si spoglia* (Ill gains, soon lost) Comedy in two acts, to be performed at the theatre of H.H. the Sovereign Prince Nicholas Esterhasi of Galantha. In the year 1786. Oedenburg, at the printing press of Giuseppe Siess.

68. Traetta, Tommaso — Coltellini, Marco
*Ifigenia in Tauride* (Iphigenia in Tauris). Drama set to music in three acts. To be performed at the theatre of H.H. the Sovereign Prince Nicholas Esterhasi of Galantha. In the year 1786. Oedenburg, at the printing press of Giuseppe Siess.

69. (Caruso, Luigi)
*L'albergatrice vivace* (The Vivacious Landlady). [Joseph Siess, Ödenburg (A.M. 4015.)]

70. Righini, Vincenzo
*L'incontro inaspettato* (The Unexpected Encounter). Comedy by Nunziato Porta set to music. To be performed at the theatre of H.H. the Sovereign Prince Nicholas Esterhasi of Galantha. In the year 1786. MLSV.

71. Sarti, Giuseppe — (Moretti, Ferdinando?)
*Idalide.* Drama set to music. To be performed at the theatre of H.H. the Sovereign Prince Nicholas Esterhasi of Galantha. In the year 1786. Oedenburg, at the printing press of Giuseppe Siess.

1787

72. Bianchi, Francesco
*Alessandro nell'Indie* (Alexander in India). Drama set to music to be performed at the theatre of H.H. the Sovereign Prince Nicholas Esterhasi of Galantha. In the year 1787. Vienna, printed by Franc. Antonio Kroyss.

73. Ponte, Abbate da — Martin, Vincenzo
*L'arbore di Diana* (The Tree of Diana). Comedy in two acts. (To be performed at the arrival of Her Royal Highness Maria Theresa, Archduchess of Austria: wife of Prince Anthony of Saxony. Printed in Vienna by Giuseppe noble of Kurzbeck, printer of H.M. JB.) The part between brackets was pasted over with the following text: To be performed at the theatre of H.H. the Sovereign Prince Nicholas Esterházy. Printed in Vienna by the Typographic Society (1789.) (Poetry by the Abbot da Ponte — Music by Vicenzo Martin.)

74. Bianchi, Francesco
*Il disertore* (The Deserter). Drama in three acts set to music. Oedenburg, at the printing press of Giuseppe Siess. (1787.) NLB.

75. Cimarosa, Domenico
*Giunio Bruto* (Junius Brutus). Tragedy set to music. At Oedenburg, printed by Giuseppe Siess. 1787. NLB.

76. Guglielmi, Pietro
*La Quaquera spiritosa* (The Lively Quaker Girl). Comedy set to music. At Oedenburg, printed by Giuseppe Siess. 1787.

77. Anfossi, Pasquale
*Il sordo e l'avaro* (The Deaf Man and the Miser). Comedy set to music to be performed at the theatre of H.H. the Sovereign Prince Nicholas Esterhasi of Galantha in the year 1787. Vienna, printed by Franc. Antonio Kroyss.

1788

78. Cimarosa, Domenico (Lorenzi, Giambattista)
*Il marito disperato* (The Desperate Husband). Comedy set to music to

Costüme Bilder zur Theaterzeitung.
No.
Schoeller, del.
And. Geiger sc.
Herr Wild
als
Don Juan
in der Oper gleichen Nahmens.
Sever
in der Oper Norma
Zu haben in Wien, im Bureau der Theaterzeitung, Wollzeil No. 780_2t Stk


78. Franz Wild as Don Giovanni and Severus

be performed at the theatre of H.H. Prince Esterhasi. At Oedenburg, printed by Giuseppe Siess. 1788.

79. Bertoni, Ferdinando — (Calsabigi, Ranieri di)
*Orfeo ed Euridice* (Orpheus and Eurydice). Play set to music to be performed at the theatre of H.H. Prince Esterhasi. At Oedenburg, printed by Giuseppe Siess. 1788. NLB.

80. Prati, Alessio
*La vendetta di Nino* (The Revenge of Nino). Tragic melodrama set to music for being performed at the theatre of H.H. Prince Esterhasi. Printed by Giuseppe Siess. 1788.

1789

81. Cimarosa, Domenico
*La Circe ossia l'isola incantata* (Circe or The Enchanted Island). Drama set to music to be performed at the theatre of H.H. Prince Esterhasi. 1789 at Oedenburg, printed by Giuseppe Siess.

82. Anfossi, Pasquale — (Livigni, Filippo)
*Le gelosie fortunate* (The Fortunate Jealousies). Comedy to be performed at the theatre of H.H. the Prince Esterhasi of Galantha. In the year 1789. At Oedenburg, printed by Giuseppe Siess.

83. Cimarosa, Domenico — (Petrosellini, Giuseppe)
*Il pittore Parigino* (The Parisian Painter). Play in two acts set to music to be performed at the theatre of H.H. the Prince Eszterhasi of Galantha. At Oedenburg, printed by Giuseppe Siess. 1789.

84. Guglielmi, Pietro
*Le vicende d'amore* (The Vicissitudes of Love). Musical drama for five voices to be performed at the theatre of H.H. the Sovereign Prince Nicholas Esterhasi. Vienna, printed by the Typographic Society. (1789.)

1790

85. Gassmann, Florian Leopold — (Goldoni, Carlo)
*L'amor artigiano* (Craftsman Love). Comedy in two acts to be performed by H.H. the Sovereign Prince Nicholas Eszterházy. Vienna, printed by the Typographic Society. (1790.)

86. Paisiello, Giovanni
*L'amor contrastato* (Thwarted Love). Comedy set to music for being performed at the theatre of H.H. the Sovereign Prince Nicholas Eszterhazy

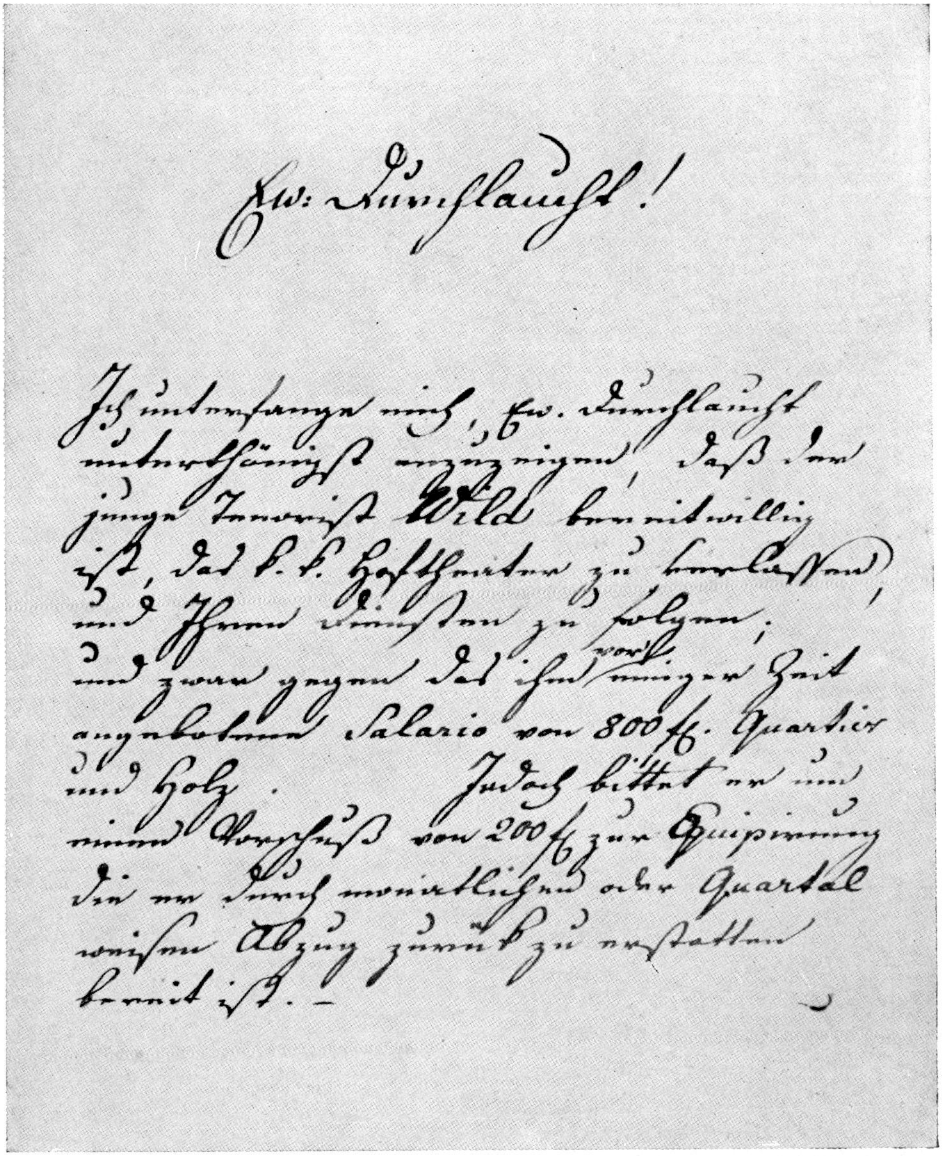

Ew: Durchlaucht!

Ich unterfange mich, Ew. Durchlaucht unterthänigst anzuzeigen, daß der junge Tenorist Wild bereitwillig ist, das k. k. Hoftheater zu verlassen, und Ihren Diensten zu folgen, und zwar gegen das ihm vor einiger Zeit angebotene Salario von 800 fl. Quartier und Holz. Jedoch bittet er um einen Vorschuß von 200 fl zur Equipirung die er durch monatlichen oder Quartal weisen Abzug zurück zu erstatten bereit ist. –

79a. J. N. Hummel's letter of 6th April 1810

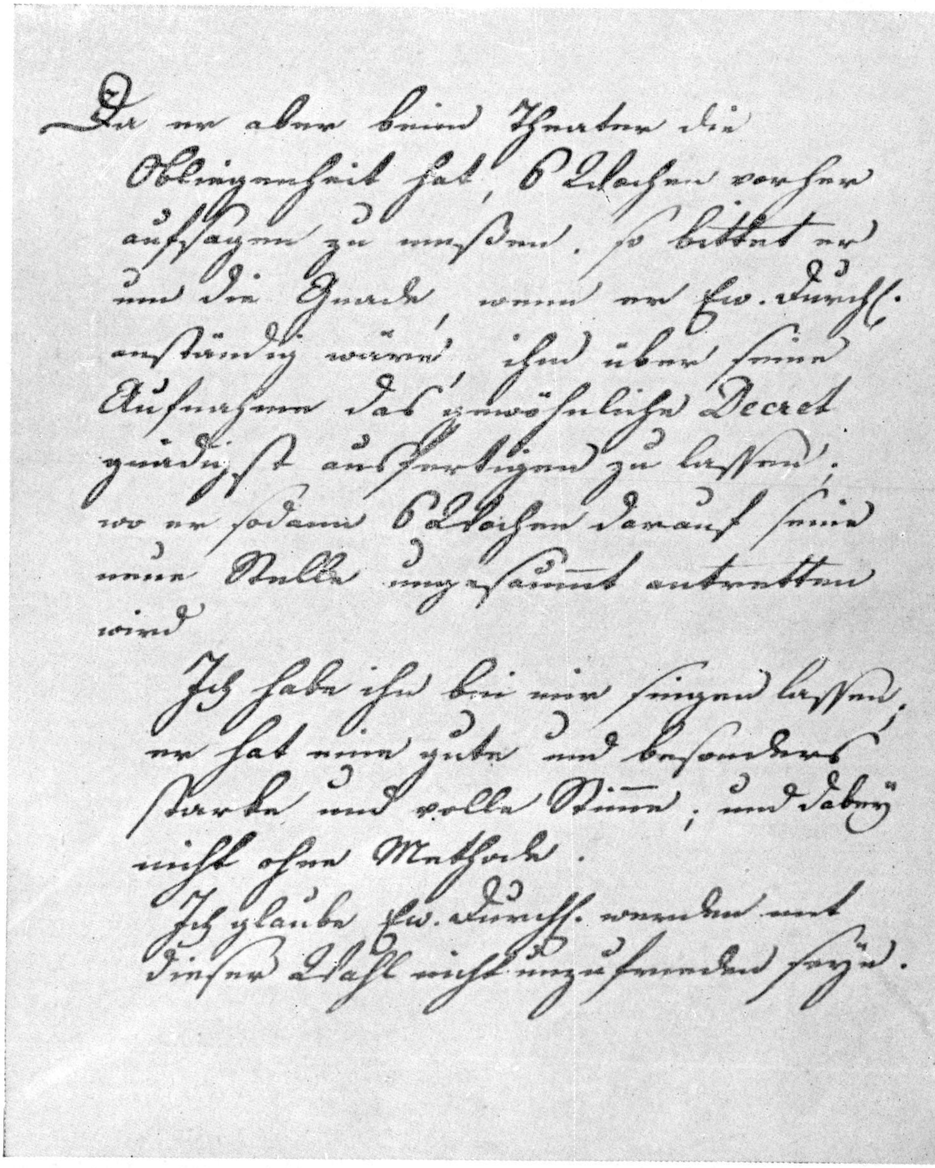

Da er aber beim Theater die
Obliegenheit hat, 6 Wochen vorher
aufzusagen zu müssen, so bittet er
um die Gnade, wenn Ew. Durchl.
anständig wäre, ihm über seine
Aufnahme das gewöhnliche Decret
gnädigst ausfertigen zu lassen;
wo er sodann 6 Wochen darauf seine
neue Stelle ungesäumt antretten
wird.

Ich habe ihn bei mir singen lassen;
er hat eine gute und besonders
starke und volle Stimme; und dabey
nicht ohne Methode.
Ich glaube Ew. Durchl. werden mit
dieser Wahl nicht unzufrieden seyn.

79b. J. N. Hummel's letter of 6th April 1810

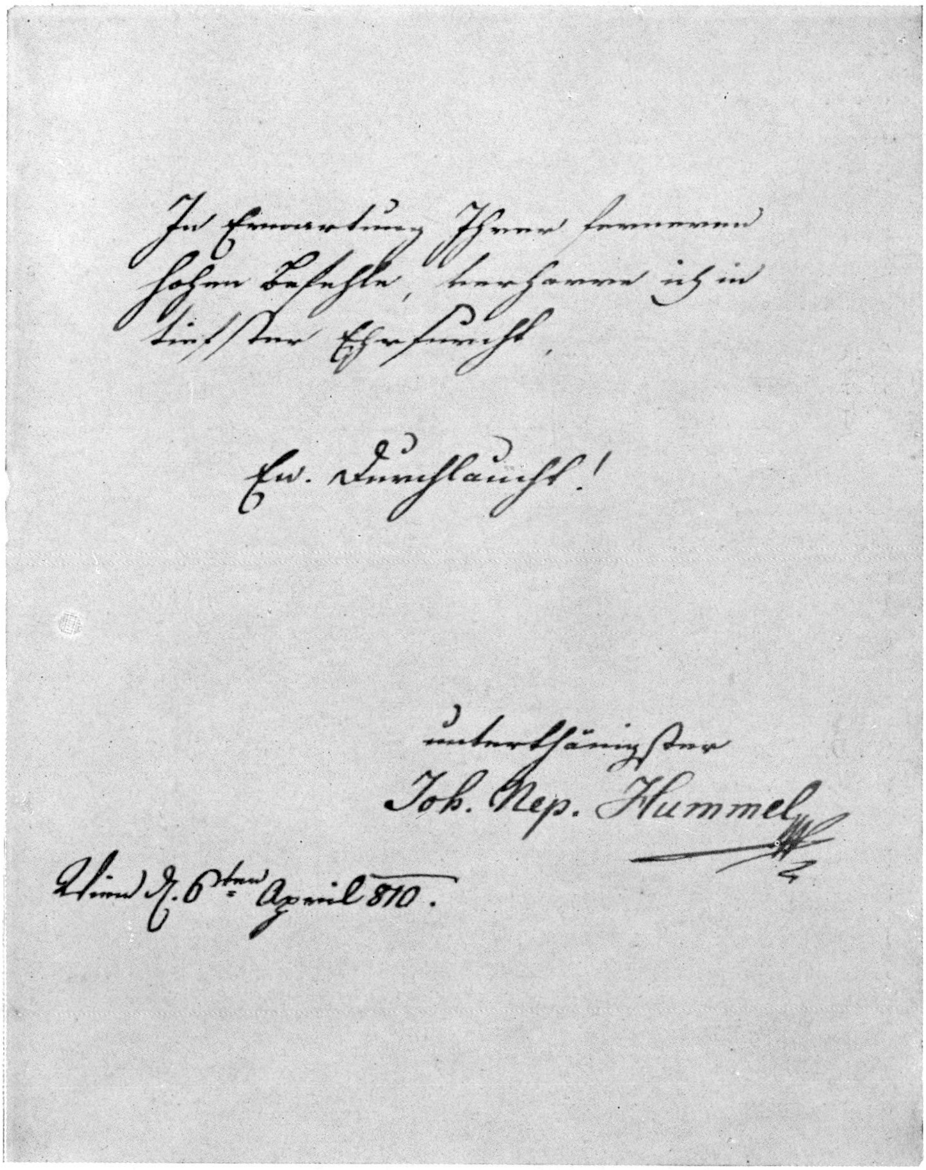

Zu Erwartung Ihrer ferneren
hohen Befehle, verharre ich in
tiefster Ehrfurcht,

Ew. Durchlaucht!

unterthänigster
Joh. Nep. Hummel

Wien d. 6ten April 810.

79c. J. N. Hummel's letter of 6th April 1810

of Galantha, In the year 1790. At Oedenburg, printed by Clara Siessin. 1790.

87. Paisiello, Giovanni
*Barbiere di Siviglia* (The Barber of Seville). (Comedy in four acts to be performed at the Court Theatre in the year 1783. Printed in Vienna by Giuseppe noble of Kurzbeck.) The text in brackets is pasted over with the following superscription: To be performed at the theatre of H.H. the Sovereign Prince Nicholas Esterhazy. Vienna, printed by the Typographic Society.

88. Cimarosa, Domenico
*Il credulo* (The Dupe). Farce set to music to be performed at the theatre of H.H. the Sovereign Prince Nicholas Eszterhazy. At Oedenburg, printed by Clara Siessin. 1790.

89. Cimarosa, Domenico
*L'impressario in angustie* (The Manager in Distress). Farce in one act to be performed at the theatre of H.H. the Sovereign Prince Nicholas Eszterhazy of Galantha. In the year 1790. Oedenburg, printed by Clara Siessin. 1790.

1796

90. *Die Worte des Heilands am Kreutze* (The Words of the Saviour on the Cross). Set to music by Haydn, Doctor of Music and Conductor in the actual service of H. Serene Highness Prince Esterhazy. Oedenburg, printed by Anna Clara Siessin. 1796.

91. *Gott erhalte den Kaiser!* (God Save the Emperor!) Written by Lorenz Leopold Haschka. Set to music by Joseph Haydn. Sung at the princely Esterházy Theatre at Eisenstadt, the 27th October of the year 1797. Oedenburg, printed by Anna Clara Siessin.

1800

92. *Die Waldmänner* (The Woodmen). Comedy with songs in three acts by Emanuel Schikaneder. The music is by the conductor, Mr. Henneberg. 1800.

1803

93. Rosenbaum, Carl
*Freuden-Gefühl* (Feeling of Joy). Cantata, sung in the princely palace at Eisenstadt, at the occasion of the august return of the Most Serene

and Illustrious of the Princes and Lords of the Holy Roman Empire, His Highness Nicholas Esterházy of Galantha, etc., etc. Set to music by Johann Fuchs, conductor to Prince Esterhazi. 1803. Colophon : Eisenstadt, printed by J. L. Stotz, court printer to Prince Esterházy.

1804

94. *Die Schöpfung* (The Creation). Set to music by Joseph Haydn, Doctor of Music, conductor in the actual service of H. Serene Highness Prince Esterházy, and member of the Royal Swedish Academy of Music. Performed by the princely chapel at Eisenstadt the 30th September 1804, for the benefit of the poor. Eszterház, 1804. Printed by J. L. Stotz, printer to His Highness. NLB.

1805

95. *Arien aus dem Fassbinder* (Arias from the Cooper). Comic opera in one act. Translated from the French. Newly set to music by Herr Schenk. Performed at the princely Esterhazy Theatre at Eisenstadt. Printed for his special princely use. 1805.

96. *Die beyden Genies* (The Two Geniuses). An original comedy in five acts. Written for the princely Esterhazy Theatre and most humbly dedicated to the Most Serene of the Princes and Sovereign Lords of the Holy Roman Empire, His Highness Nicholas Esterhazy, by Georg von Gaal. The music hereto is by the princely Esterhazy concertmaster Hummel. Eisenstadt, 1805. NLB.

97. *Der Dorfbarbier* (The Village Barber). Comic opera in one act, rewritten by Herr Joseph Weidmann, court-actor of the imperial and royal theatre. Music by Herr Schenk. Performed at the princely Esterhazy Theatre at Eisenstadt. Eisenstadt, 1805, printed by J. L. Stotz, printer to His Highness.

98. *Die Entführung aus dem Serail* (The Elopement from the Harem) Grand (opera) in three acts. Set to music by Herr Mozart. Performed at the princely Esterházy Theatre at Eisenstadt. Eisenstadt, 1805. Printed by J. L. Stotz, printer to His Highness. NLB.

99. *Der Fassbinder* (The Cooper). Comic opera in one act. Translated from the French. Newly set to music by Herr Schenk. Performed at the princely Esterhazy Theatre at Eisenstadt. Printed for His special princely use. 1805. NLB.

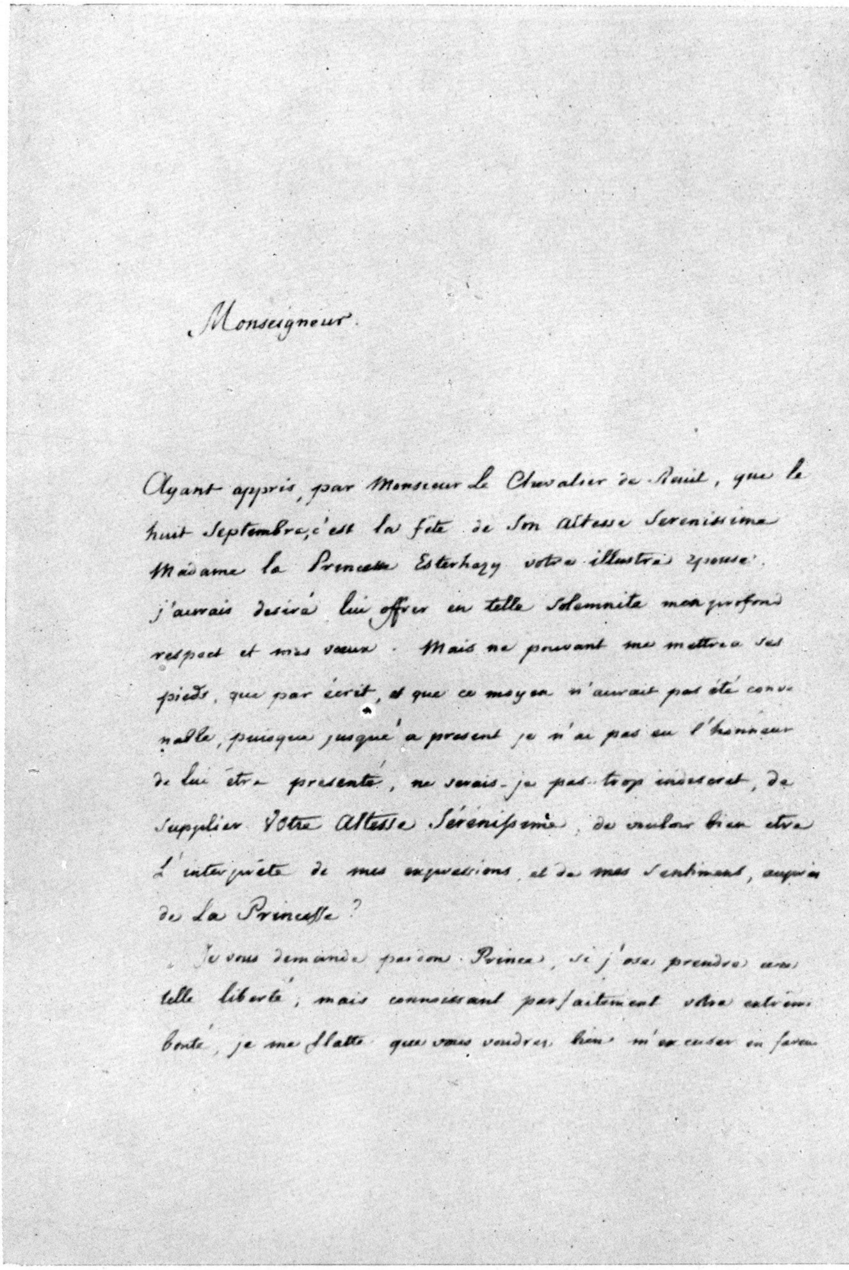

Monseigneur.

Ayant appris, par Monsieur le Chevalier de Rouil, que le huit Septembre, c'est la fête de Son Altesse Sérénissime Madame la Princesse Esterhazy votre illustre épouse, j'aurais désiré lui offrir en telle solemnité mon profond respect et mes voeux. Mais ne pouvant me mettre à ses pieds, que par écrit, et que ce moyen n'aurait pas été convenable, puisque jusqu'à présent je n'ai pas eu l'honneur de lui être présenté, ne serais-je pas trop indiscret, de supplier Votre Altesse Sérénissime, de vouloir bien être l'interprète de mes expressions et de mes sentiments, auprès de La Princesse?

Je vous demande pardon Prince, si j'ose prendre une telle liberté; mais connaissant parfaitement votre extrême bonté, je me flatte que vous voudrez bien m'excuser en faveur

80a. Cherubini's letter to Miklós Esterházy, of 21st August 1810

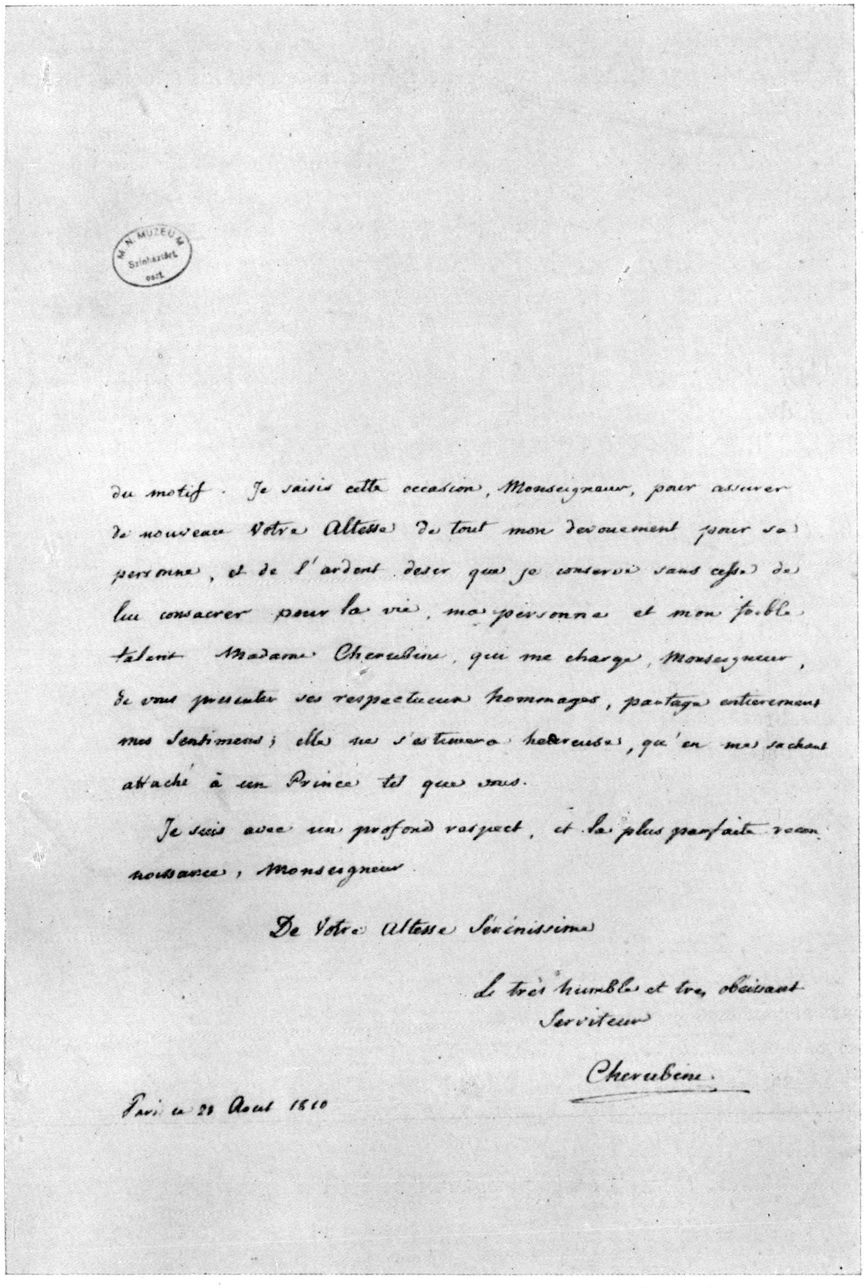

du motif. Je saisis cette occasion, Monseigneur, pour assurer de nouveau Votre Altesse de tout mon devouement pour sa personne, et de l'ardent desir que je conserve sans cesse de lui consacrer pour la vie, ma personne et mon foible talent. Madame Cherubini, qui me charge, Monseigneur, de vous presenter ses respectueux hommages, partage entierement mes sentimens; elle ne s'estimera heureuse, qu'en me sachant attaché à un Prince tel que vous.

Je suis avec un profond respect, et la plus parfaite reconnoissance, Monseigneur

De Votre Altesse Sérénissime

Le très humble et tres obeissant
Serviteur

Cherubini.

Paris ce 21 Aout 1810

80b. Cherubini's letter to Miklós Esterházy, of 21st August 1810

100. Benda, Georg [Franz]
*Das Findelkind* (The Foundling). Comedy in five acts. Performed at the princely Esterhazy Theatre at Eisenstadt. Printed for his special princely use. 1805. NLB.

101. *Der Junker in der Mühle* (The Squire in the Mill). Comic operetta in one act by Heinrich Schmidt. Music by Anton Polzelli, pupil of Herr Joseph Haydn. Most humbly dedicated by the author to the name-day of Her Serene Highness, the Princess Maria Esterhazy of Galantha, born Princess of Lichtenstein etc. Printed for His special princely use. 1805. NLB.

102. *Die Stutzperücke* (The Cropped Wig). Comedy in one act by Heinrich Schmidt. Performed at the princely Esterhazy Theatre at Eisenstadt. Printed for His special princely use. 1805. NLB.

1806

103. (*Dalayrac, Nicolas*)
*Die Beyden Savoyarden* (The Two Savoyards). [Csatkai: The princely Esterhazy Printing Presses at Eisenstadt. Burgenländische Heimatblätter (local papers of Burgenland) 1936.]

104. *Endimione e Diana* (Endymion and Diana). Cantata for five voices to celebrate the most happy wedding of His Highness Prince Maurice Lichtenstein etc. etc. with Her Highness Princess Leopoldine Esterhazy. Set to music by Sign. Hummel, and dedicated to the illustrious worth of His Highness Prince Nicholas Estrehazy, etc., etc. by his most humble servant Lodovico Brizzi. 1806. Colophon: Printed by Mattia Andrea Schmidt.

105. Passy, Franz S.
*Das Fest des Dankes und der Freude* (The Feast of Thanks and Joy). Cantata in two parts, set to music by Herr Johann Nep. Hummel, concertmaster in actual service of His Highness the Sovereign Prince Nicholas Esterhazy of Galantha. Performed in the imperial, as well as royal and imperial Augarten Hall the 29th of June 1806. For the benefit of the Charitable Institution most graciously confirmed by His Imperial, as well as imperial and royal Majesty. Vienna, 1806.

106. *Das Fest der Liebe und Freude* (The Feast of Love and Joy). A comedy with songs in two acts, by Joachim Perinet. Music by Herr Umlauf. Performed at Eisenstadt the 12th of April at the occasion of the happy consummation of marriage of Her Serene Highness the Princess Leopoldina

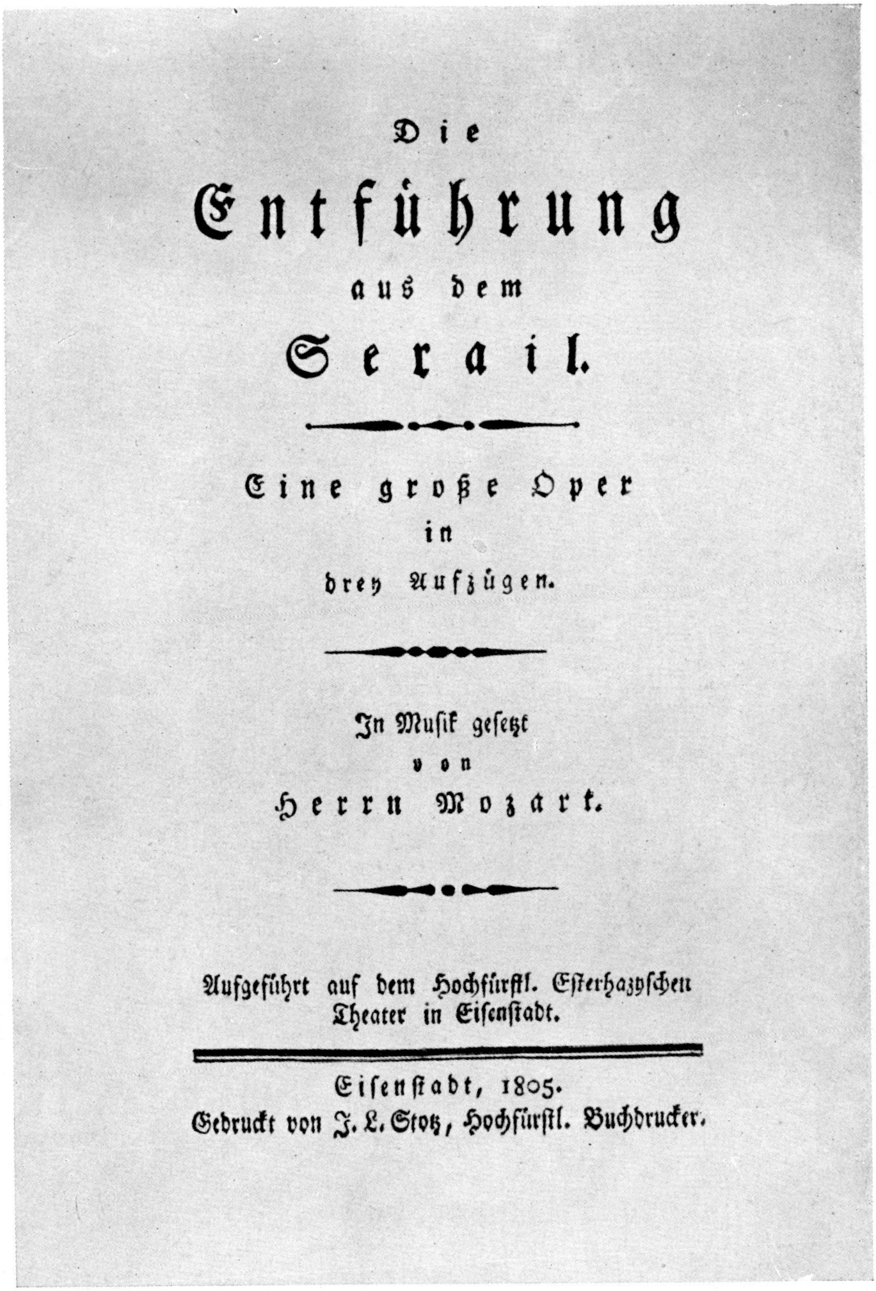

Die

Entführung

aus dem

Serail.

Eine große Oper

in

drey Aufzügen.

In Musik gesetzt

von

Herrn Mozart.

Aufgeführt auf dem Hochfürstl. Esterhazyschen Theater in Eisenstadt.

Eisenstadt, 1805.

Gedruckt von J. L. Stotz, Hochfürstl. Buchdrucker.

81. Title-page of libretto to Mozart's opera, *The Elopement from the Harem*

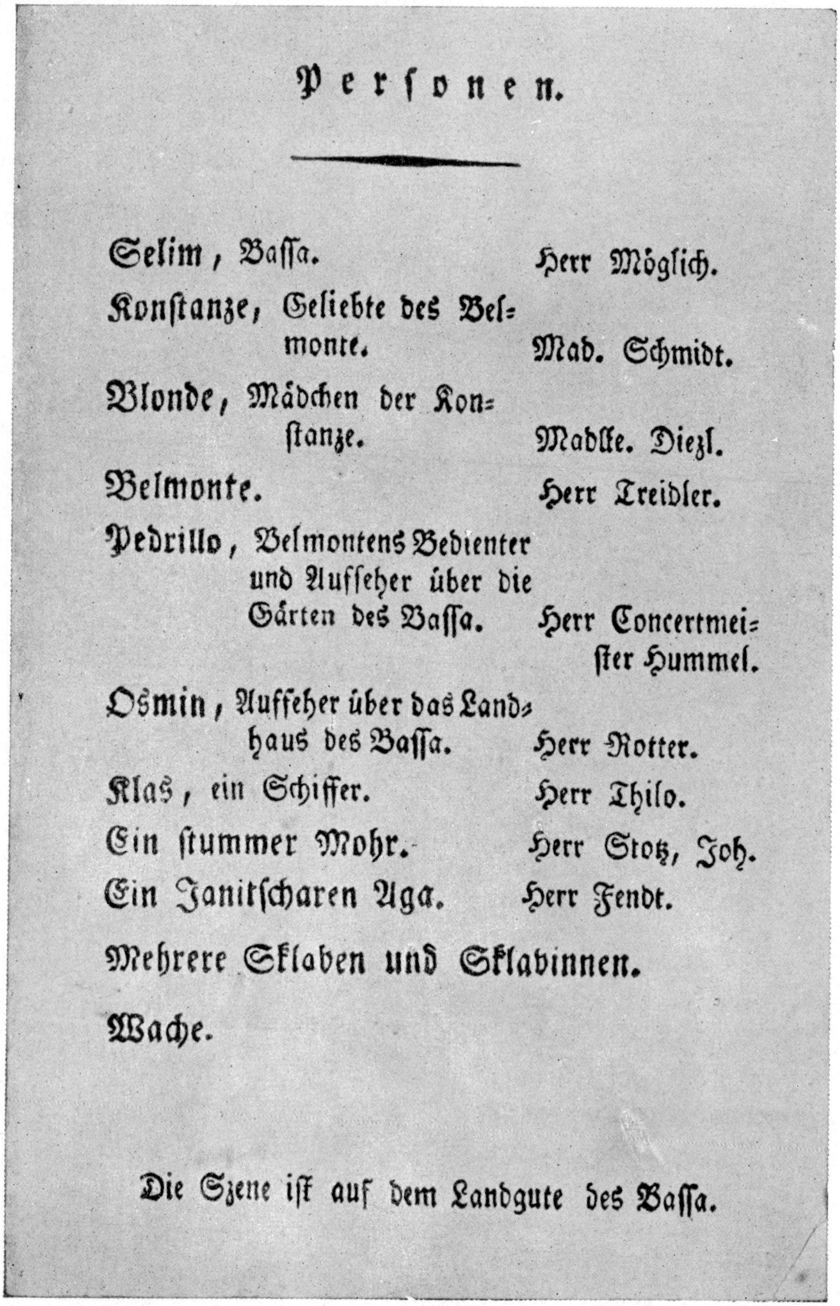

# Personen.

| | |
|---|---|
| Selim, Bassa. | Herr Möglich. |
| Konstanze, Geliebte des Belmonte. | Mad. Schmidt. |
| Blonde, Mädchen der Konstanze. | Madlle. Diezl. |
| Belmonte. | Herr Treidler. |
| Pedrillo, Belmontens Bedienter und Aufseher über die Gärten des Bassa. | Herr Concertmeister Hummel. |
| Osmin, Aufseher über das Landhaus des Bassa. | Herr Rotter. |
| Klas, ein Schiffer. | Herr Thilo. |
| Ein stummer Mohr. | Herr Stotz, Joh. |
| Ein Janitscharen Aga. | Herr Fendt. |

Mehrere Sklaven und Sklavinnen.

Wache.

Die Szene ist auf dem Landgute des Bassa.

82. Cast for Mozart's opera, *The Elopement from the Harem*

Esterházy of Galantha, and of His Highness the Prince Maurice of Lichtenstein. Eisenstadt 1806. NLB.

107. *Gulistan, oder der Hulla von Samarcanda.* (Gulistan, or The Hulla of Samarkand) Opera in three acts by Herr Etienne. Music by Herr Dalayrac. Performed at the princely Esterhazy Theatre at Eisenstadt. Eisenstadt, 1806. Printed in the princely Esterhazy Court Printing Press. NLB.

108. *Pachter Robert* (Farmer Robert). Comic opera in one act. Freely adapted from the French of Benard Valville by J. R. von Seyfried. Music by Herr Le Brun. Performed at the princely theatre at Eisenstadt. Eisenstadt, 1806. Printed at the princely Esterhazy court printing press. NLB.

109. *Die vereitelten Raenke* (Thwarted Intrigues). A musical comedy in two acts, freely adapted from the Italian, after *Le Vicende d'Amore* (Vicissitudes of Love). Music by Herr Johann Nep. Hummel, concertmaster of His Highness the Sovereign Prince Nicholas Esterházy of Galantha. Performed at the princely theatre at Eisenstadt. Eisenstadt, 1806. Printed at the princely Esterházy court printing press. NLB.

1807

110. *Der Holzerne Liebesbothe, oder: die Neuigkeitswuth* (The Wooden Messenger of Love or: The Passion for Novelty). Comic opera in two acts by Franz Gewey. Set to music by Johann Nep. Fuchs, conductor to H.H. Prince Esterhazy. Performed at the princely theatre at Eisenstadt. Eisenstadt, 1807. Printed at the princely court printing press. NLB.

111. *Der Schatzgräber* (The Treasure Seeker). Comic opera in one act, freely adapted from the French *Trésor supposé* by Hoffmann, rewritten by J. R. von Seyfried. Music by Herr Méhul. Performed at the princely Esterházy Theatre. Eisenstadt, 1807. Printed at the princely court printing press. NLB.

112. Goethe, Johann Wolfgang
*Theatralische Abentheuer* (Theatrical Adventures). Comic opera in two acts, adapted from the Italian. Music by Cimarosa and Mozart. Performed at the princely Esterhazy Theatre at Eisenstadt. Eisenstadt, 1807. Printed at the princely court printing press.

1810

113. *Cendrillon* (Cinderella). A fairy opera in three acts. Adapted from the French of Etienne by Heinrich Schmidt. Music by Nicolo Isouard. Performed at the princely Esterhazy Theatre at Eisenstadt, 1810.

# LIST*

## *of operas, academies, puppet shows and plays which were performed from the 23rd of January till December 1778 at the princely theatre of Esterház (NAB. Fasc. 2461 1-7. l.)*

January

23. *Die Grenadiere* (The Grenadiers), a comedy. Polyphemus.
27. Mr. Bienfait and Herr Christl. *Arlequin der Hausdieb* (Harlequin, the Thief in the House), a pantomime.
28. *Arlequin als Todtengerippe* (Harlequin as Skeleton), a pantomime by the same.
30. *Academie, Sinfonia*, Aria by Me. Poschwa, Concert by M. Hirsch, Aria by M. Dichtler, Sonata by Mr. Luigi, Symphonia by Vanhall, Aria by M. Prandtner, the same by M. Bianchi, Synf.

February

1. *Il finto pazzo* (Feigned Madness).
3. *Academia musica* (Musical Academy).
5. *Il finto pazzo* (Feigned Madness).
10. *Die Grenadiere* (The Grenadiers), a comedy. Bellandra.
11. *Academie, Sinfonia*, Aria by M. Bianchi, Concert by M. Rosetti, Divert. by M. Pichl; Aria by M. Dichtler, Concertino by Pichl, Aria by M. Bianchi, Synf. by Mr. Haydn.
22. *Academia musica nell'Appartamento* (Musical Academy in the Apartment).
24. The same.
26. The same.

March

10. The Pauli company began with *Die falschen Vertraulichkeiten* (The False Intimacies) in 3 acts.
11. *Arnaud*, a drama in 2 acts, and *Der Graf Althaus* (The Count Althaus), a comedy in 3 acts with Mr. Ulrich, and Bachmeyer in the cast.
12. *Il Barone di Rocca antica* (The Lord of the Old Castle).
13. *Trau, schau, wem* (Trust, Look, Whom). Played by the Schwarzwald family.
14. *William Buttler*, in 5 acts.
16. *Die verstellte Kranke* (The Sham Invalid).
17. *Emilia Galotti*, in 5 acts.
18. *Der Edelknabe* und *Jenny, oder die Uneigennützigkeit* (The Page, and Jenny or Unselfishness).
21. On the return of H. Highness: *Henriette, oder Sie ist schon verheirathet* (Henriette or She is already married).
22. *Il Barone di Rocca antica* (The Lord of the Old Castle).
23. *Der Gläubiger* (The Creditor), a touching comedy in 3 acts.
24. *Die Haushaltung nach der Mode* (Household à la mode), farce in 5 acts.
25. *Der Postzug* (The Mail-coach) in 2 acts and *Wilhelmine.*
27. and 28. (Nothing on account of the wind).
29. *La buona figliuola* (The Good Daughter). With M. Lamberti in the cast.
30. *Die Schule der Freigeister* und *Die doppelte Hinderniss* (The School of Freethinkers and The Double Impediment).
31. *Die Subordination* (Subordination).

April

1. *Die 3 Zwillingsbrüder* (The Three Twin Brothers).
2. *Das Soldatenglück* (Soldier's Luck).
3. *Der Jurist und der Bauer* (The Lawyer and the Peasant); *der Nachtwächter* (The Nightwatchman).
4. *Die Feuersbrunst* (The Conflagration).

* Foreign names and titles are given in the orthography of the original sources.

5. *Il Finto Pazzo* (Feigned Madness).
6. *Das Duell* und *Die Windmühle.* (The Duel and The Windmill).
7. *Der zu gefällige Ehemann* (The Too Obliging Husband).
8. *Der Kühehirte* und *Der dankbare Sohn* (The Cowherd and The Grateful Son).
9. *Arcifanfano.* With Mr. Pezzani in the cast.
10. *Miss Fanny* in 5 acts.
11. *Der Schneider und sein Sohn* (The Tailor and his Son).
12. *Die Mütter* (The Mothers).
No performances during Passion Week and the Holy Easter Day.
20. *Montrose und Surrey*, in 5 acts with Herr Meyer in the cast.
21. *Der Schubkarren des Essighändlers* (The Wheelbarrow of the Vinegar-Merchant).
22. *Elfriede.* With Herr Meyer's sister in the cast, the later Dittelmeyerin.
23. *Arcifanfano.*
24. *Der Todte ein Bräutigam* und *Der Bettelstudent.* (The Dead Man a Bridegroom and The Pauper Student).
25. *Miss Jenny Warton.*
26. *Der Tambour zahlt alles* und *Erispius (?) Liebesstreiche* (The Drummer Pays All and The Love Pranks of Erispius).
27. *Sophie, oder der gerechte Fürst* (Sophy, or the Just Prince) with Mad. Meyer in the cast.
28. *Der Zerstreute* (The Absent-minded Man).
29. *Der Graf von Sonnenthal* und *Der Bettler* (The Count of S. and the Beggar).
30. *Arcifanfano.*

May

1. *Burlie, Diener, Vater und Schwiegervater* (Burlie, Servant, Father and Father-in-law).
2. *Die Zwillingsbrüder* (The Twin Brothers).
3. *La sposa fedele* (The Faithful Wife). With Mad. Ripamonti in the cast.
4. *Der Deserteur* (The Deserter) and a burlesque, *Der Kapann.*
5. *Clementine*, in 5 acts.
6. *Die unähnlichen Brüder* (The Dissimilar Brothers).
7. *La buona figliuola* (The Good Daughter).
8. *Emilie Waldegrau.*
9. *Die neue Weiberschule* (The New School for Women).
10. *La buona figliuola* (The Good Daughter).
11. *Die Gunst des Fürsten* (The Favour of the Prince), in 5 acts.
12. *Nicht alles ist Gold was glänzt* (Not All is Gold that Glitters).
13. *Der Stolze, oder der Majoratsherr* (The Proud One, or The Feoffee).
14. *La buona figliuola* (The Good Daughter).
15. *Der Hausvater* (The Father of a Family), in 5 acts.
16. Puppet-show *das ländliche Hochzeitsfest* (The Country Wedding).
17. *Der Teufel steckt in ihm* und *Herkules in der Hölle* (He has the Devil in Him and Hercules in Hell).
18. *La sposa fedele* (The Faithful Wife) With M. Totti in tha cast.
19. *Das ländliche Hochzeitsfest* (The Country Wedding). Puppet-show.
20. *die 3 Zwillinge* (The Three Twins).
21. *La sposa fedele* (The Faithful Wife).
22. *Der Westindier* (The West-Indian).
23. *Gabriele von Monte Vecchio* (Gabriel of Monte Vecchio).
24. *Arcifanfano.*
25. *Der Spleen* (The Spleen) in 5 acts.
26. *Emilie, oder die Treue*, und *Lipperl der Weiberfeind.* (Emily or Faithfulness and Lipperl the Womanhater).
27. *Pamela*, Part I.
28. *La Sposa fedele* (The Faithful Wife).
29. *Der Deserteur aus Kindesliebe* (Deserter out of Filial Affection).
30. *Stella* in 5 acts, by Goethe.
31. *La Frascatana* (The Woman of Frascati).

June

1. *Minna von Barnhelm* in 5 acts.
2. Puppet show : *das ländliche Hochzeitsfest* (The Country Wedding).
3. *Der Furchtsame* (The Timid One).
4. *Arcifanfano.*
5. *Die 3 Zwillingsbrüder* (The Three Twin Brothers).
6. *Fayel* in 5 acts.
7. *La Sposa fedele* (The Faithful Wife).
8. *Der verlorene Sohn* (The Prodigal Son).
9. *Dürumel, oder der Deserteur* (D. or The Deserter).
10. *Der Ungar in Wien* (The Hungarian in Vienna).
12. *La Frascatana* (The Woman of Frascati).
12. *Darf man seine Frau lieben* (May One Love One's Wife).
13. *Tankred und Sigismunda* (Tancred and Sigismunda).
14. *Arcifanfano.*
15. *Der Bediente, Nebenbuhler seines Herrn,* und *sind Mann. od. Weibsp. standhafter in der Liebe* (The Servant, Rival of his Master or Are Men or Women More Constant in Love).
16. *Henriette, oder sie ist schon verheiratet* (Henriette or She is Already Married).
17. *Der Minister* (The Minister).
18. *La Sposa fedele* (The Faithful Wife).
19. *Der Zerstreute* (The Absent-minded Man).
20. *Die seltsame Eifersucht* (The Strange Jealousy).
21. *La Sposa fedele* (The Faithful Wife).
22. *Medon, oder die Rache des Weisen* (Medon, or The Revenge of the Wise Man).
23. *Der Edelknabe und Jenny* (The Page and Jenny).
24. *Die Stimme der Natur und der Herr Vetter* (The Voice of Nature and The Cousin).
25. *La Frascatana* (The Woman of Frascati).
26. *Der Galeren Sklave* (The Galley-Slave).
27. *Julie und Romeo* (Juliet and Romeo).
28. *Die unsichtbare Dame,* und *ein Nachspiel* (The Invisible Lady and An Afterpiece).
29. *Der Schuster und sein Freund* (The Shoemaker and his Friend).
30. *Die verliebten Zänker* (The Enamoured Quarrellers).

July

1. *Der englische Waise* und *Die Batterie* (The English Orphan and The Battery).
2. *Arcifanfano.*
3. *Pamela,* Part II.
4. *Adelson und Salvini* (A. and S.).
5. *La Sposa fedele* (The Faithful Wife).
6. *Der unvermuthete Zufall* (The Unexpected Chance).
7. *Die dankbare Tochter und Die Parodie.*
8. *Der Graf von Hohenwald* (The Count of H.).
9. *La Sposa fedele* (The Faithful Wife).
10. *Der zu gefällige Ehemann* (The Too Obliging Husband).
11. *Der Bürger* (The Burgher), a tragedy.
12. *L'Astratto* (The Distracted).
13. *Die Wahl,* und *Die Nacht* (The Choice and The Night).
14. Puppet show: *Das ländische Hochzeitsfest* (The Country Wedding).
15. *Sidney und Sylly* (S. and S.).
16. *Der gerechte Fürst* (The Just Prince).
17. *Der Krieg, oder die Soldatenliebe* (The War, or Soldier's Love).

August

On the return of H. Highness.

26. *Maria Wallburg.*
27. *La Sposa fedele* (The Faithful Wife).
28. *Der Barbier von Sevilien* (The Barber of Seville).

29. *Geschwinde, ehe man es erfährt* (Quickly, Before it is Found Out).
30. *L'Astratto* (The Distracted).
31. *Pamela*, Part III.

September

On the return of H. Highness from Vienna.
8. *Die Wohltaten unter Anverwandten* (The Good Deeds among Kinsmen).
9. *Wie man die Hand umkehrt* (In the Turn of a Hand).
10. *Il geloso in cimento* (The Jealous Man on Trial).
11. *Arist, od. der ehrliche Mann* (Arist, or the Honest Man).
12. *Der Graf von Olsbach* (The Count of Olsbach).
13. *Il Geloso in cimento* (The Jealous Man on Trial).
14. *Der Schneider und sein Sohn*, und *ein Nachspiel* (The Tailor and his Son and an Afterpiece).
15. Puppet-show: *Dido.*
16. *Die falschen Vertraulichkeiten* (False Intimacies).
17. *L'Astratto* (The Distracted).
18. *Die Poeten nach der Mode* (Poets *à la mode*).
19. *Der Hochzeit Tag* (The Wedding Day), a tragedy.
20. *La Sposa fedele* (The Faithful Wife).
21. *Die Wirtschafterin*, und *Der Kühehirt* (The Housekeeper and The Cowherd).
22. *Die verliebten Zänker* (The Enamoured Quarrellers).
23. *Der Bettler*, und *Der Bettelstudente*, (The Beggar and The Pauper Student).
24. *La Frascatana* (The Woman of Frascati).
25. *Verwirrung über Verwirrung* (Confusion upon Confusion).
26. *Stella*, by Goethe.
27. *La Frascatana* (The Woman of Frascati).
28. *Die Grafen von Sonnenfels*, und *der Herr Gevatter* (The Counts of S. and The Godfather).
29. *Minna von Barnhelm.*
30 *Wie man eine Hand umkehrt* (In the Turn of a Hand).

October

1. *La buona figliuola* (The Good Daughter).
2. *Miss Burton, oder das Landmädchen* (Miss B. or the Country Girl).
3. *Fanny, oder der Schiffbruch* (Fanny, or the Shipwreck).
4. *Der Gläubiger* (The Creditor).
5. *Die ungleichen Mütter* (The Dissimilar Mothers).
6. *Der Diener Nebenbuhler* und *der ungegründete Verdacht* (The Servant Rival and The Unfounded Suspicion).
7. *Der gute Ehemann* (The Good Husband).
8. *La Frascatana* (The Woman of Frascati).
9. *Die Unbekannte* (The Strange Woman).
10. *Adelson und Salvini* (A. and S.).
11. *La Frascatana* (The Woman of Frascati).
12. *Trau, schau, wem* (Trust, Look, Whom).
13. *Der Ungar in Wien* (The Hungarian in Vienna).
14. *Der Postzug*, und *der Selbstmord* (The Mail-Coach and The Suicide).
15. *Der Schubkarren des Essighändlers* (The Wheelbarrow of the Vinegar-merchant).
16. *Die seltsame Probe* und *die Feldmühle* (The Strange Trial and The Fieldmill).
17. *Derby*, a tragedy.
18. *Il Geloso in cimento* (The Jealous Man on Trial).
19. *Nicht alles ist Gold was glänzt* (Not All is Gold that Glitters).
20. *Clementine.*
21. *Der verlorene Sohn* (The Prodigal Son).
22. *La buona figliuola* (The Good Daughter).
23. *Der Todte ein Bräutigam, der Herr Gevatter* (The Dead Man a Bridegroom and The Godfather).
24. *Emilie Waldegrau.*
25. *La Sposa fedele* (The Faithful Wife).

26. *Das Findelkind* (The Foundling).
27. *Der Schuster und sein Freund*, und *Die Stimme d. Natur* (The Shoemaker and his Friend and The Voice of Nature).
28. The troup of Pauli and Mayer ended their performances at Esterház with *Das gerettete Venedig* (Venice Preserved).
29. *L'Astratto* (The Distracted).
30. The Diwald troup began with *Amalie oder die Leidenschaften* (Amelia or the Passions. With Mlle. Knapp and Messrs. Bartl, Schilling, Durst and Weiss in the cast.
31. *Die Wildpretschützen* und *der Tempel der Venus* (The Game-hunters and The Temple of Venus). With H. Menninger, Mad. Soliman and Mlle. Biwald in the cast.

November

1. *Der Hausregent* (The Ruler of the House).
2. *D'Arnaud* und *Pygmalion.*
3. *Der Schwätzer* (The Tatler).
4. *Die schöne Wienerin* (The Lovely Viennese Woman).
5. *La Frascatana* (The Woman of Frascati).
6. *Eugenie.*
7. *Die Bekanntschaft im Bade* (Acquaintanceship at the Bath).
8. *Der Deserteur aus Kindesliebe* (Deserter out of Filial Love).
9. *So muss man mir nicht kommen* (You need not try that on me).
10. *Der Entsatz von Wienn* (The Relief of Vienna).
11. *Der Geschmack der Nation* (The Taste of the Nation).
12. *L'astratto* (The Distracted).
13. *Die schöne Wienerin* (The Lovely Viennese Woman).
14. *Die Kindesmörderin* (The Child-murderess).
15. *L'astratto* (The Distracted).
16. *Der Westindier* (The West-Indian).
17. *Die Frau als Courier* und *Das Gespenst auf dem Lande* (The Woman as Courier and The Ghost in the Country).
18. *Die Bekanntschaft auf der Redoute*, und *Der unbekannte Wohltätige* (Acquaintance at the Masked Ball and The Unknown Benefactor).
19. *Die Verstellte Kranke* (The Sham Invalid).
20. *Montrose und Surrey*. With M. Morocz in the cast.
21. *Die Batterie* und *Der Gewürzkämer* (The Battery and The Grocer).
22. *La Locanda* (The Inn).
23. *Der Geburtstag* (The Birthday).
24. *La Locanda* (The Inn).
25. *Emilia Galotti.*
26. *La Locanda* (The Inn).
27. *Der Graf Waltron* (Count Waltron).
28. *Der betrogene Vormund* (The Deceived Guardian).
29. *Amalie, oder die Leidenschaften* (Amelia, or the Passions).
30. *Richard der dritte* (Richard III).

December

1. *La Locanda* (The Inn).
2. *Der Kobold und der Soldat* (The Goblin and the Soldier).
3. *Der Schwätzer* (The Tatler).
4. *Der Geschmack der Nation* (The Taste of the Nation).
5. *Louise, oder der Sieg der Unschuld* (Louise, or the Victory of Innocence).
6. *Il Geloso in cimento* (The Jealous Man on Trial).
7. *Alle irren sich* (All are Wrong).
8. *Il Geloso in cimento* (The Jealous Man on Trial).
9. *Alle haben recht* (All are right).
10. *Nancy, oder die Schule der Eheleute* (Nancy, or the School for Married People).
11. *Die Gunst der Fürsten* (The Favour of the Prince).
12. *Die reisende Comödianten* und *Odoardo* (The Travelling Actors and Odoardo).
13. *Der Bettelstudent* und *der todte Herr Bruder* (The pauper Student and The Dead Brother).

14. *Der Graf von Olsbach* (The Count of Olsbach).
15. *Der Teufel an allen Ecken* (The Devil at Every Corner).
16. *Die reiche Frau* (The Rich Woman).
17. *Es ist nicht alles Gold was glänzt* (All is not Gold that Glitters).
18. *Der Gefühlvolle* (The Sentimental Man).
19. *Der Schein betrügt, oder der gute Mann* (Appearances are Deceptive or the Good Man).
20. *Die Wildpretschützen* (The Gamehunters).
21. *Der Jurist und der Bauer* und *Der Einsiedler* (The Lawyer and the Peasant and The Hermit).
22. *Olivie* (Olivia), a tragedy.

### *Abbreviations*

MLSV = Library of Music-Lovers' Society, Vienna (Bibliothek der Gesellschaft der Musikfreunde in Wien)
NAB = National Archive, Budapest, Archive of the Esterházy family (Országos Levéltár, Herceg Esterházy család levéltára)
NLB = National Library, Budapest (Országos Széchényi Könyvtár)
NLV = National Library, Vienna (Österreichische Nationalbibliothek)
NMB = National Museum, Budapest, Historical Portrait Gallery (Országos Történeti Múzeum, Történeti Arcképcsarnok)
ULB = University Library, Budapest (Egyetemi Könyvtár)

## BIBLIOGRAPHY


Bartha, D.—L. Somfai
1960 *Haydn als Opernkapellmeister*, Budapest, Verlag der Ungarischen Akademie der Wissenschaften
Benyovszky, K.
1926 *Das alte Theater*, Pressburg
1929 *Theatergeschichtliche Kleinigkeiten*, Bratislava
1934 *Johann Nepomuk Hummel, der Mensch und Künstler*, Pressburg
Bubics Zs.—Merényi Zs.
1896 *Herczeg Esterházy Pál nádor* (Palatine Prince Pál Esterházy), Budapest
Confalonieri, G.
1948 *Prigionia di un artista*,
Csatkai, E.
*Beiträge zu einer Eisenstädter Theatergeschichte*. Mitteilungen des Burgenländischen Heimat- und Naturschutzvereines
1936 *Soproni iskolai szinjátékok a* 17.—18. *században* (School Dramas at Sopron in the seventeenth and eighteenth centuries). *A Szinpad.*
1793 *Geschichte der Schaubühne zu Pressburg* (reprinted in 1927), Pressburg
Gugitz, G.
1929 *Das alte Badner Theater und seine Prinzipale*, 1751—1811. Jahrbuch für Landeskunde von Niederösterreich.
Hárich, J.
1937 *A kismartoni várkert története* (History of the Castle-garden at Kismarton), MS. NLB
1941 *Szöveggyüjtemény* (Collection of Librettos), Budapest, MS. NLB
1959 *Esterházy Musikgeschichte im Spiegel der zeitgenössischen Textbücher*, Eisenstadt
*Esterházy zenetörténet* (History of the Esterházys' Music), MS, vol. I—VI. NLB
Kádár, J.
1914 *A budai és pesti német szinészet története* 1812-ig (History of German Play-acting in Buda and Pest till 1812), Budapest
1916 *Shakespeare drámái a magyarországi német szinpadokon* (Shakespeare's Dramas on the German Stages of Hungary) Magyar Shakespeare-tár.

Meller, S.
1915 *Az Esterházy-képtár története* (History of the Esterházy Picture-gallery), Budapest
Pohl, C. F.
1878—1882 *Joseph Haydn*, Leipzig
Probst, F.
1952a *Daten zur Geschichte des Hochfürstlich Esterházyschen Hoftheaters. Burgenländische Heimatblätter*, Heft 1.
1952b *Beiträge zur Geschichte des deutschsprachigen Theaterwesens in Eisenstadt*, Eisenstadt
Riesbeck,
1784 *Briefe eines reisenden Franzosen über Deutschland.*
Schmidt, H.
1856 *Erinnerungen eines weimarischen Veteranen*, Leipzig, Brockhaus
Zorn de Bulach
1901 *L'ambassade du Prince Louis de Rohan*, Strasbourg.

## NOTES

1 Pohl 1878–82.
2 Hárich 1959.
3 Riesbeck 1784.
4 Benyovszky 1934, p. 53.
5 György Bessenyei (1747–1811), poet, pioneer of Hungarian Enlightenment. As a young man he served in Maria Theresa's Body-guard at Vienna.
6 Mindenes Gyüjtemény, 1790, IV. quarter, p. 44.
7 1824, vol. III, p. 49.
8 Count István Széchenyi (1791–1860). Apart from Lajos Kossuth, the most important statesman during the era which preceded the Hungarian War of Independence of 1848 and the protagonists of which fought for the country's economic and political freedom.
9 Meller, S., History of the Esterházy Picture-gallery, Budapest 1915 (Hungarian).
10 Conspiracy of Wesselényi, a coalition of Hungarian aristocrats against Emperor Leopold under the leadership of the Palatine Ferenc Wesselényi. After his decease, Ferenc Nádassy became the leader of the organization. After a short-lived armed insurrection, the movement was suppressed by Emperor Leopold in 1671.
11 Peace of Szatmár. The unsuccessful Hungarian war of independence that had lasted nearly a decade under the leadership of Ferenc Rákóczi II, was terminated by the Peace of Szatmár in 1711.
12 Péter Pázmány (1570–1637). He was Primate of Hungary, Cardinal-Archbishop of Esztergom, a prominent figure of Hungarian counter-reformation.
13 Hárich, vol. V.
14 Bubics—Merényi 1896, p. 86.
15 op. cit., p. 87.
16 op. cit., p. 88.
17 op. cit., p. 89.
18 op. cit., p. 98.
19 Csatkai 1936, p. 267.
20 Hárich, vol. III, pp. 18–19.
21 Archives of the Arch-Abbey of Pannonhalma. Jesuit documents 119. B. 26/1–2.
22 Hárich 1959, p. 5.
23 Hárich 1937. p. 28
24 Meller 1915, p. xxv.
25 Acta Musicalia (National Library, Budapest, Department of Theatrical History) 65.
26 Hárich, vol. VI, pp. 6–70.
27 Csatkai 1936, p. 268.
28 Hárich 1941, p. 8.
29 A 'gulden' or 'forint' (florin) in Maria Theresa's time was approximately equivalent to the purchase price of two metric quintals of grain at the site of production.

30 Hárich, vol. VI, p. 5.
31 Acta Theatralia (National Library, Budapest, Department of Theatrical History) 108.
32 Acta Theatralia 108.
33 Acta Theatralia 108.
34 Acta Theatralia 108.
35 Zprávy pomátkové pece, 1958, 3–4.
36 Pohl I/1, 1878, p. 231.
37 Acta Musicalia 253.
38 Benyovszky 1929, p. 37.
39 Acta Musicalia 145.
40 Acta Musicalia 252.
41 Pohl I/2, 1882, p. 232.
42 Eszterháza was the name of the new castle and the similarly named village, near Lake Fertő, at a distance of about 18 miles. The name is spelt differently in contemporary documents: Estorhas, Estoraz, Eszterház, etc., or confounded with the name of the family — as Esterházy. — Sőtér, I., Magyar-francia kapcsolatok (Hungarian and French Interrelations). Budapest, Teleki Institute, 1946, p. 96.
43 Acta Theatralia 107.
44 Gugitz 1929.
45 Kádár 1914, p. 10.
46 Benyovszky 1926, p. 26.
47 Gugitz 1929, p. 329.
48 Pohl I/2, 1882, p. 37.
49 Aus der Zeit Maria Theresias. Tagebuch des Fürsten Johann Josef Khevenhüller-Metsch kaiserlichen Oberhofmeisters. 1742–76. Holzhausen—Engelmann, Leipzig 1925.
50 Acta Musicalia 451.
51 Acta Musicalia 740.
52 I. Cs. Katona, Constructional Progress of the Castle at Fertőd (Eszterháza). Építés- és Közlekedéstudományi Közlemények 1959, Nos. 1-2, pp. 77-130 (Hungarian).
53 It was B. Péczeli who called attention to M. Dallos' extensive rhymed description of Eszterháza. Soproni Szemle 1957.
54 NAB. Maps, plans XXXXIV/1542–5.
55 'Il fait venir toutes les raretés de Paris'. Zorn de Bulach 1901.
56 Zprávy památkove pece, 1958, No 3–4.
57 Entwurf zu stärkerer Heizung des Hochfürstl. Opern Hauses zu Esterhaz. NAB (Maps, plans), XXXVIII/1222.
58 Entwurf zu einem Fürstl. Winter Theater in Esterhaz. NAB (Maps, plans), XXXVIII/1223.
59 Ground plan from the beginning of the nineteenth century. Acta Musicalia 3315.
60 Acta Theatralia 1.
61 Benyovszky 1926, p. 27.
62 Probst 1952, p. 27.
63 Acta Theatralia 11.
64 Acta Theatralia 12—15.
65 Acta Theatralia 12.
66 Acta Theatralia 24.
67 Acta Theatralia 22.
68 Acta Theatralia 16.
69 Benyovszky 1926, p. 28.
70 Pohl I/1, 1878, p. 45.
71 Acta Theatralia 20.
72 Acta Theatralia 18.
73 Acta Theatralia 17.
74 Acta Theatralia 23.
75 Acta Musicalia 2520.
76 Hárich 1959, p. 34.
77 Acta Theatralia 25.
78 Acta Theatralia 30.

79 Acta Theatralia 31.
80 Benyovszky 1926, p. 29.
81 Egyetemes Philológiai Szemle (Universal Philological Review), 1919, p. 197.
82 Zorn de Bulach 1901.
83 Pohl I/2, 1882, p. 91.
84 Pressburg 1793. Reprinted in 1927.
85 Pressburger Zeitung, 11th September 1773.
86 Pressburger Zeitung, 5th January 1774.
87 Acta Musicalia 196.
88 Pohl I/2, 1882, 9. 62.
89 Acta Musicalia 2244.
90 Acta Musicalia 610/a.
91 Acta Musicalia 610/b, c.
92 Acta Musicalia 196.
93 Probst, 1952b, pp. 28–30.
94 Acta Theatralia 27.
95 Acta Theatralia 28.
96 1775, 3. Vierteljahr, p. 94.
97 Kádár 1916, p. 69.
98 Pressburger Zeitung, 23rd November 1774.
99 Acta Musicalia 1354.
100 Acta Musicalia 87.
101 Acta Musicalia 1366, 1367, 1368.
102 Acta Musicalia 1366.
103 NAB, Fasc. 2461, 1–7.
104 Acta Theatralia 58.
105 Pohl I/2, 1882, p. 19.
106 Acta Theatralia 4.
107 Acta Theatralia 10.
108 Acta Theatralia 33.
109 v. pp.
110 Acta Theatralia 45.
111 Acta Theatralia 36.
112 Acta Theatralia 37.
113 Although the name of Sacchini is printed on the libretto, extant musical documents show the music to have been taken from Felici's opera of the same title (Bartha—Somfai, p. 82).
114 Acta Musicalia 3754.
115 Acta Theatralia 89.
116 Acta Musicalia 3983.
117 Acta Musicalia 3983.
118 Acta Musicalia 3983.
119 Acta Musicalia 4023.
120 Acta Musicalia 4006, 4027.
121 Acta Musicalia 4003, 4004.
122 Acta Theatralia 40.
123 Acta Theatralia 39.
124 Acta Theatralia 38.
125 Acta Theatralia 32.
126 Acta Musicalia 3968.
127 Acta Theatralia 50.
128 Acta Theatralia 48.
129 Acta Theatralia 49.
130 Acta Theatralia 43.
131 Acta Theatralia 44.
132 Acta Theatralia 54.
133 Acta Theatralia 55.
134 Acta Theatralia 51.
135 Acta Theatralia 52.
136 Acta Theatralia 60.

137 Acta Theatralia 53.
138 Acta Theatralia 60.
139 Acta Theatralia 60.
140 Almost the entire monograph of D. Bartha and L. Somfai *Haydn als Opernkapellmeister* (Akadémiai Kiadó, Budapest, 1960), deals with the subject treated in this chapter. The German version of the present book was amply utilized by the authors who have enabled us, at the same time, to make important corrections in and necessary additions to this edition. It should, however, be noted that the monograph in question leaves much to be desired in respect of sources and philological authenticity. Although the work pretends to be complete, the authors seem to ignore the archival material of whole periods, while their data needs revision on account of many erroneous references and numerous faulty quotations of sources. Even their references to the German version of this book contain many erroneous data.
141 Acta Musicalia 4008.
142 Eisenstädter Commissions Prothocoll 1777–90. No. 1338, NAB.
143 Acta Musicalia 4008, 4009, 4010.
144 Eisenstädter Commissions Prothocoll 1770–90. No 1235, NAB.
145 Al merito incomparabile di sua Altezza il Principe Nicolo Esterhazi di Galantha . . . In segno di profondissimo rispetto e particolare venerazione, Luigi Rossi. NAB (Aprónyomtatvány Tár 1779/81. Fol.
146 NAB 799.
147 Acta Musicalia 1186.
148 Acta Musicalia 4021.
149 Acta Musicalia 4014–19.
150 Acta Musicalia 4012.
151 NAB XLII. 1376.
152 NAB 799 Nos. 46, 138.
153 Acta Musicalia 3997.
154 NAB 799, No. 110.
155 NAB 799 Proth. 3, 156.
156 Sürgöny, 6th September 1865; Fővárosi Lapok No. 33, 1875.
157 NAB Fasc. 2461, p. 102.
158 Acta Musicalia 217.
159 NAB Fasc. VI., p. 369.
160 NAB Fasc. VI., p. 370.
161 NAB Fasc. 2461, p. 115.
162 NAB Fasc. 2461, p. 78.
163 NAB Fasc. 2461, p. 118.
164 NAB Fasc. 2461, p. 129.
165 Acta Musicalia 1972.
166 Tudományos Gyüjtemény, 1924, vol. III, pp. 40—56. Utazásbeli jegyzetek Óvárról, Kis-Martonról, Fraknóról, 's Eszterházáról (Travel notes on Óvár, Kis-Marton, Fraknó and Eszterháza. — Hungarian).
167 Csatkai, Beiträge III/16.
168 NAB Fasc. 2461, p. 10.
169 NAB Fasc. 2461, pp. 8–9.
170 NAB Fasc. 2461, p. 14.
171 NAB Fasc. 2461, p. 26.
172 NAB Fasc. 2461, p. 60.
173 NAB Fasc. 2461, pp. 79, 115, 117.
174 NAB Fasc. 2461, p. 118.
175 NAB Fasc. 2461, p. 113.
176 NAB Fasc. 2461, pp. 227–8.
177 NAB Fasc. 2461, p. 111.
178 NAB Fasc. 2461, p. 110.
179 NAB Fasc. 2461, p. 123.
180 NLV Handschriftensammlung.
181 Wiener Zeitung 1797, No. 88.
182 Rosenbaum: 'Die Illumination war die schönste die man noch je in Eisenstadt sah'.
183 1797, vol. II, pp. 574–6.

184 1801, vol. II. pp. 428–431.
185 Hárich 1937, p. 58.
186 Alsókubin, Csaplovics Library.
187 Theater Dekorationen nach den original Skitzen des k. k. Hof Theater Mahlers Anton de Pian. Gestochen und verlegt von Norbert Bittner. Wien 1818 pp. 19, 70.
188 Acta Musicalia 1427, 1422.
189 Acta Musicalia 1427.
190 Acta Musicalia 1383/a.
191 Acta Musicalia 3344.
192 Schmidt 1856, pp. 123–4.
193 op. cit. pp. 130—131.
194 Acta Musicalia 1624.
195 Acta Musicalia 2541.
196 Schmidt 1856, pp. 126–7.
197 Acta Musicalia 220, 221.
198 Acta Musicalia 3354.
199 Acta Musicalia 2780.
200 Schmidt 1856, p. 7.
201 op. cit. pp. 124–125.
202 Acta Musicalia 3161, 3102.
203 Acta Musicalia 3191.
204 Confalonieri 1948, II, p. 151.
205 Acta Musicalia 3191.
206 J. Hárich is mistaken in stating that the librettos were transferred to the National Library Budapest (Hárich 1959, p. 4).

# OPERA SINGERS AT ESZTERHÁZA AND KISMARTON

There are two available sources for the determination of the time the singers spent in the service of Prince Esterházy: the casts and the pay bills. The data supplied by these sources are not always in agreement. Before their disappearance at the end of World War II, the printed libretti were still at the disposal of Pohl so that, with their aid, he was able to ascertain the cast of almost every performance. It was presumably on these casts that he relied when compiling the list on which the earlier editions of the present book were based. The list of contracts for the years 1776 to 1790, compiled by Bartha and Somfai, was based on pay bills. As we are no longer in a position to check up the data of Pohl, we too have to rely on the pay bills: we want to present here Bartha-Somfai's list minus its details and plus the data concerning the period between 1763 and 1776. It should be noted that the pay bills are not quite reliable since those contained in the 'Chor' and 'Kameral Music' are sometimes contradictory, and show gaps if compared with the casts. Besides, there exist only 'Chor Music' lists from 1763–1764 and 1766–68 and only joint 'Chor' and 'Kammer Music' lists from 1769 to 1772, so that it is rather difficult to separate singers who performed only in the church choir from those who sang both in the church and the opera.

Our list includes only those members of the church-choir who appeared at least once on the stage also, as well as those who — without appearing on the stage — were obliged (according to a statement of 1765) to do theatre service as well. Only annual statements for the period up to 1772, and monthly ones for the first half of 1772 as also for the period from 1773 to 1790 are available. Therefore, the first and last months of the term of service are indicated (by Arabic numerals) only where we could rely on monthly statements. Cases where the singer's name occurred in the cast only, are indicated in the corresponding year by means of a circle instead of an asterisk.

List of Opera Singers at Eszterháza

| Female singers | 1763 | 1764 | 1765 | 1766 | 1767 | 1768 | 1769 | 1770 | 1771 | 1772 | 1773 | 1774 | 1775 | 1776 | 1777 | 1778 | 1779 | 1780 | 1781 | 1782 | 1783 | 1784 | 1785 | 1786 | 1787 | 1788 | 1789 | 1790 |
|---|---|---|---|---|---|---|---|---|---|---|---|---|---|---|---|---|---|---|---|---|---|---|---|---|---|---|---|---|
| Benvenuti, Barbara | . | . | . | . | . | . | . | . | . | . | . | . | . | . | . | . | . | . | . | . | . | . | . | . | . | 8— | * | —9 |
| Bologna, Maria | . | . | . | . | . | . | . | . | . | . | . | . | . | . | . | . | . | . | 5— | . | . | —8 | . | . | . | . | . | . |
| Bologna, Mathilde | . | . | . | . | . | . | . | . | . | . | . | . | . | . | . | . | . | . | 5— | * | * | * | * | * | * | * | * | —9 |
| Bon, Rosa and Anna | . | . | * | . | . | . | . | . | . | . | . | . | . | . | . | . | . | . | . | . | . | . | . | . | . | . | . | |
| Cellini, Gertrude | . | . | . | . | . | . | 8— | . | . | . | —4 | . | . | . | . | . | . | . | . | . | . | . | . | . | . | . | . | . |
| Delicati, Margherita | . | . | . | . | . | . | . | . | . | . | . | . | . | . | . | . | . | . | . | . | . | . | 4— | * | —6 | . | . | . |
| Dichtler (Fux), Barbara | * | * | * | * | * | * | * | * | * | * | * | * | * | —9 | . | . | . | . | . | . | . | . | . | . | . | . | . | . |
| Friberth (Spangler) | | | | | | | | | | | | | | | | | | | | | | | | | | | | |
| Magdalena | . | . | . | . | . | 8— | * | * | * | * | * | * | * | —4 | . | . | . | . | . | . | . | . | . | . | . | . | . | . |
| Jäger, Eleonora | * | * | * | * | * | * | * | * | * | * | * | * | . | . | . | . | . | . | . | . | . | . | . | . | . | . | . | . |
| Jermoli, Anna | . | . | . | . | . | . | . | . | . | . | . | . | . | . | 3—6 | . | ○ | 4— | —3 | . | . | . | . | . | . | . | . | . |
| Melo, Theresia | . | . | . | . | . | . | . | . | . | . | . | . | . | . | . | . | . | . | . | . | . | . | . | . | . | . | . | 7—8 |
| Polzelli, Luigia | . | . | . | . | . | . | . | . | . | . | . | . | . | . | . | . | 3— | —12 | 3— | * | * | * | * | * | * | * | * | —9 |
| Poschwa, Katharina | . | . | . | . | . | . | . | . | . | . | . | . | . | 1— | * | * | —8 | . | . | . | . | . | . | . | . | . | . | . |
| Prandtner (Swoboda), | | | | | | | | | | | | | | | | | | | | | | | | | | | | |
| Maria El. | . | . | . | . | . | . | . | . | . | . | . | . | 10 | 1— | * | * | * | —10 | . | . | . | . | . | . | . | . | . | . |
| Puttler, Anna | . | . | . | . | . | . | . | . | . | . | . | . | . | 1— | * | —12 | . | . | . | . | . | . | . | . | . | . | . | . |
| Raimondi, Anna | . | . | . | . | . | . | . | . | . | . | . | . | . | . | . | . | . | . | 4— | —7 | . | . | . | . | . | . | . | . |
| Ripamonti, Barbara | . | . | . | . | . | . | . | . | . | . | . | . | . | . | . | 1— | * | —3 | . | . | . | 6— | * | —6 | . | . | . | . |
| Sassi, Barbara | . | . | . | . | . | . | . | . | . | . | . | . | . | . | . | . | . | . | . | . | . | . | . | 5— | * | * | —9 | . |
| Sassi (Nencini), Palmira | . | . | . | . | . | . | . | . | . | . | . | . | . | . | . | . | . | . | . | . | . | . | 9— | * | * | * | * | —7 |
| Scheffstoss, A. M. | ○ | . | * | . | ○ | * | * | . | . | . | . | . | . | . | . | . | . | . | . | . | . | . | . | . | . | . | . | . |
| Speccioli, Maria Antonia | . | . | . | . | . | . | . | . | . | . | . | . | . | . | . | . | . | . | . | 9— | * | * | —8 | . | . | . | . | . |
| Tauber, M. Anna | . | . | . | . | . | . | . | . | . | . | . | . | . | . | 1— | —12 | . | . | . | . | . | . | . | . | . | . | . | . |
| Tavecchia (Taveggia), | | | | | | | | | | | | | | | | | | | | | | | | | | | | |
| Theresia | . | . | . | . | . | . | . | . | . | . | . | . | . | . | . | . | . | 8— | —7 | . | * | . | . | | . | . | . | . |
| Trever, Marie Elisabeth | . | . | . | . | . | . | . | . | . | . | . | . | . | . | 1— | —12 | . | . | . | . | . | . | . | . | . | . | . | . |
| Valdesturla, Constanza | . | . | . | . | . | . | . | . | . | . | . | . | . | . | . | . | 8— | * | * | * | * | * | —7 | . | . | . | . | . |
| Zannini, Anna | . | . | . | . | . | . | . | . | . | . | . | . | . | . | . | . | 1—8 | . | . | . | . | . | . | . | . | . | . | . |
| Zecchielli, Maria | . | . | . | . | . | . | . | . | . | . | . | . | . | . | . | . | . | . | . | . | . | . | . | . | . | . | 4— | – |

## List of Opera Singers at Eszterháza

| Male singers | 1763 | 1764 | 1765 | 1766 | 1767 | 1768 | 1769 | 1770 | 1771 | 1772 | 1773 | 1774 | 1775 | 1776 | 1777 | 1778 | 1779 | 1780 | 1781 | 1782 | 1783 | 1784 | 1785 | 1786 | 1787 | 1788 | 1789 | 1790 |
|---|---|---|---|---|---|---|---|---|---|---|---|---|---|---|---|---|---|---|---|---|---|---|---|---|---|---|---|---|
| Amici, Giuseppe ...... | . | . | . | . | . | . | . | . | . | . | . | . | . | . | . | . | . | . | . | . | . | . | . | . | . | . | . | 3—9 |
| Bianchi, Benedetto ... | . | . | . | . | . | . | . | . | . | . | . | . | . | 4— | * | * | * | * | —4 | . | . | 7— | * | * | * | * | * | —6 |
| Bon, Girolamo ...... | . | . | * | . | . | . | . | . | . | . | . | . | . | . | . | . | . | . | . | . | . | . | . | . | . | . | . | . |
| Braghetti, Prospero ... | . | . | . | . | . | . | . | . | . | . | . | . | . | . | . | . | . | . | 7— | * | * | * | * | * | * | * | * | —9 |
| Crinazzi, N. .......... | . | . | . | . | . | . | . | . | . | . | . | . | . | . | . | . | . | . | 7—9 | . | . | . | . | . | . | . | . | . |
| Dichtler, Leopold .... | * | * | * | * | * | * | * | * | * | * | * | * | * | * | * | * | * | * | * | * | * | * | * | * | * | * | * | * |
| Ernst, Michael ....... | . | . | . | . | . | . | . | . | . | . | * | * | * | * | . | . | . | . | . | . | . | . | . | . | . | . | . | . |
| Friberth, Karl ....... | ○ | . | * | . | ○ | ○ | . | ○ | . | 1—7 | * | * | * | —4 | . | . | . | . | . | . | . | . | . | . | . | . | . | . |
| Gherardi, Pietro ...... | . | . | . | . | . | . | . | . | . | . | . | . | . | 6— | * | —1 | . | . | . | . | . | . | . | . | . | . | . | . |
| Griessler, Melchior .... | * | * | * | * | * | * | * | * | * | * | . | * | . | . | . | . | . | . | . | . | . | . | . | . | . | . | . | * |
| Jermoli, Guglielmo ... | . | . | . | . | . | . | . | . | . | . | . | . | . | . | 3—6 | . | ○ | 4— | —3 | . | . | . | . | . | . | . | . | . |
| Lambertini, Giac. ... | . | . | . | . | . | . | 8— | —8 | . | . | . | . | . | . | . | 3— | —3 | . | . | . | . | . | . | . | . | . | . | . |
| Majeroni, Pietro ...... | . | . | . | . | . | . | . | . | . | . | . | . | . | . | . | . | . | . | . | . | . | . | . | . | . | . | . | 3—9 |
| Mandini, Paolo ....... | . | . | . | . | . | . | . | . | . | . | . | . | . | . | . | . | . | . | . | . | 1— | —10 | . | . | . | . | . | . |
| Martinelli, Filippo .... | . | . | . | . | . | . | . | . | . | . | . | . | . | . | . | . | . | . | . | . | . | . | . | . | . | . | . | 8—9 |
| Moratti, Vincenzo .... | . | . | . | . | . | . | . | . | . | . | . | . | . | . | . | . | . | . | 5— | * | * | * | —4 | . | 3— | * | —5 | . |
| Morelli, Bartholomeo . | . | . | . | . | . | . | . | . | . | . | . | . | . | . | . | . | . | . | . | . | . | . | 5— | * | —4 | . | . | . |
| Negri .............. | . | . | . | . | . | . | . | . | . | . | . | . | . | . | . | . | . | . | . | 9— | * | —8 | . | . | . | . | . | . |
| Nencini, Santo........ | . | . | . | . | . | . | . | . | . | . | . | . | . | . | . | . | . | . | . | . | . | . | 9— | * | * | * | * | —7 |
| Paoli, Gaetano de ... | . | . | . | . | . | . | . | . | . | . | . | . | . | . | . | . | . | . | . | . | . | . | . | . | . | 6— | * | —9 |
| Pasquale, di Giovanni | . | . | . | . | . | . | . | . | . | . | . | . | . | . | . | . | . | . | 5—9 | . | . | . | . | . | . | . | . | . |
| Peschi, Antonio ...... | . | . | . | . | . | . | . | . | . | . | . | . | . | . | . | . | 3— | * | * | —7 | . | . | . | . | . | . | . | . |
| Pezzani, G. ......... | . | . | . | . | . | . | . | . | . | . | . | . | . | . | . | 3— | —3 | . | . | . | . | . | . | . | . | . | . | . |
| Prizzi (Brizzi), Aloysius | . | . | . | . | . | . | . | . | . | . | . | . | . | . | . | . | . | . | . | . | . | . | . | . | . | 5— | . | —9 |
| Rossi, Luigi ......... | . | . | . | . | . | . | . | . | . | . | . | . | . | . | . | . | 3— | . | —2 | . | . | . | . | . | . | . | . | . |
| Speccioli, Antonio..... | . | . | . | . | . | . | . | . | . | . | . | . | . | . | . | . | . | . | . | 9— | * | * | —8 | . | . | . | . | . |
| Specht, Christian .... | . | . | . | . | . | * | . | . | . | . | . | . | . | . | . | . | . | . | . | . | . | . | . | . | . | . | . | . |
| Totti, Andrea ........ | . | . | . | . | . | . | . | . | . | . | . | . | . | . | . | 6— | * | * | * | —5 | . | . | . | . | . | . | . | . |
| Ungricht, Vitus ...... | . | . | . | . | . | . | . | . | . | . | . | . | . | 6— | * | * | * | * | * | * | * | * | * | * | * | * | * | * |

## *List of Opera Singers at Kismarton*

| Male singers | 1800 | 1801 | 1802 | 1803 | 1804 | 1805 | 1806 | 1807 | 1808 | 1809 | 1810 | 1811 | 1812 | 1813 |
|---|---|---|---|---|---|---|---|---|---|---|---|---|---|---|
| Bader, Johann | . | . | . | . | . | * | . | . | . | . | . | . | . | . |
| Forti, Franz Anton | . | . | . | . | . | . | . | . | * | * | * | . | . | . |
| Grell, Otto | . | . | . | . | . | . | . | . | * | * | * | . | . | . |
| Lendvay, Gabriel | . | . | . | . | . | * | * | * | * | * | * | . | . | . |
| Michalesi, Wenzeslaus | . | . | . | . | . | . | . | . | . | . | * | * | * | * |
| Möglich | . | . | . | . | . | * | . | . | . | . | . | . | . | . |
| Posch, Johann | . | . | . | . | . | . | . | . | * | * | * | . | . | . |
| Rathmayer, Richard | . | . | . | . | * | * | * | * | * | * | * | * | * | * |
| Rotter, Joseph | . | . | . | . | * | * | * | * | * | * | * | * | * | * |
| Schmidt, Heinrich | . | . | . | . | * | * | * | * | * | * | * | * | * | * |
| Schuster, Anton | . | . | . | . | . | . | * | * | * | * | * | * | * | * |
| Specht, Christian | . | . | . | . | . | . | . | . | * | . | . | . | . | . |
| Tillo, Carl August | . | . | . | . | . | . | . | . | * | . | . | . | . | . |
| Treider, Joseph | . | . | . | . | . | * | * | * | * | * | * | . | . | . |
| Wild, Franz | . | . | . | . | . | . | . | . | . | . | * | * | . | . |
| *Female singers* | | | | | | | | | | | | | | |
| Cornega, Anna | . | . | . | . | . | . | . | . | * | . | . | . | . | . |
| Höld, Carolina | . | . | . | . | . | . | . | . | * | * | * | . | . | . |
| Marr, Mlle | . | . | . | . | . | * | . | . | . | . | . | . | . | . |
| Schneider, Elisabeth | . | . | . | . | . | . | . | * | * | * | * | * | * | * |
| Schöringer, Josepha | . | * | * | * | * | * | * | * | * | * | * | * | * | * |
| Siebert, Elisabetha | . | . | . | . | . | . | . | * | * | * | * | * | * | * |
| Stotz, Theresia | . | . | . | . | . | . | . | * | * | * | * | * | * | * |
| Tommasini, Josepha | . | . | . | . | . | . | . | . | * | * | * | . | . | . |
| Vadász, Josepha | . | . | . | . | . | . | . | . | * | * | * | * | * | * |

# LIST OF ILLUSTRATIONS

# INDEX OF NAMES

# INDEX OF OPERAS, PLAYS AND OTHER WORKS REFERRED TO IN THE TEXT